# MAKE iPHONE MOVIES

# EVERYONE LOVES

## ALLEN BRONSTEIN

Allen Bronstein Publishing, California

Library of Congress Cataloging-in-publication Data is available.

ISBN 978-0-9861986-1-8 (paperback)

eISBN 978-0-9861986-0-1

ALLEN BRONSTEIN PUBLISHING

PO Box 215

Inverness, CA 94937-0215

*guru@mobilemoviemaking.com*

# DEDICATION

*For Murray, without whom this book*

*would never have existed.*

.

# CONTENTS

MAKE iPHONE MOVIES EVERYONE LOVES

MAKE iPHONE MOVIES EVERYONE LOVES

# 1 INTRODUCTION

Ever thought about making a movie with your smartphone, tablet, or GoPro but haven't?

If so, I'm here to help you do it. You don't need to go to film school. But there are a few tricks to learn. It's easier than you think, and mastering the techniques is also fun.

Think about it. You already own the camera; it's right there in your pocket – all the time. In terms of experience, you've clocked in hours and hours of time watching movies on TV and YouTube. You may not understand everything about how they're put together. But, when I point out how to do it, you'll say... oh yeah! That's right.

I believe we are on the cusp of a revolution in filmmaking. Smartphone videography is democratizing the making of films. There are powerful video camera apps that can be purchased for less than ten dollars. TEN DOLLARS!!!! And, the cost of other equipment like add-on lenses, accessories, and applications is 40% to 90% lower than a DSLR or HD Video camera. You've already made the most expensive investment, your phone or tablet. Everything you need to get started is right there on your phone.

So, start exercising your brain, because we're going to take it on a creative adventure you and your smartphone will never forget.

I love movies! I love watching them, learning about them, making them, and most important, coming up with fun ways to talk about how they're made. There is something magical about understanding how something works... and learning how to do it myself. That's what this book is all about. How to do it in small, fun, easy to understand steps. By the end of our journey, you will be familiar with the techniques and tools needed to make movies that your friends and family will ask to watch, over and over.

We'll start out slow, talking about your smartphone's camera and how it works. Building a foundation of knowledge that will free you up, so you can unleash your creativity unhampered by the technology. I've taken a novel approach to helping you become a better filmmaker. For example:

• There is a chapter about "Lens Personalities" that explains the different types of lenses and the how to use them creatively.

1

- A chapter titled "Little Did They Know", about how to create surprise and suspense.
- A chapter titled, "Where do I stand" all about staging actors.
- A chapter titled, "Video Scrabble" to help you understand how to use the power of editing in your movies.

Over the last 25 years as a filmmaker, artist, and teacher, I've developed the knack of making technical and artistic topics understandable and accessible to everyone.

In addition to how the camera works, we'll discuss:

- What apps (applications) you should use
- What equipment and accessories you'll need, and how they work.
- How to light a scene and record great sound
- What are the aspects of visual story telling you'll need, and how to use them.
- How to edit
- How to create all kinds of videos including a child's birthday party, a travelogue, a local commercial, a video blog, and even a suspense flick.
- And, most important, whatever kind of movie you make, you'll learn how to create a finished product that everyone will love.

With YouTube, everyone can post their creations for the world to see. Who knows, maybe you'll be the next filmmaker to enchant millions of viewers? Or, just entertain close family and friends.

The idea behind this book is to have fun learning about smartphone videography and making movies your customers, friends and family will want to watch over, and over again. Let's get started!

Allen Bronstein
Cofounder, MobileMovieMaking.Com magazine

P.S. I want to invite you to participate by asking questions, recommending tools, or suggesting techniques. visit me at:    http://mobilemoviemaking.com/bronstein-home-page/ or email me at:     Guru@MobileMovieMaking.com

# 2 UNDERSTANDING IMAGE QUALITY

The video camera on your smartphone is absolutely amazing, it is capable of taking excellent High Definition video images, some with 4k resolution and large Mega Pixel capabilities. Wonderful as these cameras are, they all have their limitations. Limitations, that you need to understand so you don't waste time trying to do things your camera it's not suited for.

Why is image quality so important? Well, the bigger the screen you're planning to show your videos on, the more obvious issues, like noise (grainy or fuzzy images) or banding, which is abrupt changes in a smooth graduated of tone.

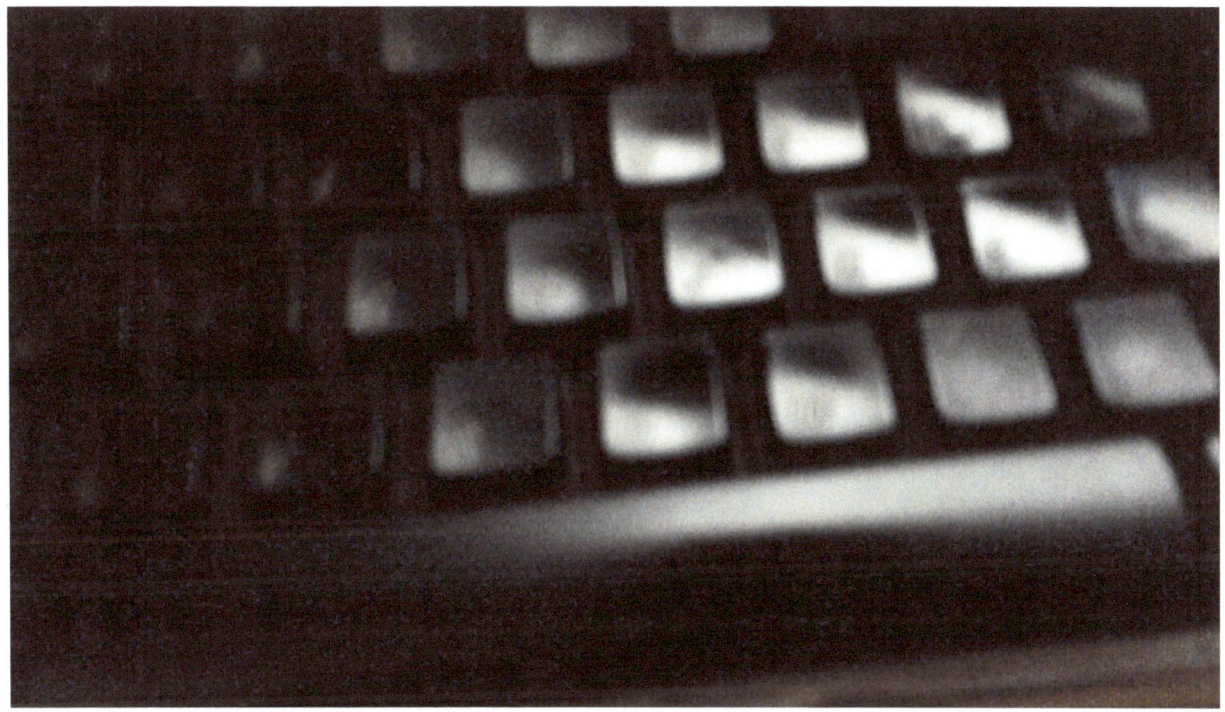

Video noise in an image is caused by shooting in either low light, or when using the digital zoom.

Both noise and banding can be caused by shooting in low light, using a digital zoom, a high

ISO setting, or a low a capture rate. Given the low light limitations of your camera, care should be taken when shooting at night, or in low light situations. In the chapters that follow, we'll be showing you specifically how to overcome and correct for these limitations by using lights, or by shooting dusk-for-night or day-for-night.

One of the best way to maintaining image quality is to utilize optical lenses rather than the digital zoom on your camera.

**The Standard Smartphone:** Most smartphones come with the equivalent of a standard DSLR 28mm to 33mm camera lens with a f/2.2 to f/2.8 aperture, a 4x to 6x digital zoom, (which is the equivalent of a 132mm to 198mm telephoto lens) and small 1/3 inch sensor. Having a small size sensor limits your camera's ability to control depth-of-field. (See Lens Personalities for more details)

Your phone comes with both FRONT AND REAR FACING CAMERAS. For now, we'll only discuss the rear facing camera.

**28mm to 33mm Equivalent lens:** The millimeter measurement on a lens defines its *focal length* and *field of view*. For example in the photo below the 28mm lens has a wider *field of view* than a normal 50mm lens. A 50mm is considered normal because it is thought to match what the human eye sees. The smaller the *focal length* of the lens the wider its *angle-of-view*.

Using lenses like telephoto, fisheye, close-up, and macro offers you an amazing range of image size and *angle-of-view*. Using these lenses you can photograph anything from ants to a 747. Many of these lenses come as combination lens kits, allowing you to have a wide angle, fish-eye and 10x or 15x macro all in the same kit (see lens attachments below).

The focal length of Smartphone and tablet attachment lenses are not measured in millimeters like a DSLR camera, instead they are measured using an "X" multiplier to indicate their focal length:

• A TELEPHOTO LENS is described as being a 2.5X Telephoto lens. *(denoted by a number larger than one before the decimal point)*

• A WIDE ANGLE LENS is described as being a 0.45X Wide Angle lens. *(denoted by a number smaller than one. The smaller the fraction the wide the lens)*

• A FISHEYE LENS is a 0.3X Ultra Fisheye lens

• MACRO LENSES are designated by the power of their magnification, such as 10X or 15X *(with no decimal point).*

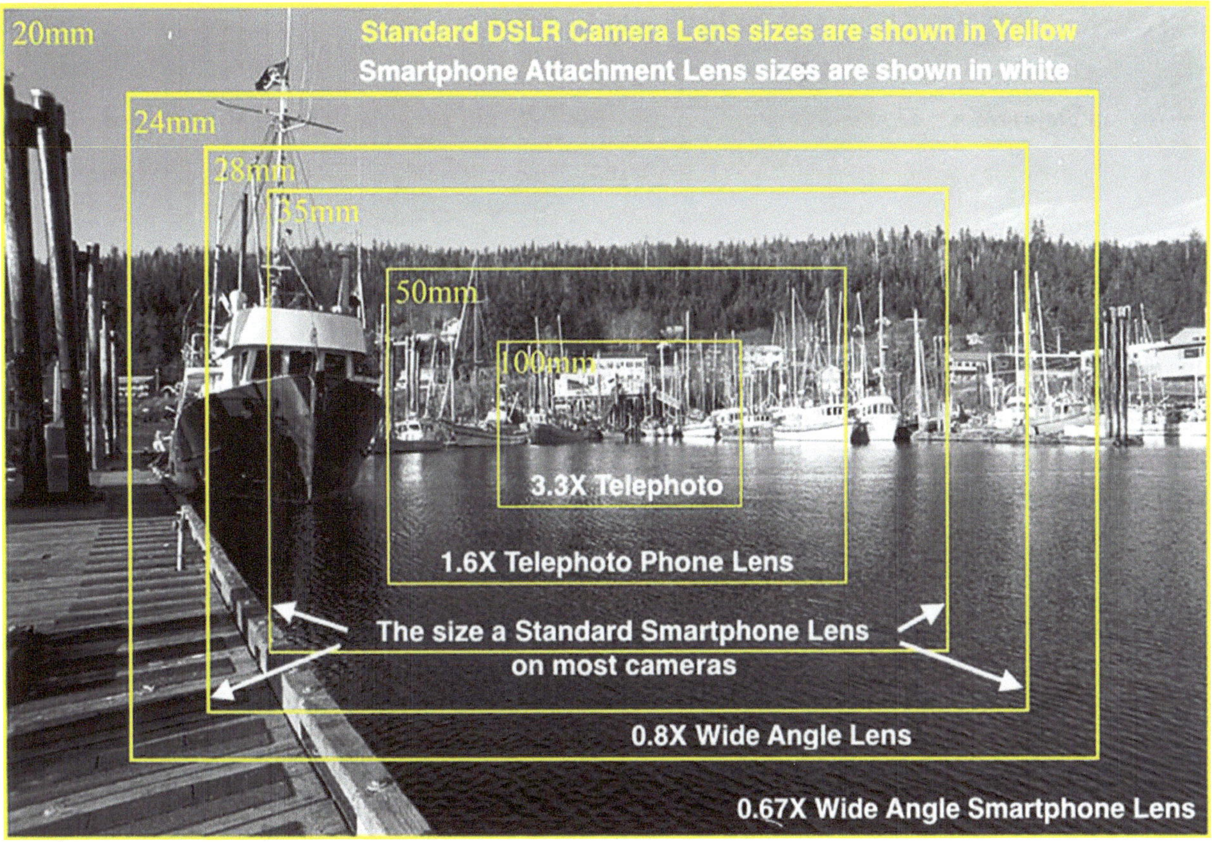

20mm
24mm
28mm
35mm
50mm
100mm

**Standard DSLR Camera Lens sizes are shown in Yellow**
**Smartphone Attachment Lens sizes are shown in white**

**3.3X Telephoto**

**1.6X Telephoto Phone Lens**

**The size a Standard Smartphone Lens on most cameras**

**0.8X Wide Angle Lens**

**0.67X Wide Angle Smartphone Lens**

Above is a photo by Neal Currie showing the angle-of-view for different size standard 35mm DSLR and Smartphone Lenses

**F/2.2 to f/2.8:** Your camera comes with a very fast f/2.2 to f/2.8 aperture. Camera apertures range from f/1.4 to f/22. The smaller the f/number the more light the lens is able to capture and focus on the camera's sensor (see diagram below).

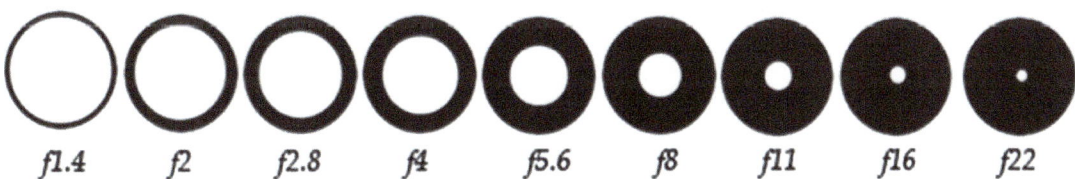

| f1.4 | f2 | f2.8 | f4 | f5.6 | f8 | f11 | f16 | f22 |

Unlike many point and shoot and DSLR cameras which have adjustable apertures, your phone's aperture is fixed. So any brightness or light adjustments are controlled by the camera's light sensitivity (ISO settings) and the shutter speed, not by changes in the aperture. Some camera applications, including some apple apps, allow you to manually adjust the light level of the image, and ISO settings. Some of the later iphone or iPad cameras allow changes in exposure.

**4x to 6x digital zoom**: This is the equivalent of a 132mm to 198mm telephoto lens. A Digital zoom works by enlarging a standard size image electronically, using your cameras software. It does not actually enlarge the image, but instead spreads the pixels of a normal size image further apart, manufacturing pixels to fill-in the empty spaces.

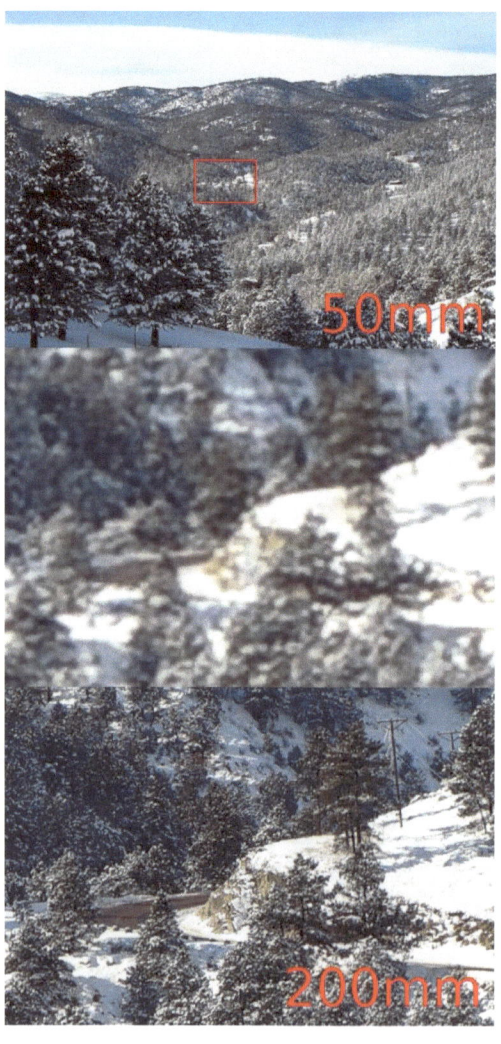

It guesses at what those missing pixels look like. This lowers image quality. And, produces banding and noise in the image. How much depends on what the magnification of the zoom is.

That noisy image may look just fine on your smartphone or tablet, but imagine what it will look like blown up on a large screen TV or movie screen. The average viewer seeing a soft fuzzy image, will believe that the film is slightly out of focus and shot on an inferior camera, or by an inexperienced cameraman. If you want to capture sharp images, forget about using the digital zoom, use lens attachments instead.

**Lens Attachments:** Lenses for Smartphones and pads are not expensive when compared to lenses for a DLSR or a video camera. There are many different kits and mounting systems for attaching lenses to your camera.

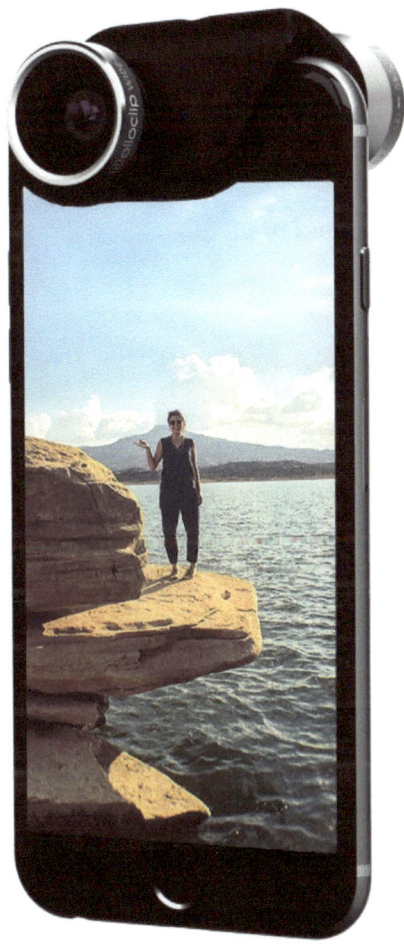

Some clip onto your phone, like the OlloClip 4-in-1 kit (iPhone 6 version shown above, Samsung Galaxy shown below), which includes a wide angle, fisheye, and 10X and 15X macro lenses.

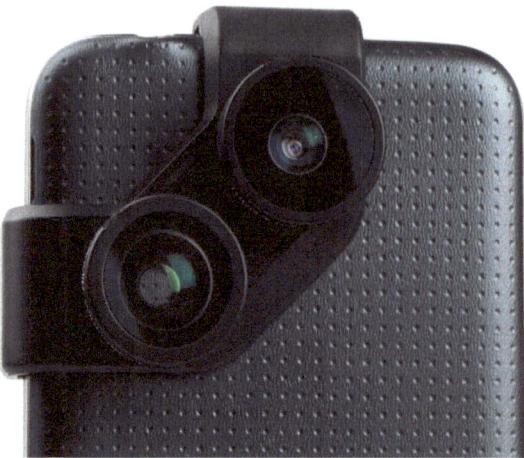

Others attach to a case or frame that holds the phone and allows the lenses to be screwed on to it. Like the BeastGrip smartphone case shown below with a 37mm fisheye lens (*37mm refers to the thread size of the lens, not its field of view.*)

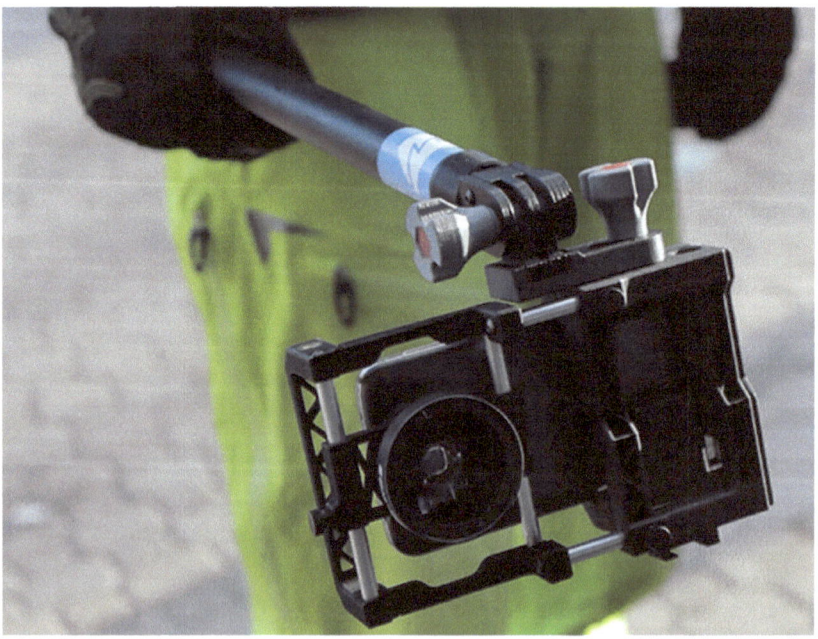

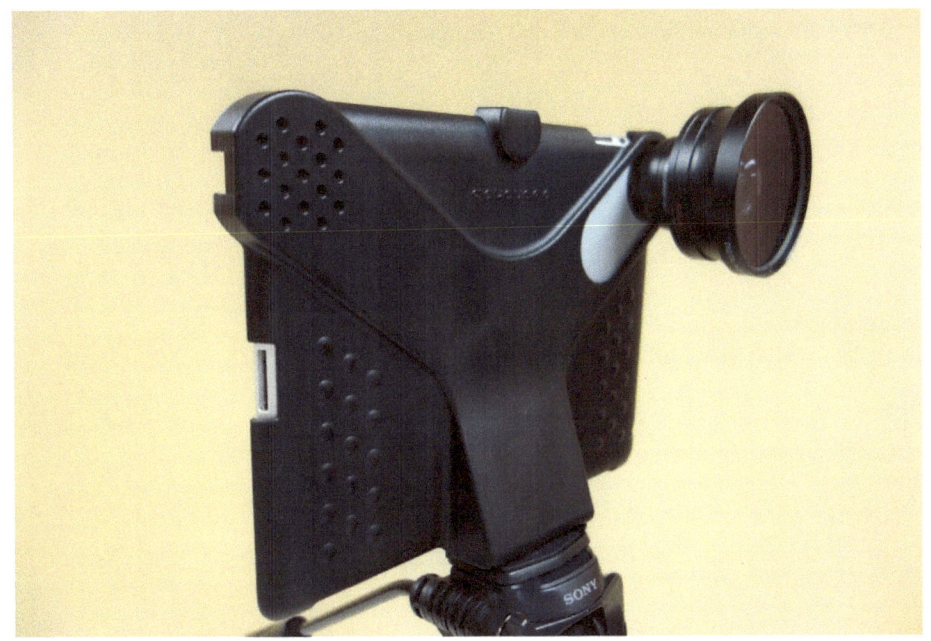

Makayama iPad Movie Mount with 37mm lens

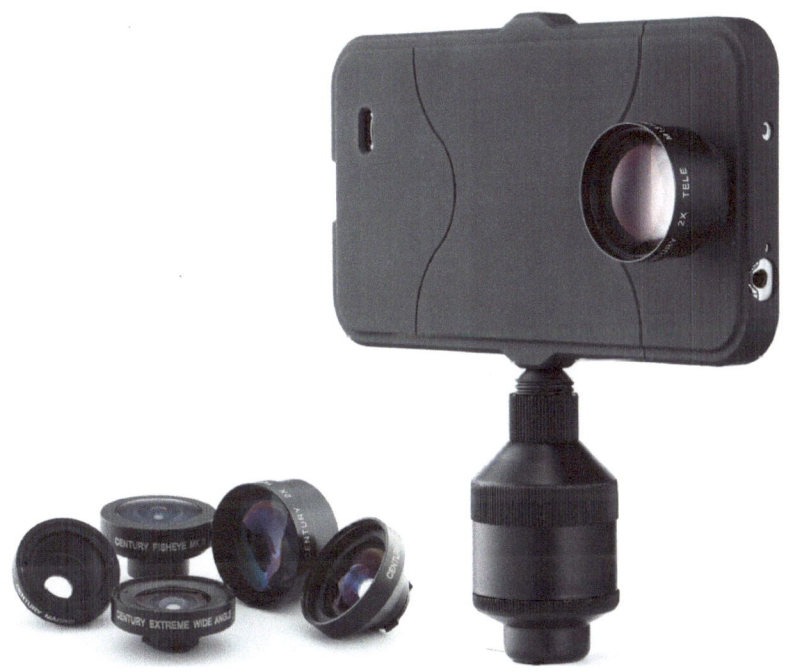

Schnider iPro Lens System for iPhone, iPad, and Galaxy S4

In the next chapter, we'll be discussing the expressive attributes of each type of lens. *(See Lens Personalities, for more details)*

**THREE TIPS:**

1.  Experiment with your digital zoom so you have an idea of how much noise you're getting in your images. (I suggest viewing these images on a large computer screen or TV, rather than on your phone)

2.  To get familiar with your lenses, keep your tripod and camera in one location, and shoot the same scene or object with different lenses. Experiment with how a telephoto, close-up, or fisheye changes the size of the image and the *field-of-view* in the frame.

3.  Repeat tip two, but this time move your camera so that the image is the same size in the frame with each lens change. How does this affect the depth of the image? Notice any distortion?

# 3  LENS PERSONALITIES

I spend a lot of time researching the topics I write about, always looking for new ways to think about a subject, which is what happened when I read cinematographer Mark Wood's article about Lens Personalities.  My perspective is different, but I was so impressed with Mark's concept I've included a link to his original article. https://www.cameraguild.com/member-resources/techtips/lens-personalities.aspx

Lenses like people... have their own personality.  Some are friendly, outgoing, and inclusive, inviting everyone to come and join the party.  Others are introverts, living in their own worlds and keeping to themselves.  Each lens distorts reality in some manner; some, more than others.  Utilizing different lenses is a powerful tool that can increase the expressive power of your videos.

There are three factors that determine a lens's character.

1.  ANGLE-OF-VIEW, or how much of the world the lens sees at one time — from the left side of the frame to the right side, and from the top to the bottom.

2.  DEEP FOCUS, or how that lens portrays and distorts the illusion of depth, along the "Z" axis in the image. (See photo below)

3.  SELECTIVE FOCUS, or how deep or shallow can the lens focus on an object to isolate it from the background.

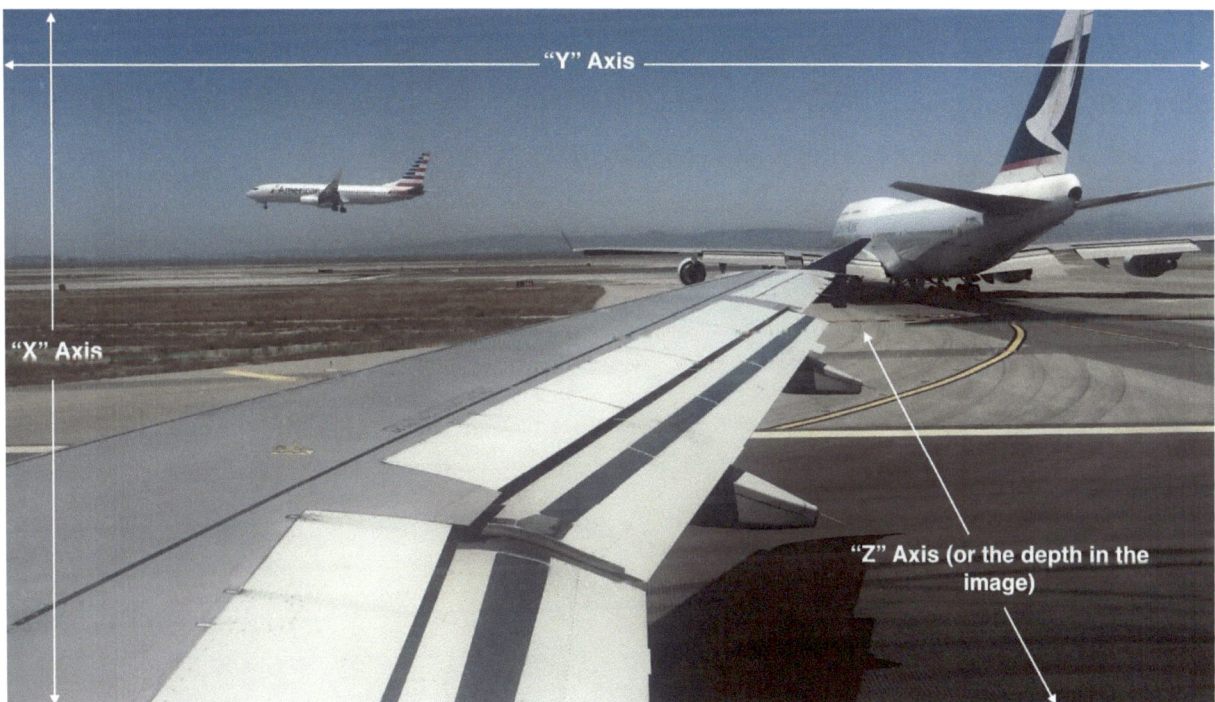

**Standard smartphone camera lens**: You know this lens — it's your buddy. It's the lens that comes with your smartphones or tablet. With it you can select an object, within your picture frame, and lock focus on it so that does not change while you film.

Ideally, you would like it to have the option of using *selective focus* of a subject against an out-of-focus background. But, that's not going to happen with this lens. Its depth-of-focus is limited by the camera's design.) The best you'll be able to achieve is some degree of partial blurring of the background.

When used for filming close-ups, it will portray the world as it is. And distort reality the least. Use it for any shot, from extreme close-up to landscape

**Telephoto Lens:** Telephoto's are shy and introverted. Because of their narrower angle-of-view, they're exclusive and keep what they see to themselves.

They're described as beauty lenses, because when used for shooting close-ups they tend to flatten space, and won't exaggerate facial features, like the length of your nose or the size of your chin. Because they have a short focal distance, it is easier to achieve *selective focus* while blurring the background. They tend to flatten depth-of-field in a composition and diminish perspective.

An excellent example of this effect is the scene in the movie The Graduate (1967), where Dustin Hoffman's character, Ben, is racing down the street to stop Elaine from getting married. Shot with a long telephoto, Ben runs and runs, but appears to get nowhere, because the telephoto lens has obliterated any sense of depth in the shot

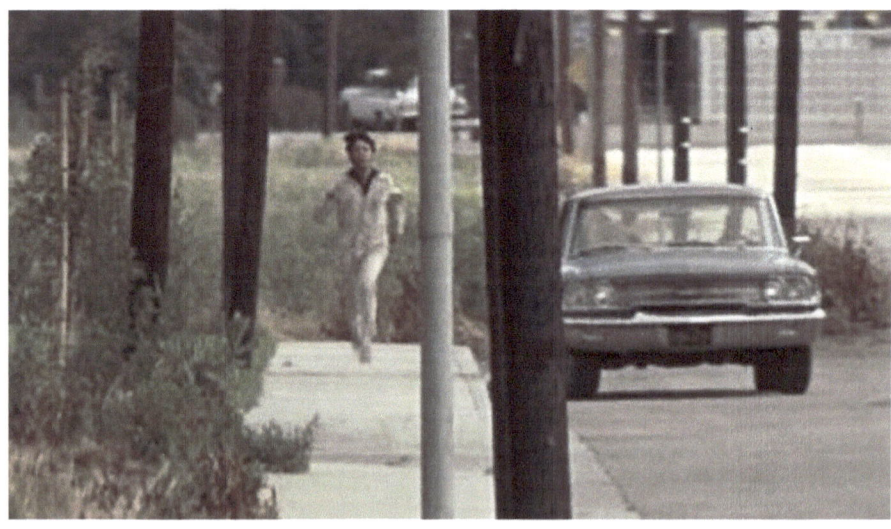

Most lens attachment kits come with a 2.0X telephoto lens, which is the equivalent of a 60mm to 70mm lens.

In addition, there are some very inexpensive zoom lens attachments on the market that go from 8X to 17X magnification, equivalent to a 240mm to 500mm telephoto lens. Be careful, image quality is low, especially considering that an equivalent 300mm DSLR telephoto lens would cost anywhere from $900 to $5,000.

Another alternative that offers quality optics at a reasonable price is to use a digiscoping adapter for either binoculars or a bird spotting scope. There are many adaptors on the market that you can choose from, ranging in price from $12 to over $100. Below is iPhone Digiscope Adapter on a pair of binoculars.

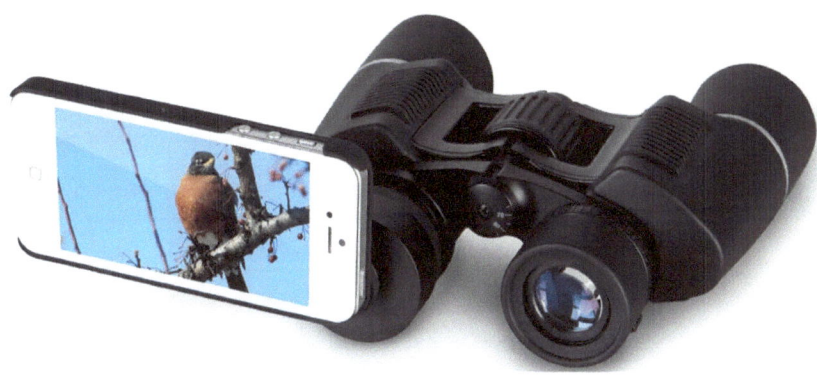

**Lens Field-of-View:** in the four photos below notice how the field-of-view narrows as the lens size increases from Fisheye #1, Wide Angle #2, Normal #3, to Telephoto #4.

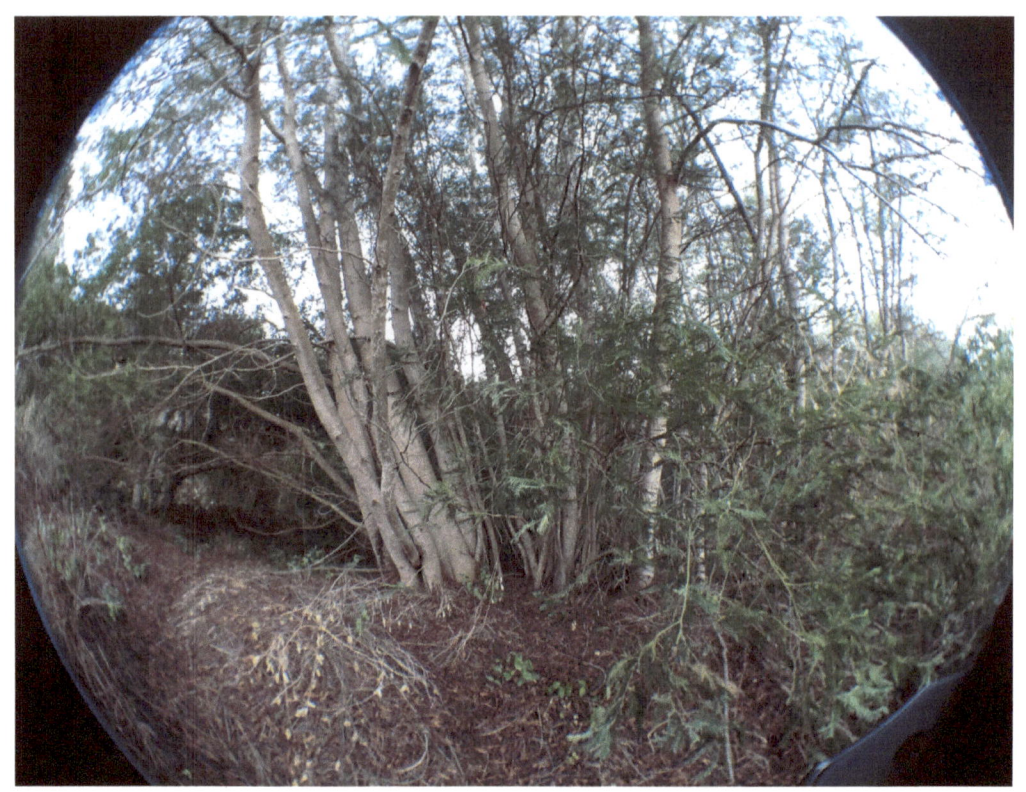

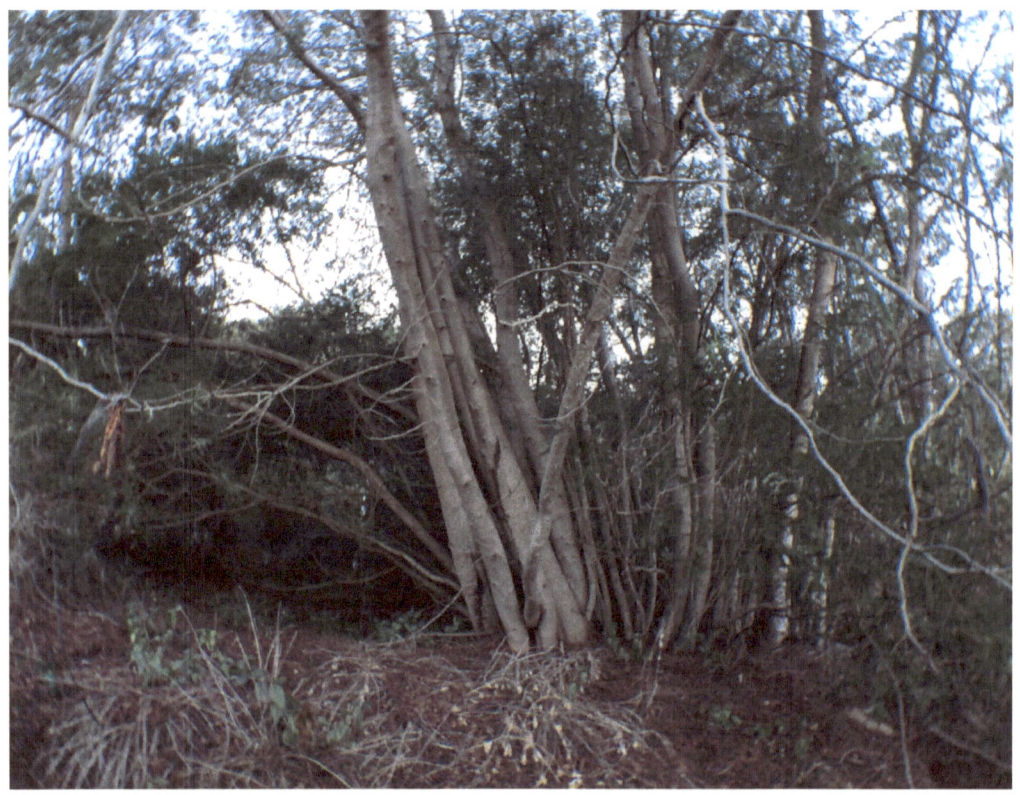

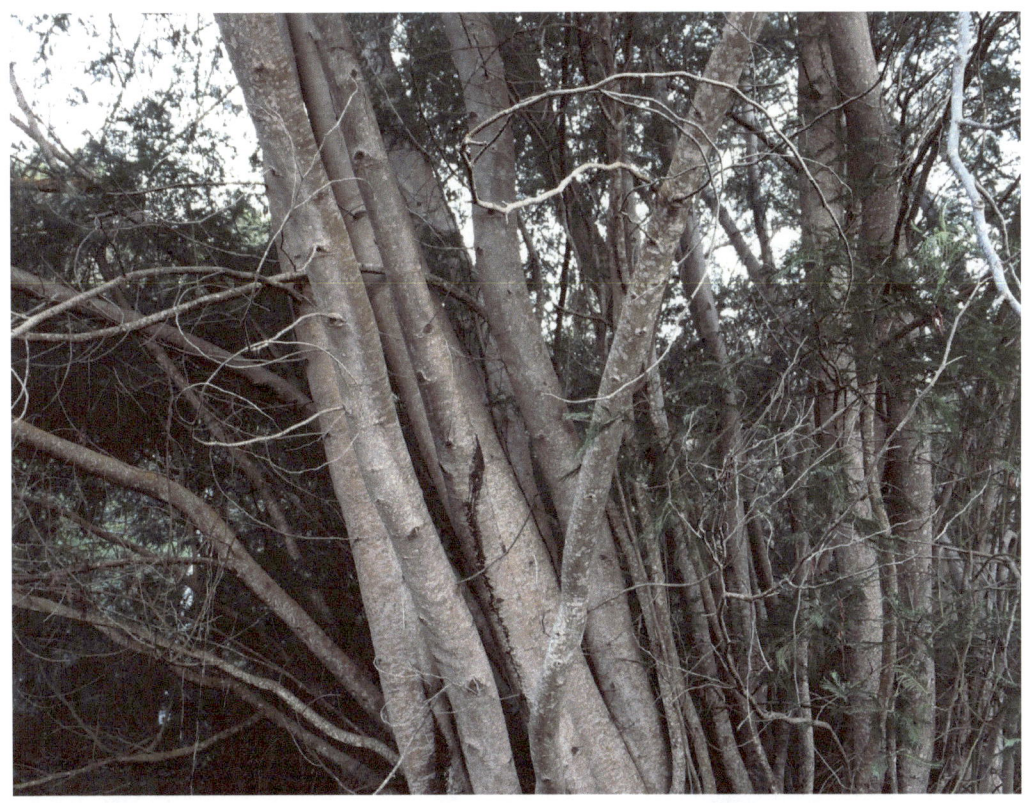

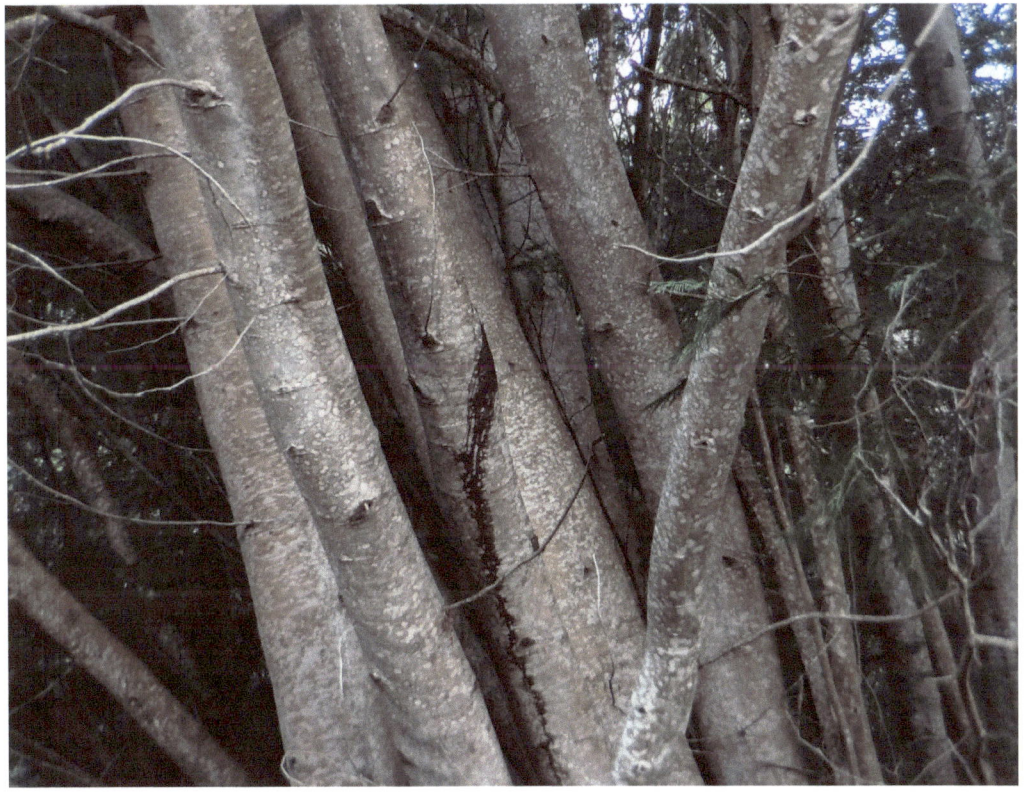

In addition to narrowing the field-of-view, the perspective or depth-of-field is reduced, flattening the image in "Z" space.

**Wide-Angle Lens:**  Because of their wide field-of-view, they are extroverts, and want to reach out and include everyone in what's going on.

They add a sense of drama to whatever they do.  They exaggerate depth on the  "Z" axis of the picture plane by making objects seem further apart.  They also tend to distort whatever they see. The wider the lens, the greater is this distortion. For example: If you were to photograph an hand pointing straight at the camera, like the photo below, with a 0.5X wide angle lens, the hand would seem to be many times larger than it really is.

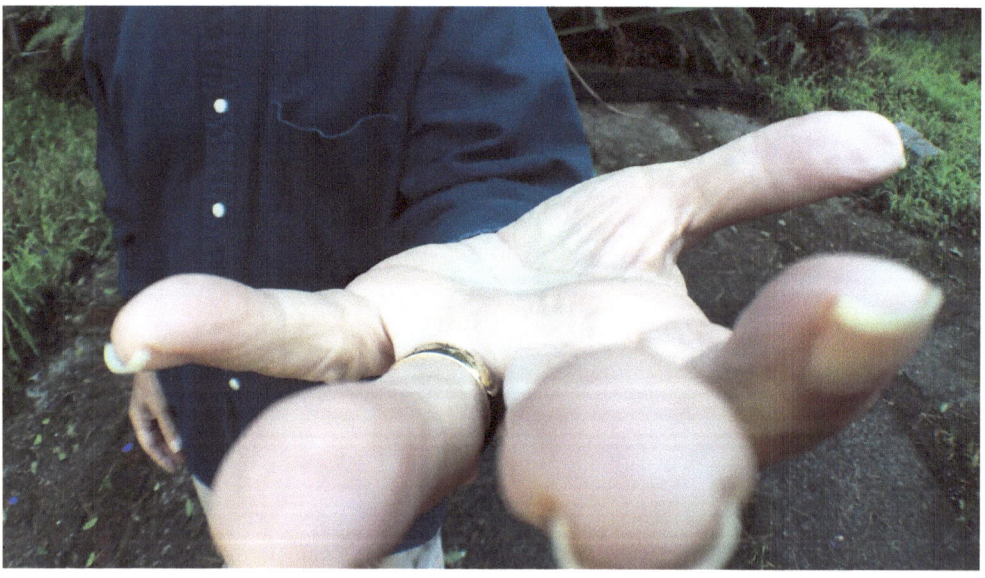

When used to shoot up at a subject a wide-angle lens can enhance a subject's status or sense of power and control, making them seem taller than they are.  On the other hand, shooting down communicates lowly status, rejection, or defeat.

Wide-angle lenses also possess the ability to create deep focus.  You can utilize this to your benefit when shooting chase scenes.  Because of the exaggerated illusion of depth along the "Z" axis, objects, especially ones that are moving toward or away from the camera, appear to move faster in the frame.  Where as, shooting an object moving along the "Y" axis with a wide lens will not have the same illusion of speed.

**Smartphone lens attachments** incorporate an "X" multiplier to indicate lens size. The placement of the lens's number before the decimal point (for Telephoto) or after (for Wide-angle) distinguishes what kind of lens it is. The greater the angle-of-view a lens has the smaller is its number. For example:

• A telephoto lens might have 2.0X designation. (The number is in front of the decimal point)

• A wide-angle lens might be 0.45X (the number is behind the decimal point)

• A fish-eye lens, which has a greater angle-of-view than the wide-angle lens, would be a 0.3X or lower.

If the standard lens on your phone is the equivalent of a 30mm lens, adding a 0.45X wide-angle attachment converts it to the equivalent of a 13.5mm wide-angle lens.

30mm x 0.45 = 13.5mm

**Fish-eye lens:** These are the freaks of the camera world. Nothing about them is normal. They were called fish-eye because biologists once thought that's how fish saw the world. Forget normal perspective, there are no straight lines on buildings, streets, or landscapes. With an angle of view somewhere between 100 to 180 degrees, they are known for their playfulness, they love to skydive, skateboard, and bungee jump. And, because they distort so much, they can be used in genres like horror movies to portray a sinister or evil point of view. Use them on close-up shots and you'll get a mash-up of features, eyes, nose, ears, teeth, where nothing is normal. Below are the different lenses found in Olloclip 4-in-1 attachment

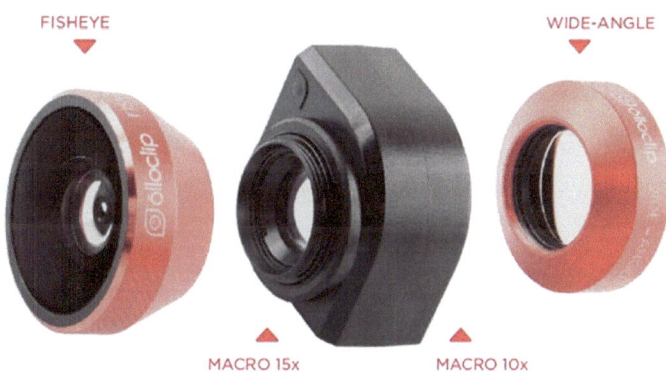

FISHEYE     WIDE-ANGLE

MACRO 15x     MACRO 10x

**Macro Lenses**:  These are the nerds of the camera world.  They are specialist, understanding and revealing specific aspects of the world in fine detail.

Macros have a very *selective focus*, measured in fractions of an inch.  They prefer to limit what they see, rejecting anything outside of their field of view, blurring extraneous details.  Their ability to concentrate is unlimited, they are capable of revealing hidden details of plants, insects, and other small objects.  Below is a photo of 37mm wide and macro combination lens.

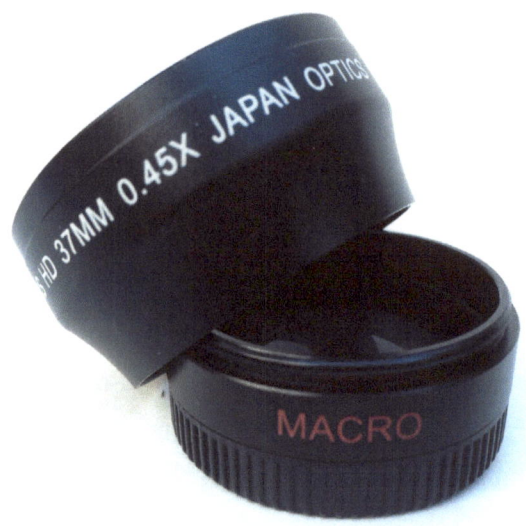

Most wide-angle and fish-eye lens attachments include a Macro lens section that can be unscrewed from the body of the lens and used separately. (See the photo above).  Macros are designated by an "X" factor which indicates their power of magnification.  This is usually somewhere between 10X  for Wide-Angle lenses, to 15X for Fish-eye.

**Three Tips on Lens Personalities:**

1.  Wide Angle lenses tend to include everyone, with a large field-of-view which exaggerate perspective and creates the illusion of speed of an objects moving in "Z" space

2.  Telephoto lenses are introverts and keep to themselves, with a narrow field-of-view they flatten perspective, and are used as beauty lenses.

3.  Fisheye lenses know how to work a room, they are everywhere, distorting perspective they have a 100° to 180° field-of-view.

# 4 WHAT COLOR ARE YOU?

Orange colored people... what's up with that? Unexpected results can occur when you allow your camera to control the video palette.

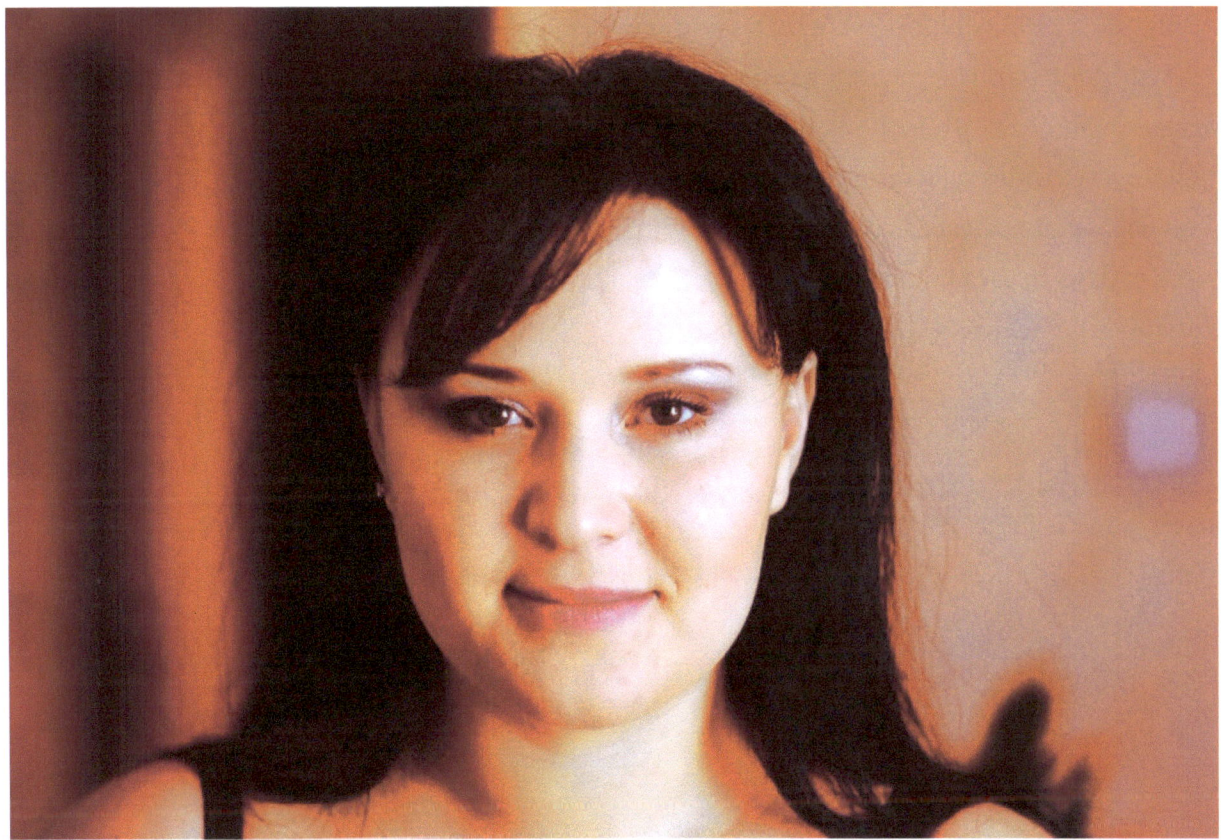

In the photo above Di by Liviuss76 (2010) We've intentionally shifted the image color to illustrate the result of incorrectly white balancing your camera.

Whether you're indoors or outside, our eyes automatically adjust to the changes in the color of the light. Your camera doesn't. What it does do, is guess, and sometimes not very intelligently.

Despite which phone you have, the camera needs to be told what the color temperature of the light you're shooting is. Is it warm? Cool? Or, some color in between? This is usually controlled by the camera setting called "*White Balance*". *White balancing* allows you to tell the camera what type of light (incandescent, sunlight, shade, or fluorescent) you're shooting in.

Setting the white balance before you shoot will make editing your footage later much easier. Otherwise, when it comes time to edit, everything you've shot will have a slightly different color cast and you'll have a difficult time combining the shots together. There is always the possibility of doing color correction in your editing app, but it's a lot of work, and I've found that the footage never quite matches.

Below is an illustration of how changing your camera's white balance settings effects the color cast of your video when shooting in daylight. The Incandescent setting (warm light) gives your images a blue cast; while the cloudy (cool light) setting yields images that have a warm orange or yellow cast. Unless you have your camera set to "Automatic White Balance", it's a good idea to manually white balance every time you're starting a new sequence, or shooting at a different time of day. In the photo below we can see the effects of using Incandescent, Daylight, and Cloudy white balance settings when shooting.

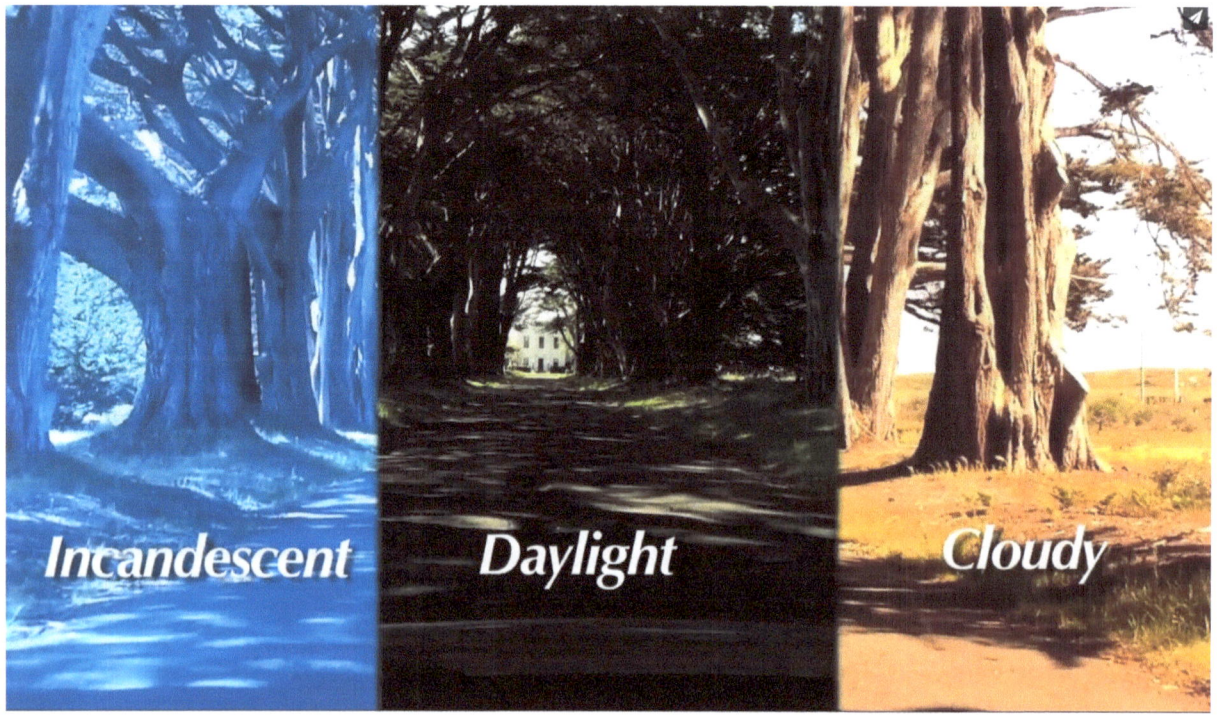

The camera that comes with your iPhone or iPad has automatic white balance. It cannot be adjusted manually. If you want control over *White Balance*, you'll need to install a third party camera app, like Filmic Pro.

Filmic Pro has proven to be one of the most powerful video camera apps available for Apple devices. It offers the user the same level of adjustment and control as a DSLR camera including; white balance, shutter speed, ISO, video resolution, frame rate, zoom speed adjustments and controls, slow motion and time-lapse, audio metering, framing guides, video encoding, and much more.

Below is a screen shot of FilimicPro's main control screen, illustrating some of the many camera controls available within this app.

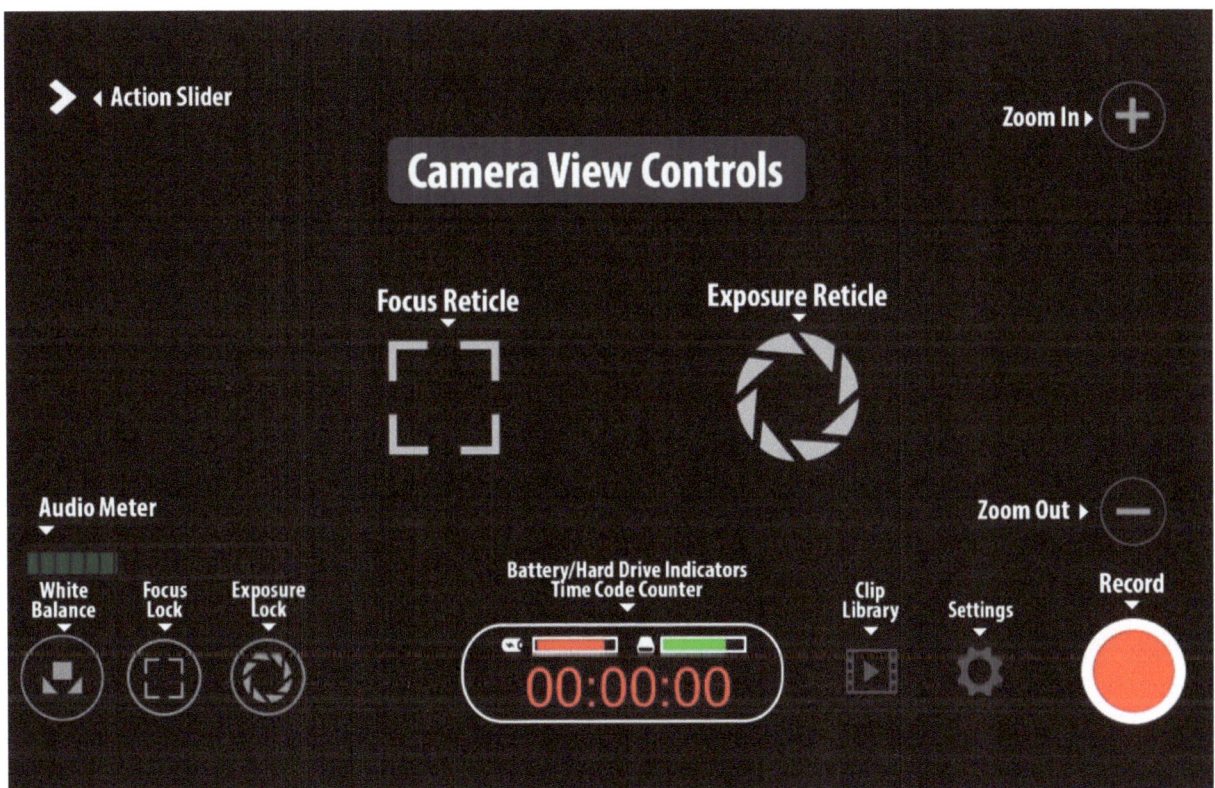

There are three different ways of manually set white balance in Filmic Pro.

1. Use a white card and lock the white balance by tapping the white balance icon.
2. Adjustment by Color Temperature (in degrees K)
3. Adjustment by Tint of the image.

Adjusting by color temperature or tint is acquired by holding down the *White Balance* icon for 2 seconds revealing either the manual adjustment "K" for color temperature or the word "Tint". Below is a screen shot of the main control screen in Filmic Pro, illustrating some of the many manual controls available within this app.

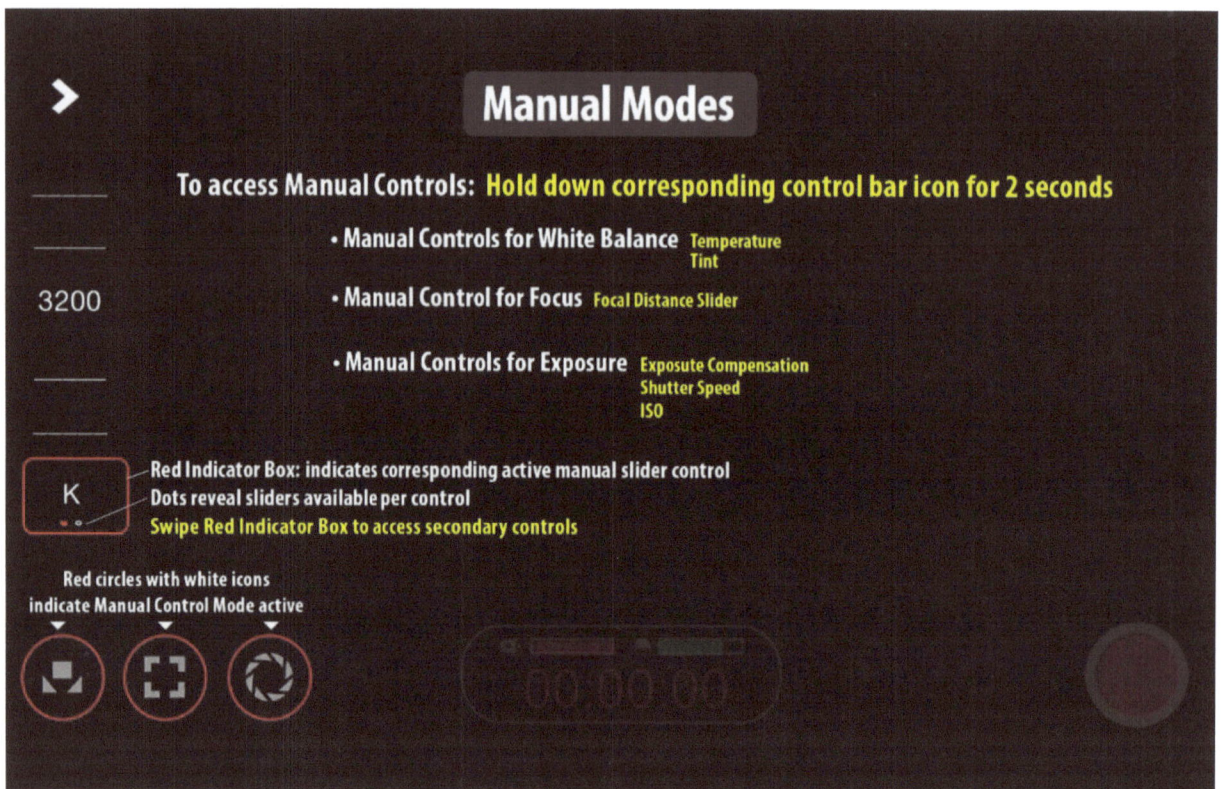

Most Android, Windows, and other smart phones come equipped with cameras that allow you to choose how you're going to *white balance* your camera. The different *white balance* settings are: Automatic, Daylight, Cloudy, Incandescent, Fluorescent, and Custom. See the table below.

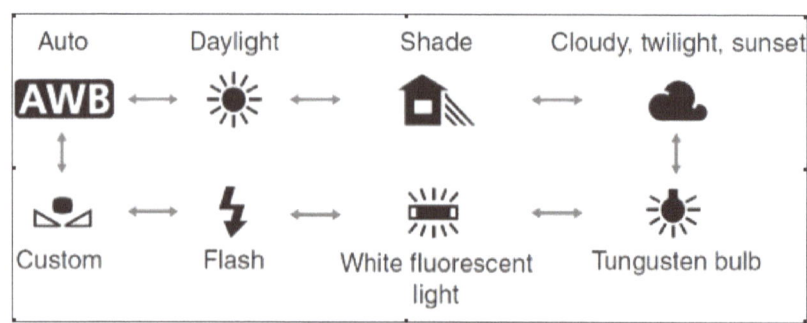

Many of the Apple, Android, Window, and other phone camera apps allow you to manually set *white balance* yourself. Depending on the app, Custom White Balance might be shown as a camera icon you press or just as the letters "WB".

To white balance, hold a sheet of white paper in front of the camera so that it fills the frame, while being illuminated by the lighting source in the scene you're shooting. Pressing the white balance icon on your screen will lock white balance for that lighting situation. Pressing it again will unlock it.

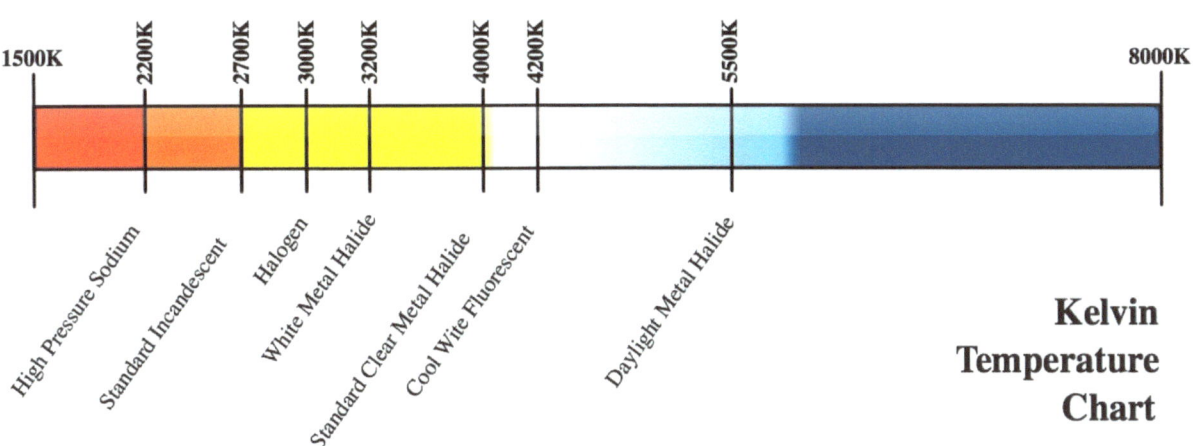

Above is a table that illustrates how the color of light changes throughout the day and for different types of light sources.

If you're doing an extended shoot outdoors—over several hours— you will need to white balance your camera frequently because the color and intensity of the light will change, especially during the morning and late afternoon.

White balancing is crucial for maintaining consistent color rendition in the images that you shoot throughout the day.

**Here are three tips:**

1. Instead of using a white card, you can manipulate the colorcast of your images by using a different colored card. Experiment. To get the color you want think in terms of opposites, using the complement of the color you want. To get a warm look, use a cool (blue) colored card. Or, to get a cool look, use a warm (orange) card. This allows you tremendous control over the color of the images you're shooting.

2.  To capture the warm brilliance of a sunrise or sunset, change the *white balance* setting on your camera from automatic to daylight (5500 K).  Or if you're working with an Apple phone, use an application with manual white balance, and use either a slightly blue tinted card, or white balance in the shade.   That way the camera records everything with a brilliant warmer look.

3.  Try shooting a horror or love scene with a setting that turns your image a different color than usual.  Here's where that orange face might be just want you want.

BONUS:  Most pros don't like to shoot at mid-day when the color of the light is very cool and there are no cast shadows to help define the shape of objects .

# 5 HOW LONG CAN I LAST?  Battery life, resolution, bit rate, and memory

You're all set – the battery is fully charged, you've bought that lightweight carbon tripod plus a set of snap-on lenses, and you have a great video camera app loaded on your phone.  You've come clear across the country to attend Becky's fifth birthday party and film it for your family and friends.  It starts in five minutes.  But rattling around in the back of your mind is the question, "How long can I shoot for?"   Will your camera have enough power in the battery and memory to get all the shots you want?

So how long can you shoot for?  The answer to that question is – it depends on four factors:

1. The amount of memory (storage) available
2. The resolution (size in the number of pixels) of the image you are shooting
3. The bitrate, which controls the quality of the image and the size of the video files.
4. Your phones battery capacity.

Shooting 1080p High Definition (HD) video your camera consumes approximately 102 MB/minute, or 6 GB/hour of storage capacity (memory).

With your phone set to airplane mode and the screen's brightness set as low as possible, you can record for approximately 2.5 hours, or a total of 16 GB on a full battery.  Older smartphones use from 149 MB/minute to 160 MB/minute, or record for a total of 2 hours.

Some of newer phones come with cameras that can shoot in 4K video (which is 3840 pixels wide x 2160 pixels high) and requires 5.3 times more storage space than 1080 HD.  Given the amount of memory in most smartphones, that's only a half hour of recording time.

The most of the world has not caught up to 4K video yet, so we're not going to discuss 4K now, and leave it for some time in the future.

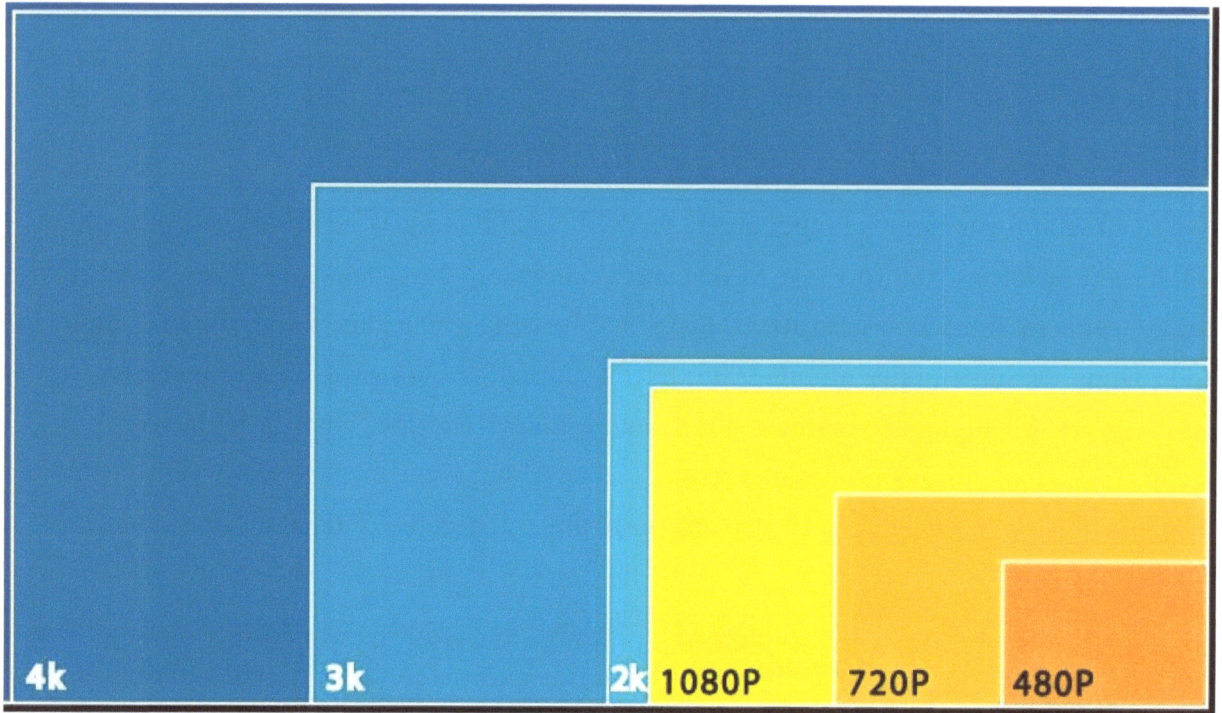

**Resolution and bitrate** (They're interrelated.) *Resolution* is the size of the video image measured in pixels. A video shot 1080 HD is 1920 pixels wide x 1080 pixels high. It has four times more pixels than a 720 x 480 Standard Definition video image.

*Bitrate* controls image quality and file size. The higher the bitrate, the better the image quality and the larger the file size that needs to be stored. For example the Filmic Pro app will let you shoot 1080 HD at four different bitrates:

- Economy (12.0 mbit/sec)
- Standard (24.0 mbit/sec)
- Quality (32.0 mbit/sec)
- Extreme (50.0 mbit/sec)

Each higher bitrate increases image quality, and file size.

The iPhone 6, Samsung Galaxy S5, and many other smartphones shooting HD 1080 video have an average bitrate between 16Mbps to 17Mbps, which consumes 6GB/hour of memory. Audio adds another 128Kbps.

Not all cameras are alike. For example: the iPhone camera, that comes with each phone, has a fixed resolution and bitrate, which you cannot adjust. So do many other types of smartphones. If you find that your camera doesn't have settings for Resolution and bitrate (also called Image

Quality) I suggest purchasing a video camera app that will allow you to have control over these functions, and many more. Among the many apps out there, I recommend:

- Filmic Pro for iPhone and iPad owners
- Cinema FV-5 for Android phones.

Both offer professional level control of your camera. Below is a table for the iPhone/iPad app FilmicPro that shows the bitrates for different video resolutions and quality settings. This table gives us an excellent approximation of data rates for many other smartphones, tablets, and their camera apps.

### Hourly Data Rate for the Filimic Pro Camera Application

| Resolution | Economy | Standard | Quality | Extreme |
|------------|---------|----------|---------|---------|
| 960 x 540 | 0.9 GB/hr | 1.8 GB/hr | 2.7 GB/hr | 3.6 GB/hr |
| 1280 x 720 | 2.7 GB/hr | 3.6 GB/hr | 6.3 GB/hr | 10.8 GB/hr |
| 1920 x 1080 | 5.4 GB/hr | 10.8 GB/hr | 10.8 GB/hr | 22.5 GB/hr |
| | | | | |

Changing the resolution and/or the bitrate can extend or shorten the amount of video you can record. For example if you need to shoot for four hours, instead of the 2.5 hour limit at 1080 you might choose to down grade the bitrate from Quality to Standard.

Downsizing the resolution from 1080 HD to 720 HD reduces your file size by approximately half, allowing you to film for twice as long. Going to 540 will reduce it even more. Consider this, the reduction in resolution from 1080 to 720 is negligible, if the finished product is to be displayed on YouTube and watched on a smartphone or laptop. Of course, if image quality is a paramount concern, this strategy won't work. If anything, you'll probably go in the opposite direction, increasing the bitrate and resolution.

**MEMORY (STORAGE)** How much storage you have on your phone is the most inflexible part of this equation. Especially considering all the apps, photos, and music already stored there. All that stuff is already using approximately 10 GB of memory. On a phone with a 16 GB memory card you have room for approximately one hours worth of 1080 HD video (6 GB/hr). My iPhone 5S has 64 GB of memory, so theoretically I can record for approximately 8 or 9 hours. If you're going to be shooting lots of video, you might consider getting a device with a larger memory card.

Another option is a wireless media hub. These compact devices let you add your own storage in the form of either SD cards or USB drives, thus affording you lots of extra space for your documents and media. About the size of a deck of cards, they connect to your phone either with a wireless or USB connection, so that you can down load your videos and keep on shooting. Many come with a back-up battery that allows you to recharge or power your phone while you're shooting.

**BATTERY** The battery in the average smart phone or tablet lasts approximately 2.5 hours when shooting video. Adding an external battery can extend your recording time. For example, I have 16,000 mAh backup battery that I can plug into my phone with a USB power cord, that offers me up to an additional 120 hours of operation. That's a little extreme, but as you can see using an external battery can solve the limited power supply issue.

This has been a long but important chapter. Knowledge is power. May you have sufficient memory and backup battery power so that your mobile never quits before you get all the shots you need.

# 6 MAKE IT STEADY – Tools for holding the camera

Everybody loves new toys, at least I do!  So let's put together a birthday, Xmas, Chanukah, or you deserve a gift list of equipment that is guaranteed to put a smile on your face and also raise the "production value" of your videos. The good news is that the gear for mobile devices is affordable, with most items costing less than $100.

**Mounts:**  Starting at the top you'll need a tripod mount to attach your phone or tablet to the tripod's head.  The mount attaches to the tripod's head with the 1/4"-20 threaded screw.   Below are a few of the many different mounts available like the Ivation Universal Tripod Mount.

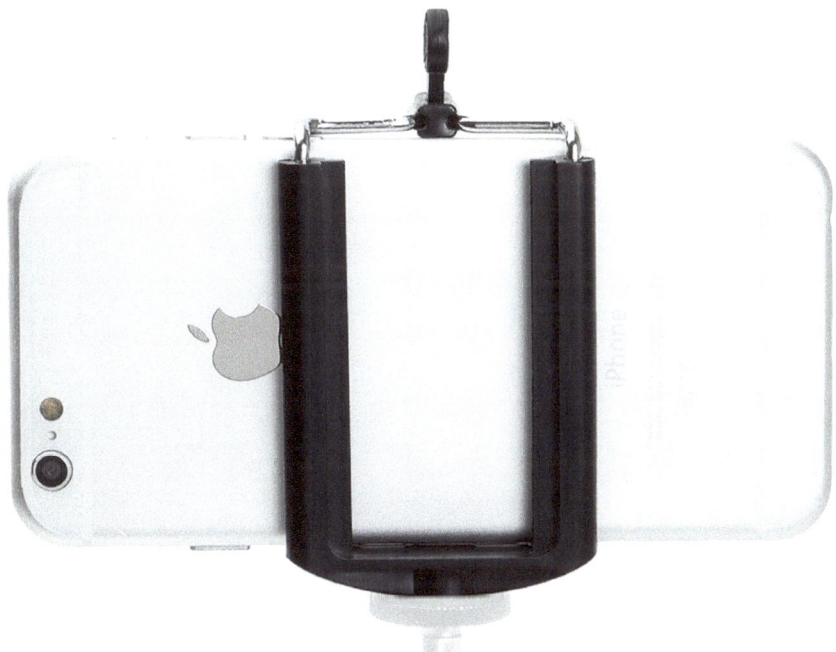

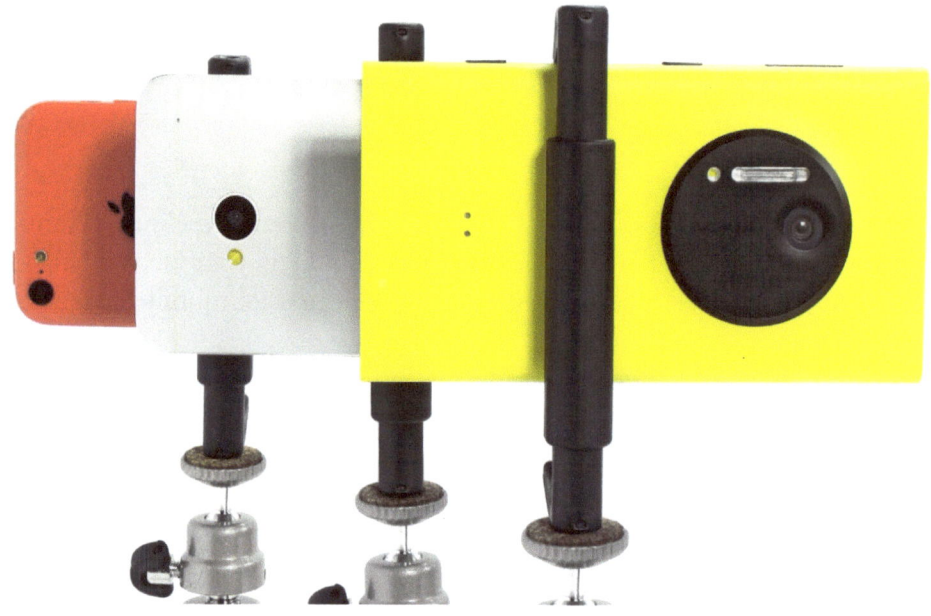

*Or the Glif Adjustable Smartphone Mount*

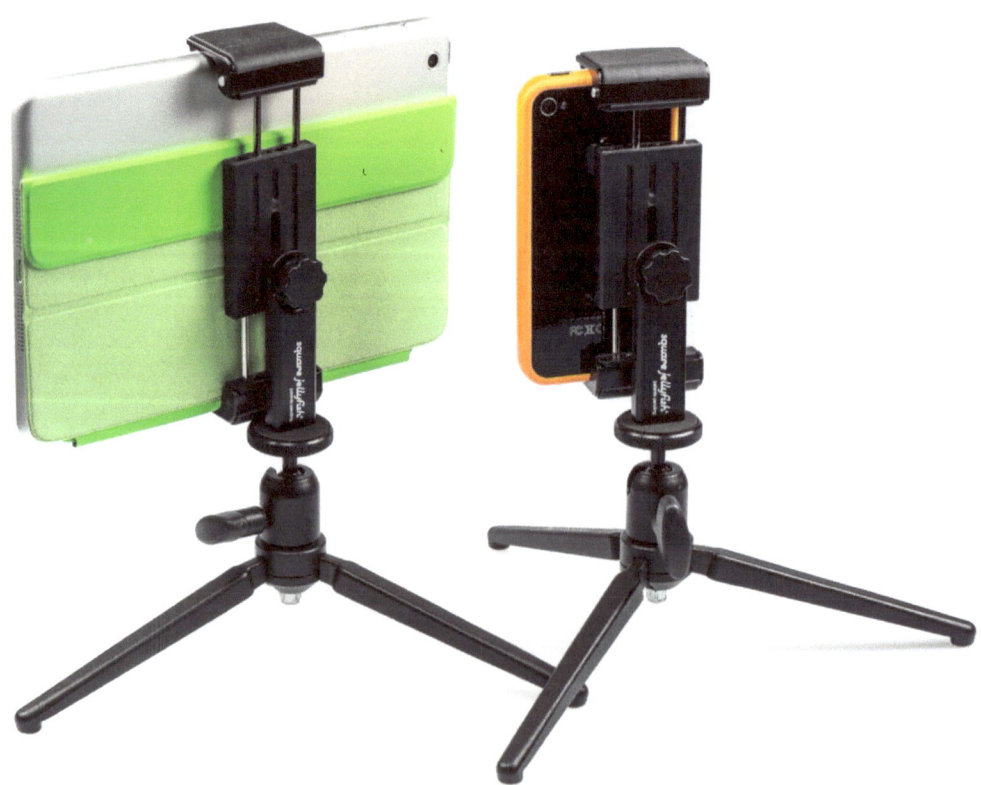

*Or the Square Jellyfish Adjustable Tablet or Phone Tripod Mount*

**Tripods:** Tripods come in all sizes, shapes, and prices. Designed to hold a camera steady, the most important features for smart device users are: portability, flexibility, and cost.

There are aluminum, ultra-light weight carbon fiber, miniature, large, photo, and video tripods, varying in price from $8 to thousands. Actually there are too many choices, so let's talk about what's the most important features you'll need when considering which to buy.

**3 Way Pan and Tilt Head:** Pan/Tilt heads attach to the top of a tripod and allow independent rotation of the camera around two or three axes. The head offers tremendous flexibility: you can quickly move the camera in any direction and then lock it in place; or you can lock the camera in one or two axes while rotating it in the third, allowing you to smoothly pan or tilt. Some pan and tilt heads come either built into the tripod, like the Amazon Basic tripod shown below, or are purchased separately.

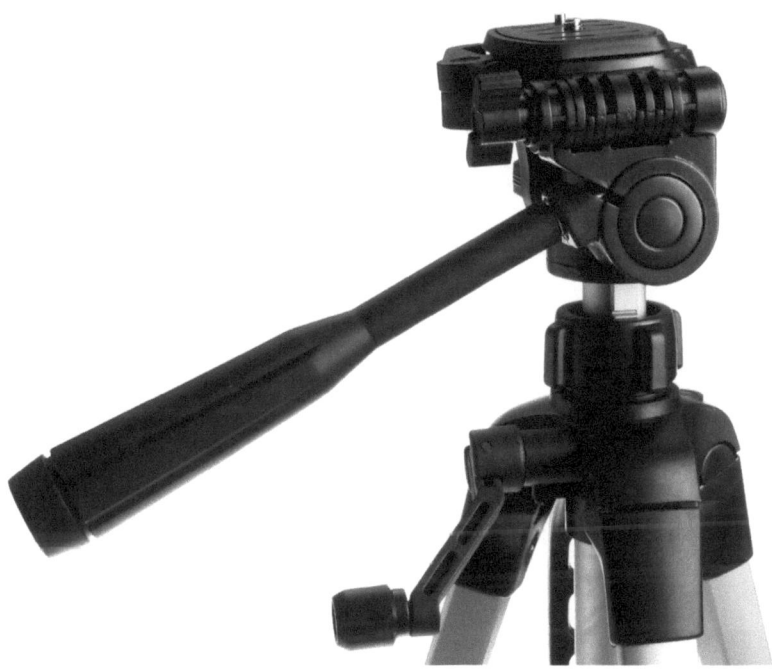

**Fluid Heads** are used in the professional film and video business. The fluid in the head provides dampening and reduces vibration allowing extremely smooth movement in two axes. They are usually more expensive because they are sold separately from the tripod legs. Below is a picture of the Magnus VPH-10 2 Way Pan/Tilt Fluid Head

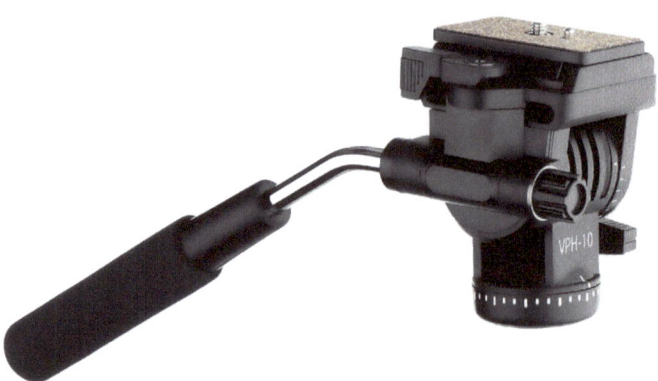

**Ball Heads** are designed to maneuver in almost 360-degrees of rotation.  Despite the fact that they do not offer pan and tilt capabilities, they offer quick and easy adjustment of the camera's position. Below is the Joby Ballhead with level and quick-release plate.

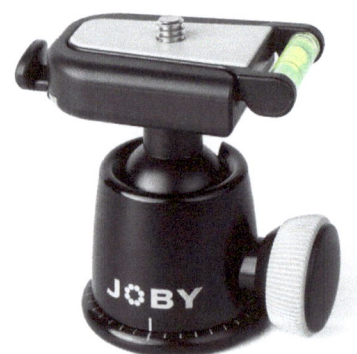

**Three Tips:**

1. To get a smooth pan with no abrupt changes in speed use an elastic band as a shock absorber.  Stretch one end around the handle of your tripod's pan head and the other around a finger.  Then begin your pan, pulling the handle with the elastic band while maintaining a uniform tension on it as you move.  The stretched elastic will absorb any changes in tension and give you a smooth pan.

2. Retract one of your tripod's legs to turn it into a quasi slider.  By tilting the tripod either forward or back on its two legs, you can slide the camera in for a close-up, or back for a pull out.

3. Fold up the legs and use the tripod as a steadicam.  The weight of the tripod will help stabilize your shots as you move.

# 7 MAKE IT MOVE – Tools for moving the camera

Dolly, slider, steadicam, gimbal, jib (crane), and drones are all professional filmmaking tools used to enable the camera to get smooth shots while moving through space. What's amazing about this technology is that allows you to capture high quality professional footage with your smartphone at a very modest cost. Lets take a look how it works.

**Dolly:** A dolly is designed to create smooth horizontal movements using a wheeled platform to hold your camera. In some cases, the wheels run on a track; in others, they can move on any smooth surface. Below is a picture of a Revolve iPhone Table Top Dolly with articulating (Israeli) arm and Glif Mount.

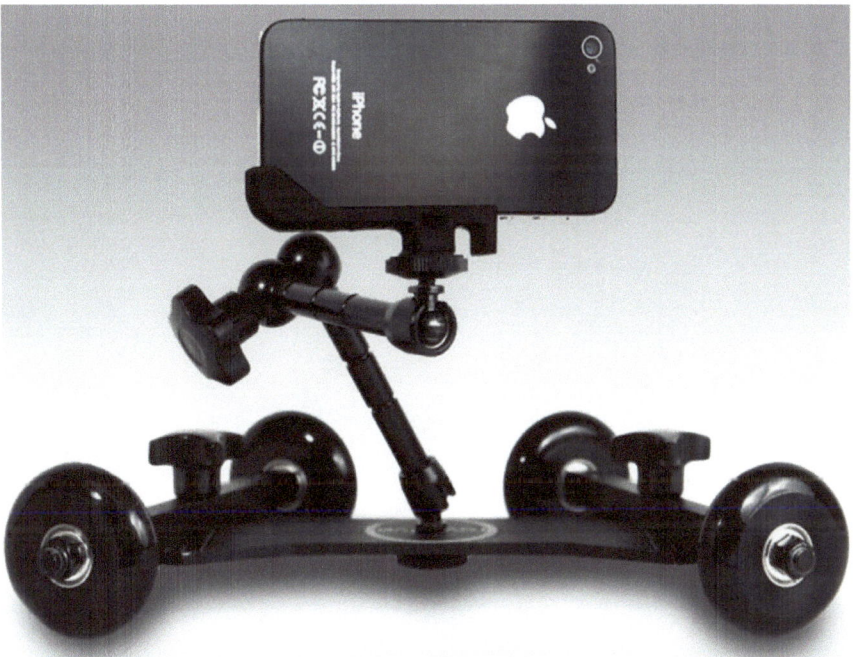

Dollies don't have to be expensive. As a matter of fact you're only limited by your imagination and resourcefulness in ways to make your own dolly. For example any wheeled device such as: a bicycle, rolling cart, wheel chair, or hand truck can be converted into a dolly using a super clamp.  The superclamp is designed to clamp onto both cylindrical and flat surfaces and allows you to attach a camera tripod mount or head, either with a threaded stud or 1/4" Male to 1/4" male threaded screw adapter.

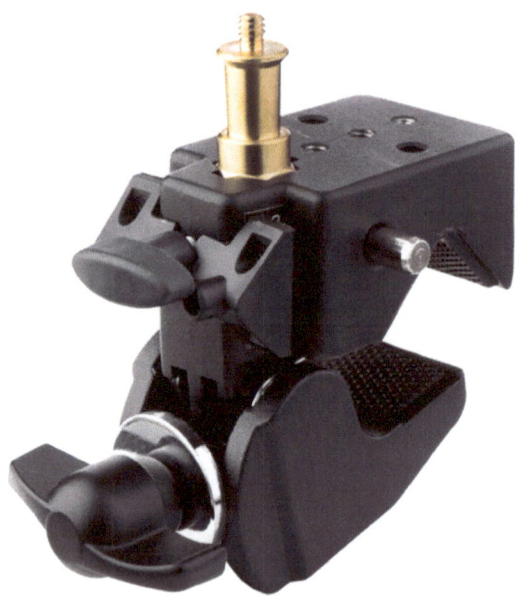

Shown above is the Impact Super Clamp with threaded Stud

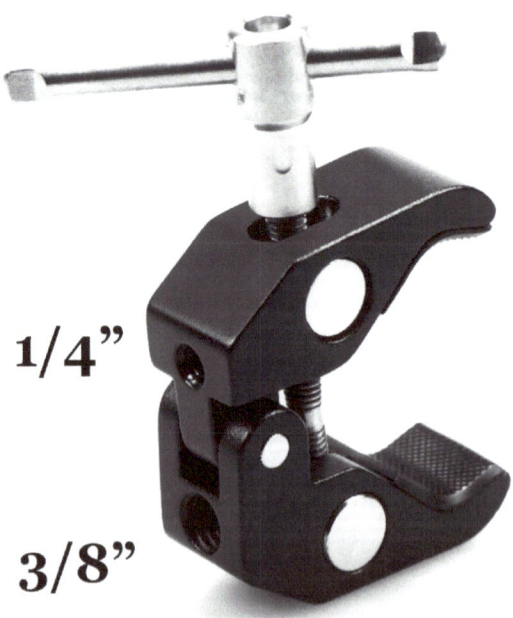

Smallrig Super Clamp with 1/4" and 3/8" threaded holes

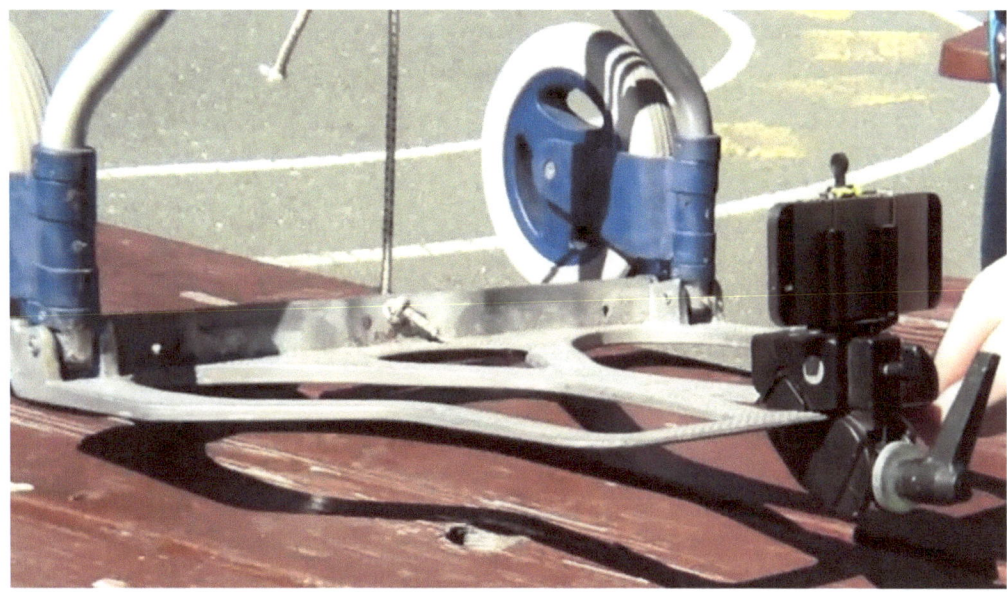

Shown above is a Do-it-yourself Dolly made with hand truck, super clamp, threaded stud, mount, and iPhone 5S

One of my favorite tools is the Joby GorillaPod. (Shown below) Using it you can attach your camera to everyday wheeled devices such as bicycles and baby carriages. It comes with stiff yet flexible legs that you can bend around just about anything.

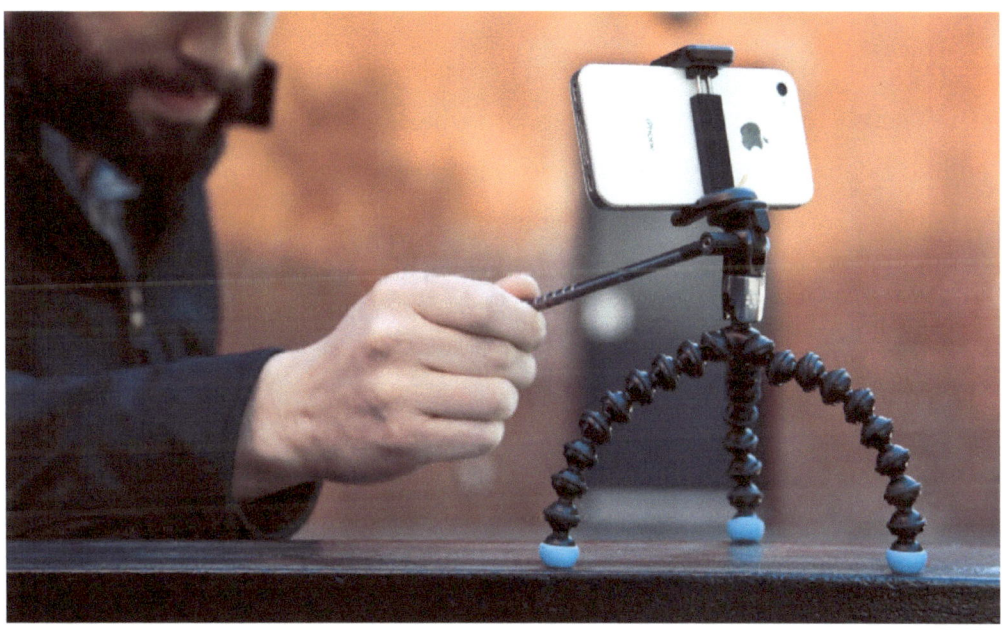

I personally like the larger SLR-Zoom version (shown below), because of its versatility of attaching wheels and suction cups to it. The SLR-Zoom comes with an adjustable ball head and a quick release mount attachment that allows me to quickly switch from my iPhone to my iPad without having to unscrew the mount.

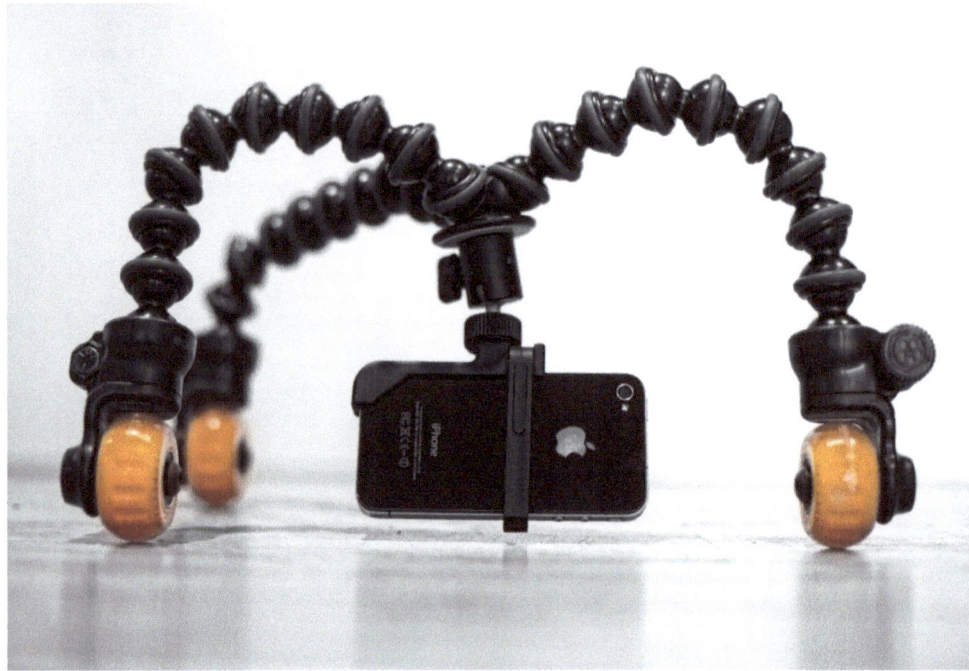

In addition, the accessories for this GorillaPod have allowed me to get some amazing moving shots. Cinetics sells a set of attachable skateboard wheels, shown above, that turn my GorilliaPod into a dolly. They also have a set of suction cups that allow me to mount my camera on any hard smooth surface, like a car windshield, the side of a boat, or even the outside of an airplane. The amazing thing about this is how inexpensive all this equipment less than $100.

Check out this video about the cinisquid, the big brother of the minisquid.

https://vimeo.com/37177985

**Sliders:** Are similar to dollies, in that they run on a track and allow smooth horizontal linear camera movement. Some are designed to sit on a flat surface like a table or sidewalk, while others are mounted on a tripod. There are even motorized sliders that allow you to program their movement. Shown below is the Glidetrack Mobislyder Portable Camera Slider.

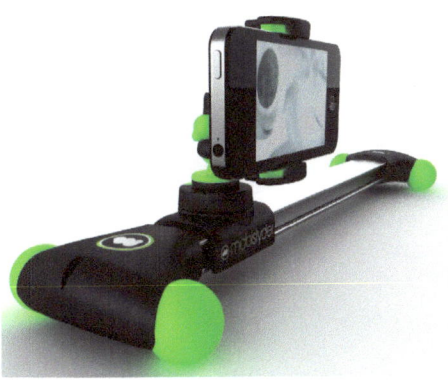

**Steadicam (Camera Stabilizer):** Steadicam is a brand that has become a generic term for a camera stabilizer. The steadicam is designed to isolate the camera from the operator's movements. It provides smooth shots even when the operator is climbing up or down stairs or moving quickly. The hand-held steadicam offers the smartphone filmmaker infinite possibilities of movement. It can crane up or down, dolly high or low, track a subject from either the side, in front, or behind giving the audience the illusion that the camera is floating in space. We've all seen the shots where two lovers kiss and the camera circles round and round them as they embrace. That's a steadicam shot. Click the link below to see the steadicam in action.

https://vimeo.com/17099117

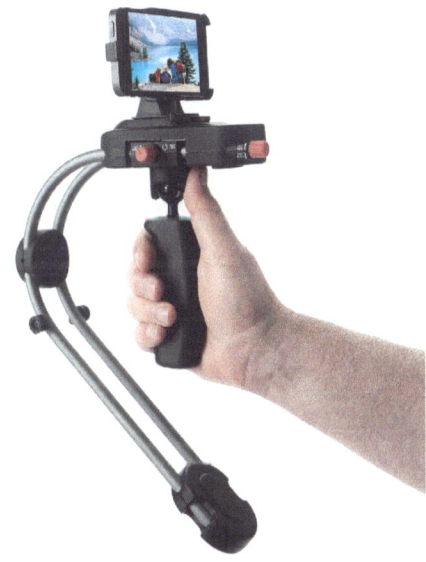

Tiffen's Steadicam Smoothee with an iPhone 5.

**3 Axis Motorized Gimbal:**  The gimbal is a computer controlled camera stabilizer that yields amazingly smooth images that appear to fly through space.  The gimbal comes with rechargeable batteries that power the internal computer and three small motors.

Turning one of these devices on is an amazing experience.  The gimbal feels lifeless and floppy in your hand until it's turned on, then it springs to life, becoming rigid and knowingly taking control of the camera by adjusting the balance and fine-tuning the level.  It's almost like it's alive.  Once activated, no matter how you move your body, the gimbal counteracts your movements.  It's rock steady.  Like the steadicam, the gimbal offers the smartphone filmmaker infinite possibilities of movement.   Here's the URL for a video of a gimbal in action.

https://vimeo.com/94567020

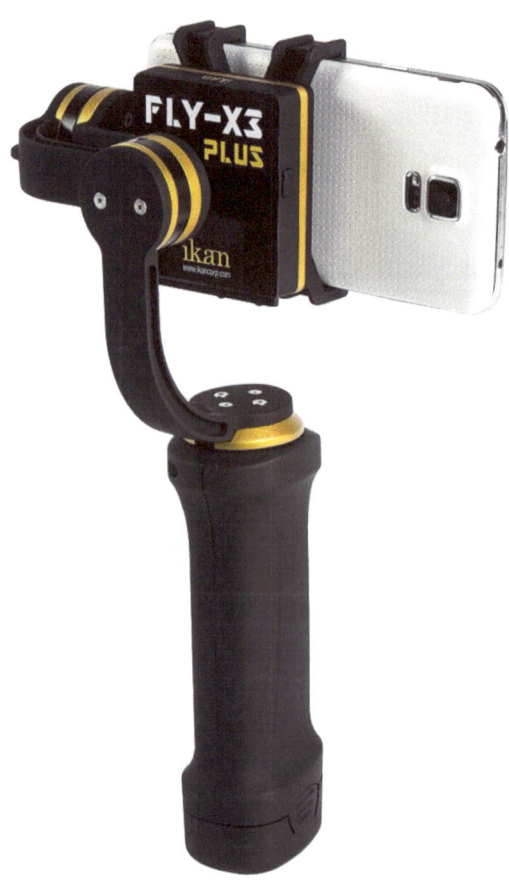

The Fly-X3-Plus Gimbal

**Camera Jib (Crane)** is a balanced arm with a camera on one end and a counter weight on the other. It works like a seesaw. The jib is usually mounted on a tripod so the operator can pivot the counter weighted camera effortlessly in any combination of vertical and horizontal movements.

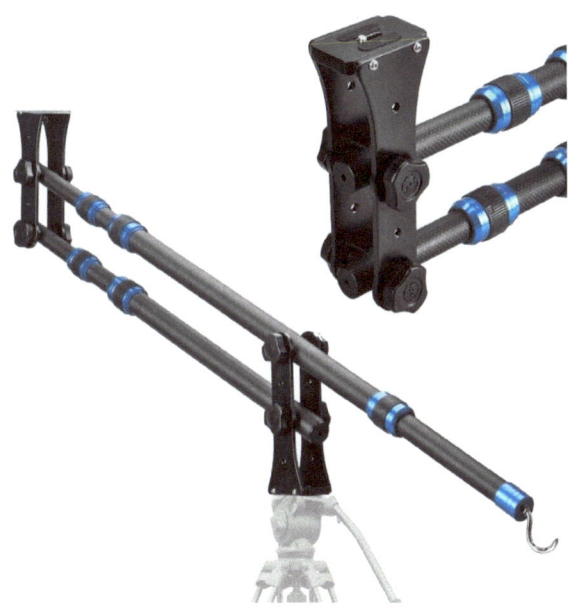

Shown above is the Fancierstudio Carbon Fiber Mini Jib Crane Portable. Once set up, the camera remains level at all times, regardless of position, because of the parallel linkage in its arms.

**Three tips:**

1. For those of you who like do-it-yourself projects, there are many instructional videos on YouTube about how to make jibs, dollies, and sliders. Here is one that I really like by Chad Bredahl.     https://www.youtube.com/watch?v=40e7T1x8s3A

2. DYI Slider. I've made a do-it-yourself slider by placing a dish towel on a table or counter, and them piling some heavy books on top of the towel to give the slider some weight and mass, then mounted my camera on top of the books using a mini tripod or gorillapod. The whole affair slides smoothly across the table, surprisingly it works quite well.

3. Another alternative is to use a monopod with a ball head attachment as a jib. The monopod can be held in one hand while shooting. Because it's so lightweight, it will require some practice to perfect your technique. But it's a low cost portable alternative.

# 8 GETTING THE SOUND IN — Understanding connectors

I never thought that I'd start a chapter about sound recording talking about connectors, but I am.  Whenever you use an external microphone, and I highly recommend that you do, you'll need a special connector for that mic, otherwise it won't work.  So let's talk about connectors and get that out of the way.

There are three ways to attach an external microphone to your smart device:

1.  Through the headset port with a 2.5mm TRS (for older phones) or 3.5mm TRRS earphone jack connector

2.  Through the phone's power/USB connector

3.  Via Bluetooth.

**Tip, Ring, Sleeve (TRS)**  Phone jack connectors are commonly used with audio equipment. They typically come with two to four contacts  (electrical connections).  The three-contact male version, shown below, is known as a **TRS** connector, where the **T** stands for "tip", **R** stands for "ring", and **S** stands for "sleeve".

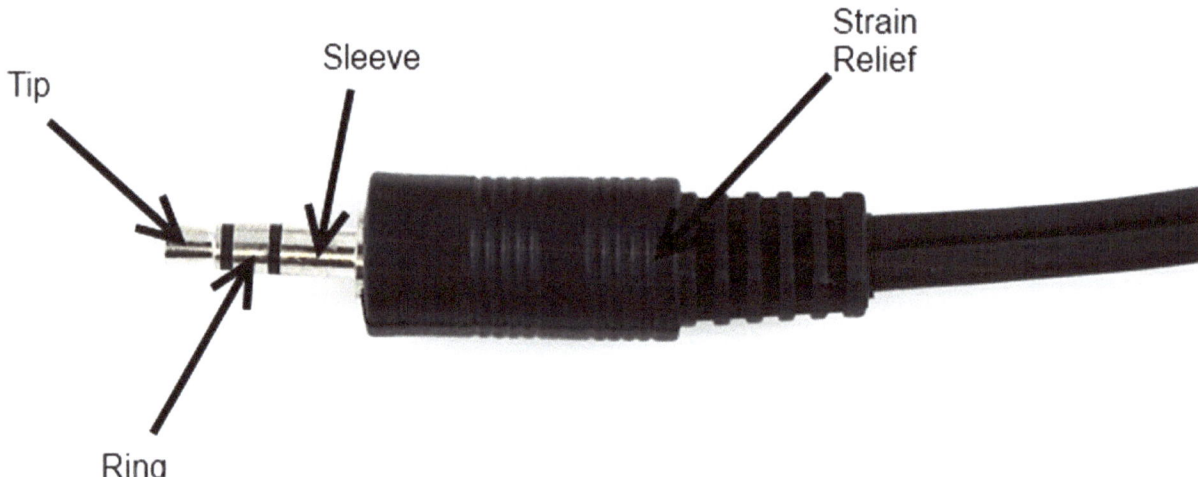

Various TRS connectors can be found for mono, stereo, or stereo headphones that include audio:

- A two contact version called **TS** used for mono connections
- A three contact version called **TRS** used for stereo connections.
- A four contact version called **TRRS** used for a combined stereo headphone, microphone, and on/off switch connections.

## All TS & TRS connectors require an adaptor when used with smartphones or tablets.

**Smartphone headset connectors:** The four-conductor 3.5mm **TRRS** jacks are common on most smartphones. They allow you to listen with stereo headphones and talk or record at the same time. They providing stereo sound and a microphone input, together with signaling (e.g., push a button to answer a call). The three-conductor 2.5 mm **TRS** connectors are particularly common on older phones, while four-conductor 3.5 mm TRRS connectors are more common on newer phones.

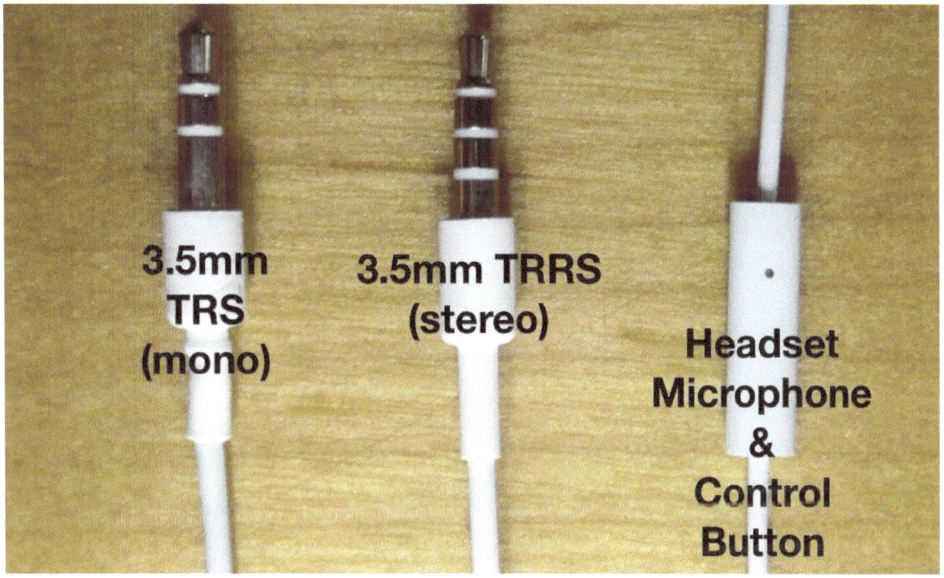

**Standard Connectors for Microphones and Headsets.** Most mics and headphones come with either mono **TS** connectors, or stereo **TRS** connectors. Shown below are different size standard phone connectors: 2.5 mm mono TS, 3.5 mm mono TS, 3.5 mm stereo TRS, and 1/4 inch TRS. ALL REQUIRE AN ADAPTOR TO WORK WITH YOUR SMARTPHONE.

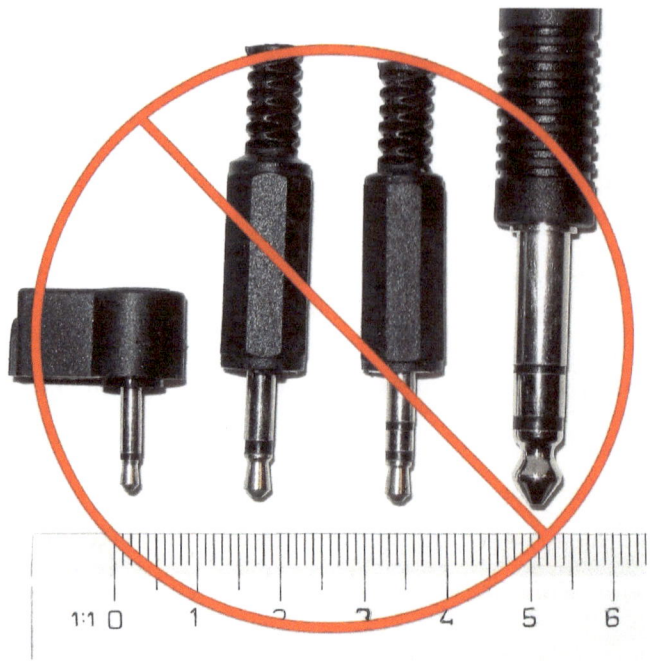

**Adapters:** You can purchase adaptors that will allow you to connect any standard phone connector such as a **TS, TRS, 1/4 inch**, or **XLR** connectors to the **3.5mm TRRS** female connector on your phone. Some adapters come with a second 3.5 TRS female end which allows you to plug in headphones so you can hear what your recording. Shown below is a 3.5mm TRRS male to 3.5 mm Headphone (TRS female) and 1/4 inch microphone (guitar) adapter.

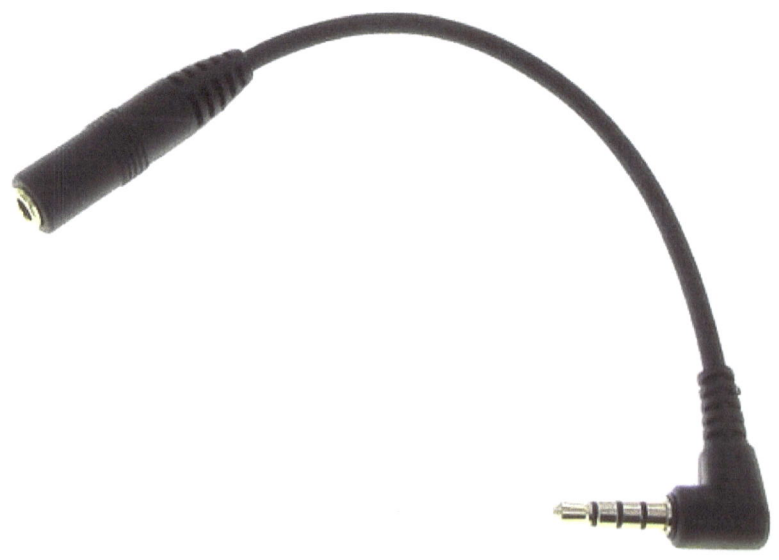

MAKE SURE THAT THE ADAPTER COMES WITH MICROPHONE IMPEDANCE MATCHING CAPABILITIES SPECIFICALLY DESIGNED FOR SMARTPHONE USE

**Extension Cables:** in addition to adapters, extension cables should be included in your smartphone sound kit.   These come in varying lengths from 3' to 12' and allow you to separate the microphone from the recording device, offering you tremendous flexibility.

If you're going to be utilizing professional audio microphones with XLR connectors, I recommend using Star-Quad type, dual twisted pair cables (Either from Canare or Beldon).

You'll still need an adapter between your microphone cable and your smart device.  The balanced cables come shielded with a twisted pair, which allows for long cable runs, while reducing or eliminating external noise and hum in the line.

**Power Port USB Adapters** allow you to connect another device like a microphone interface, USB mixer, or external hard drive, to your phone's charging port via a USB connector.  There are different kinds of connectors for the different types of smartphones and tablets. Shown below are three such adapters.

Apple lightning to USB female adapter for  iPhone 5, 6, 6+, and various iPads

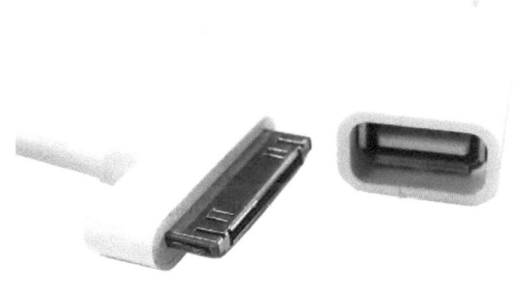

30 Pin male to USB female Adapter for older iPhone and iPad models.

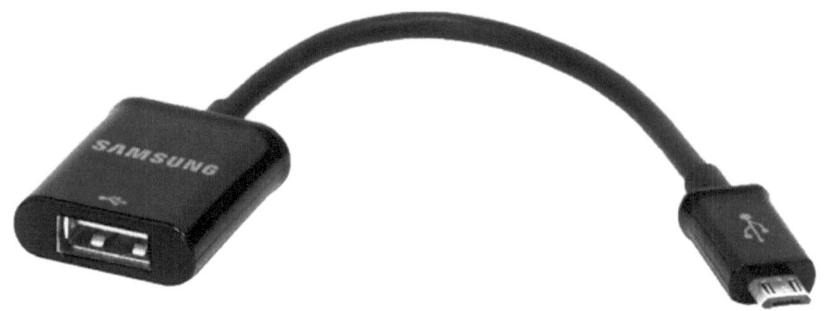

Micro USB male to USB female Adapter for Samsung phone and tablets.

**Bluetooth Wireless Connection:** To be quite honest there aren't a lot of options available in terms of either microphones or apps for utilizing Bluetooth technology for professional quality sound. A better alternative would be to use an adapter or a wireless microphone transmitter/receiver, which we'll discuss in the next chapter.

**How To Monitoring your recording.** Whenever you're recording sound, I would suggest that you monitor what's being recorded. You'd be amazed at how noisy a refrigerator or lawn mower three houses down from you can be. The best way to do this is with an adapter that has a separate headset connection capability like those shown in this chapter.

In addition to wired adapters shown above, Rode Microphones manufactures an adapter, they describe as a break-out box, that allows you to connect two of their Smartlav+ lavaliere microphones and a pair of headphones to your device through the headphone jack on phone. Shown below is the Rode SC6 Duel TRRS input and headphone output adapter for smartphones.

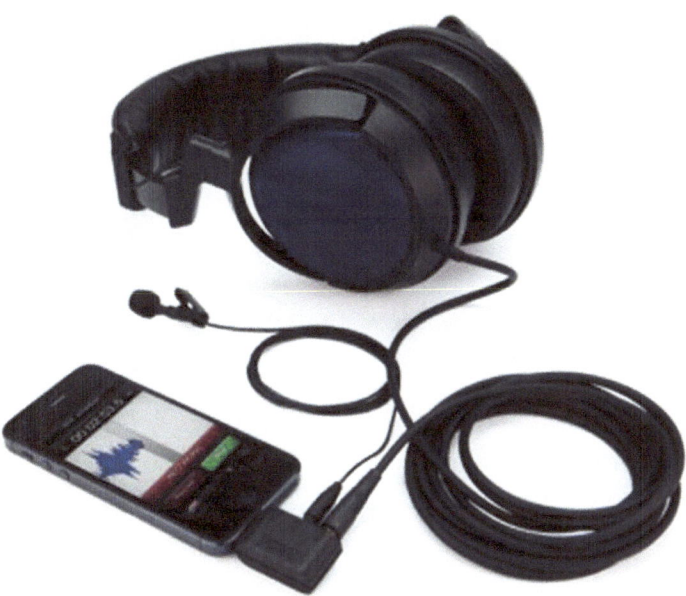

In the next chapter we'll discuss various sound recording applications, microphones, mixers, and other interfaces that allow you to utilize professional quality microphones.

**Three Tips:**

1. A good source for all types of cables and adapters for smart devices is:
http://www.kvconnection.com/

They offer a wide variety to adapters for every type of application including: External microphones, audio output, headset, and line-level recording. The website has a helpful "Mobile Device Adapter Guide" and "Adapter Selection Helper".

2. Microphone Output: It is important to understand whether your microphone's output is at mic-level or line-level. If it's line-level you'll need an adapter to "ATTENUATE" (reduce) the output signal from line-level down to mic-level for your phone. (see the chapter on Microphones for more information about different types of mics)

3. There are XLR adaptors with a Pre-Amplifier (*like the VeriCorder XLR to iPhone Adapter with Pre-Amplifier)* for your iOS devices that boosts the gain of low-impedance dynamic XLR microphones and wireless microphone receivers by 6.1 dB, thereby giving you a high quality audio source for recording on your phone.

# 9 RECORDING APPS AND MICROPHONES

There are many ways of recording sound on a smart device. Let's take a look at the apps (software applications) and the equipment. The apps first.

**Apps for Apple Devices:** iPhone, iPad, iPod. There are hundreds of audio recording apps for iOS devices. Some are designed for taking dictation, others for music composition, and a few for professional sound recording. Of those, I recommend the following:

1. The **"Camera"** application that came with your device. Be warned, there is no audio meter display or volume control. Volume is controlled automatically.

2. **Filmic Pro -** $7.99 (available on the Apple App Store) is a video application that has an audio gain (volume) level control and audio meter. It offers multiple compressed and uncompressed from 44.1 kHz to 48.0 kHz. It doesn't have audio editing capability.

3. **Garage Band -** sound recording and music editing application. It comes free with your phone or tablet.

4. **TwistedWave Editing App $9.99** (available on the Apple App Store) It offers real-time waveform display and volume level control as well as a variety of editing options to: amplify or normalize the sound level; fade in and out, trim, paste, and copy; and various filters to adjust levels and frequencies. It offers multiple audio formats from 8.0 kHz to 96.0 kHz. Shown below is TwistedWave Audio Editor screen showing duel waveform display, audio meter, and editing icons.

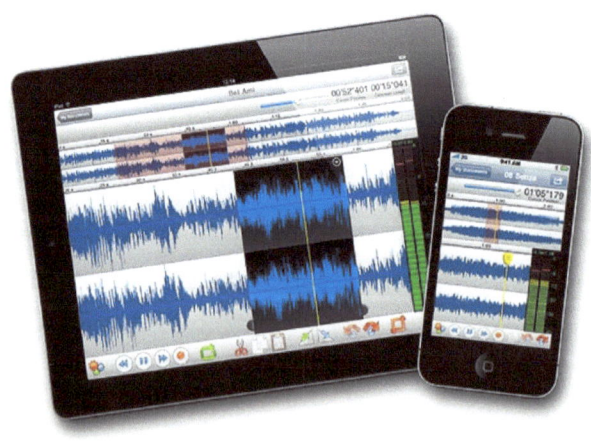

**APPS FOR ANDROID & WINDOW PHONE AND TABLET :**   (For more information go to the Google Play)

- Use the **"Camera"** app that came with your phone or tablet.  Be warned, there maybe no control over the audio's volume level or and audio meter display.

- Use the **Audio Recorder** on your phone as separate recorder.

- **RECForge II - $3.99**   It offers real-time waveform display and volume level control.  It offers multiple audio formats from 8.0 kHz to 48.0 kHz.

- **nTrack Studio - Recording audio with Android - $6.99**  Multi-Track recorder, records up to four devices simultaneously, requires android compatible USB device adapter.

- **WavePad** Audio Editor Free  - Sound Recording and Editing Software on Google Play. It offers real-time waveform display and volume level control as well as a variety of editing options to:  amplify or normalize the sound level; echo, fade in and out, trim, paste, and copy; and various filters to adjust levels and frequencies.  It offers multiple audio formats from 8.0 kHz to 44.1 kHz.

**Microphones:**  Starting with the basics, let's look at microphones.

**Built-in Microphone:**  using the built-in microphone on your phone or tablet is a fast and simple solution for sound recording.  The problem with this approach is quality. More than likely, your camera and the microphone will be located some distance from your subject. If the microphone is not located within 6" to 18" to your subject's mouth, the sound quality is going to suffer.  You'll be forced to increase the recording volume, thereby picking up more of the surrounding ambience, which probably includes: lawn mowers, refrigerators, airplanes, and barking dogs.

An external microphone with an extension cable, or even a separate dedicated recorder, can solve this problem. (*See the chapter,"Put Your Hands Together" for more details.*)

**External Microphones** come in all shapes and sizes, but they all can be reduced to two basic types:
- Dynamic microphones that requiring no external power
- Condenser microphones require power to operate, either with a battery powered or by

phantom powered. *(usually by an independent power supply, providing 48 Volts DC).* Phantom Power is used in professional audio equipment to power condenser type lavaliere, cardioid, and shotgun microphones. It's called "Phantom Power" because it works invisibly by sending DC power to the microphone using the same cable that carries the audio signal. Phantom power is used in conjunction with balanced XLR connectors and cables, which allow long cable runs without creating any hum or static in the line. Phantom power can be provided by a special adaptor, separate power supply, pre-amp, or mixer.

Shown below is the Tascam iXZ Mic & Guitar Interface for Smartphones. It is a Portable adapter that provides 48 volt phantom power. It accepts XLR & 1/4" phone connectors and has a 3.5mm TRRS male jack for connection to a smart device. It runs off of two AA batteries.

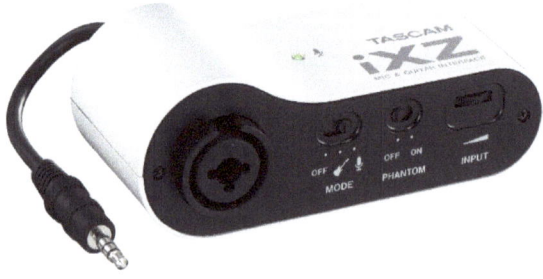

The Behringer Q502USB 5-Channel Mixer shown below has a built-in USB Interface, connects to your iPad or Tablet using a USB adapter and requires a power cable to operate

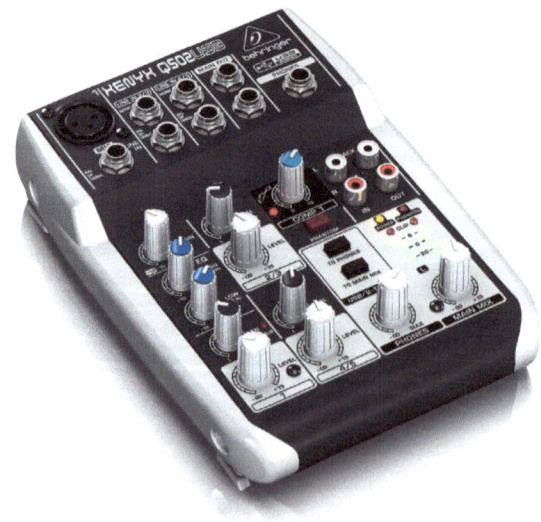

**Microphone pick-up patterns.** Microphones are designed to have a directional sensitivity to sound arriving at different angles to its pick-up axis.   Shown in the illustrations below as a polar pattern, which illustrates the directionality or sensitivity of the microphone to sounds arriving at different angles about in central axis).   Microphones vary in how much sound they pick up from their sides and back.   It should be pointed out that unlike a camera's lens, the microphone cannot limit its field of view, and regardless of it pickup pattern, they cannot completely block out or eliminate unwanted sounds, regardless of its pickup pattern.

The most important concept about sound recording is this:  the closer you get the microphone to the sound source the higher the sound quality will be.  Sometimes, especially when filming dramatic projects, it will be important to keep the mic out of the shot; that's exactly where understanding a microphone's pickup pattern can help you.

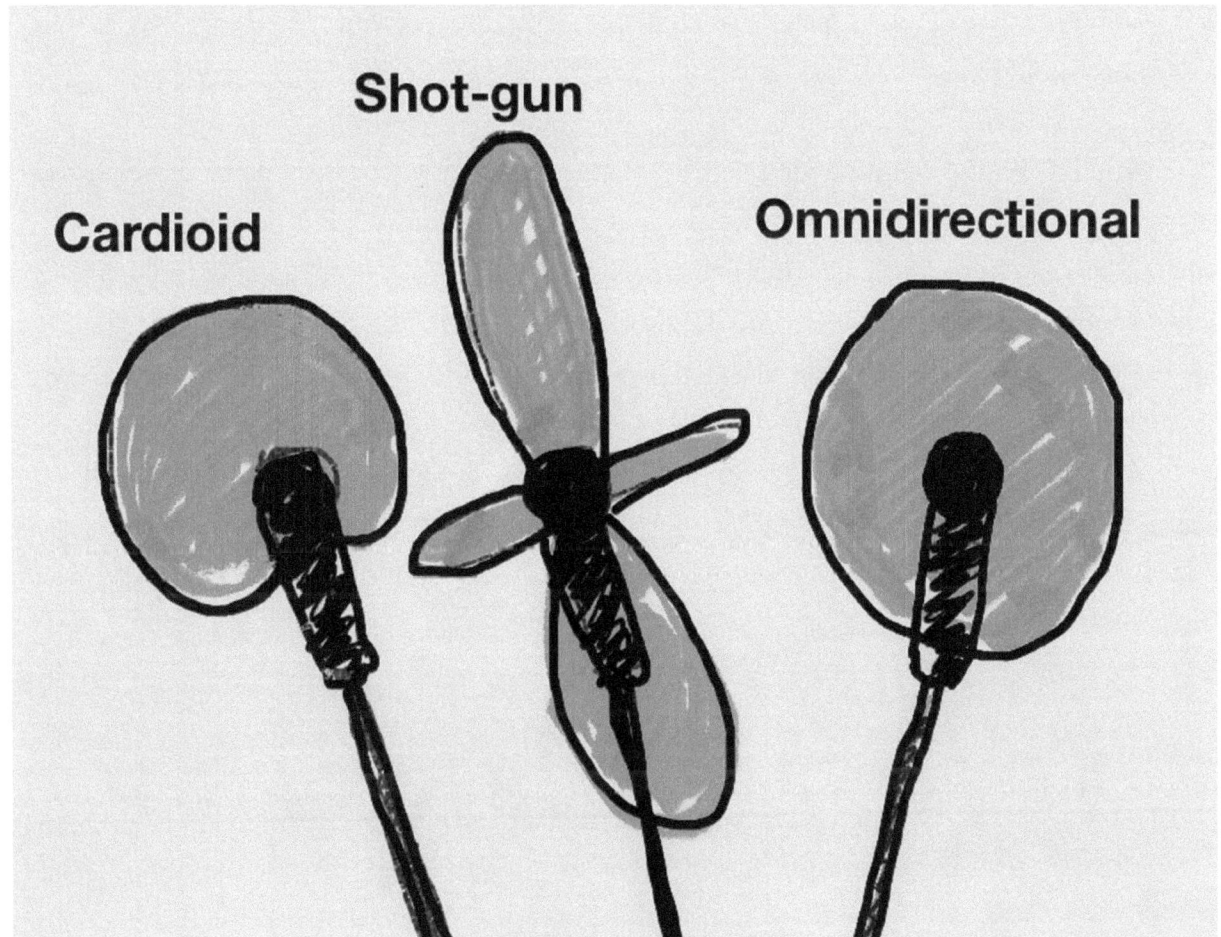

**Microphone patterns:**

• Cardioid (heart shaped): greatly reduces sound coming from the rear of the microphone, while also lowering the sensitivity to sound coming from the sides.

• Shot-gun: is extremely sensitive to sound coming from directly in front and behind it, with-in a narrow angle of view, while greatly reducing sound coming from the sides. Usually used in conjunction with a boom pole.

• Omni Directional: picks up sound coming from every direction. (many lavaliere mics have an Omni pattern, allowing them to be placed upside down, slightly to the side, or above, if necessary. This mic works best in close proximity to the sound source.

Choosing the right microphone depends on the situation, but the list is pretty short:

• Cardioid pattern for most indoor studio work using a boom pole.

• Shot guns mic for both studio or outside work, especially when you need to limit the sound coming from the surrounding environment.

• Lavaliere mics are primarily used for interviews, presentations, and other applications or where you need a small inconspicuous microphone. They are frequently used with wireless transmitters and receivers.


**Dynamic microphones** work via electromagnetic induction, which is the same principle as a loudspeaker in reverse. They require no external power, are relatively inexpensive, and very tough. They can be connected to your phone with an extension cable and adapter. When used some distance from your phone, it is advisable to use balanced microphone cables. (*see the "Getting the Sound In" chapter for more information*)

AKG - D5 Supercardioid Handheld Dynamic Microphone below has a supercardioid polar pattern that reduces sound coming from the sides and rear of the microphone. It uses XLR connectors, so you'll need a XLR to TRRS adapter to connect this mic to your smart device.

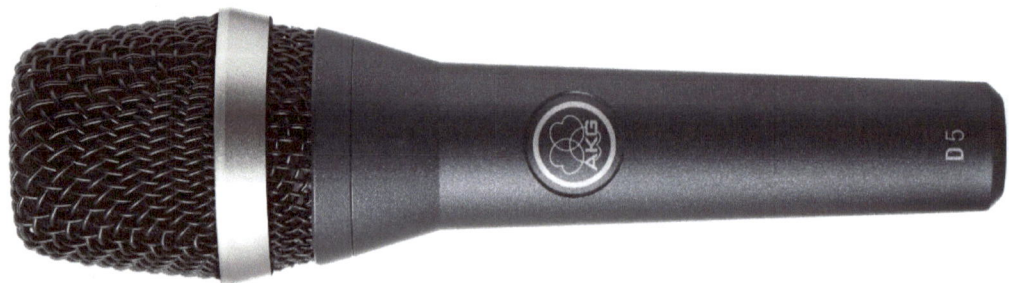

The major issue with dynamic microphones is their low sensitivity. They need to be held close to the sound source.  They are great for musicians and singers because they offer tremendous volume control.  They are also used as a handheld interview microphone,  but as soon as you need to move the mic out of the shot and away from the sound source, you'll need to use a condenser type microphone that will offer you greater sensitivity and reach.

**Lavaliere Mics** (lapel mic):  are small inconspicuous microphones that get attached to a person's clothing to record their voice.  Most have an Omni directional pattern, allowing them to be placed anywhere in close proximity to a sound source.  They allow hands-free operation and are located 6 to 8 inches away from the speaker's mouth, providing excellent sound quality. Because of their small size, it's a great microphone for hiding either in an actors clothing, on a prop like a vase of flowers, or a car's sun visor.

Lavaliere mics come in all flavors.  Some like the Rode SmartLav+ are a dynamic type, which doesn't require a power source, and comes a male TRRS connector so it can be connected directly to your smart device.  I especially like the Rode SmartLav+, shown below, because it is well made, works great, and is not as expensive as other professional microphones costing hundreds of dollars.

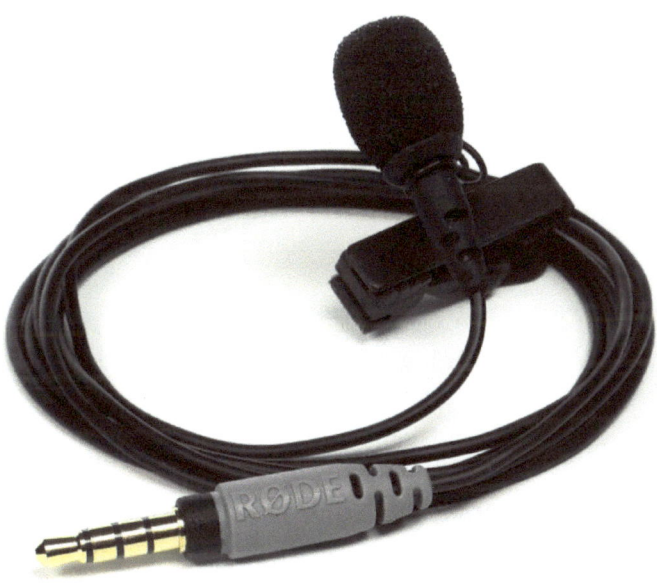

The Audio-Technica ART3350 shown below, is an inexpensive mic that uses a small button battery to provide internal power and requires an TRS to TRRS adapter.

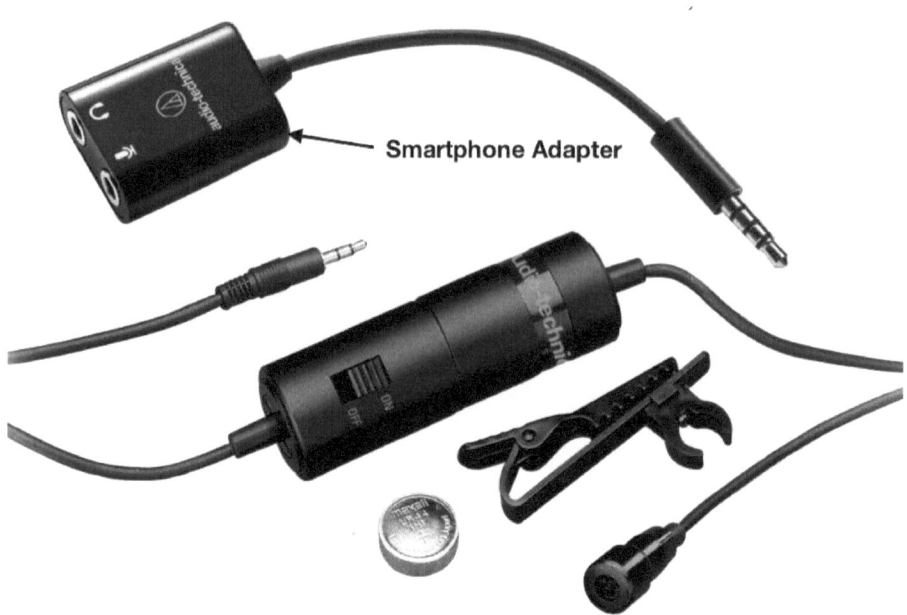

If you have the money, purchasing a professional microphone can be a great investment. Good microphones don't go out of style or get replaced by newer ones. Some of the best microphones have been around for decades. You'll find that they are a sound investment that will last year after year.

Profession lavaliere microphones are expensive and need phantom power to operate. They are either used with a power supply or with a wireless transmitter. When used in conjunction with a power supply they are called wired lavs. The wired lav is connected to a recorder, mixer, or interface like the Tascam iXZ interface, which provides phantom power to drive the mic.

**Wireless Microphone Transmitters**: Wireless systems allow the user tremendous flexibility in movement. The subject being mic'd is not tied to one location by a cable, but is free to move around at will. Wireless systems are often used in conjunction with lavaliere microphones. Once the lav is attached to a persons clothing, the mic's cable is hidden from view by running the cable under a shirt or jacket to the transmitter, which is clipped onto the subject's belt or pocket. The receiver is attached to the camera or a separate recorder. Below is the Audio Technica Pro88W-R35 Wireless system with Lav microphone.

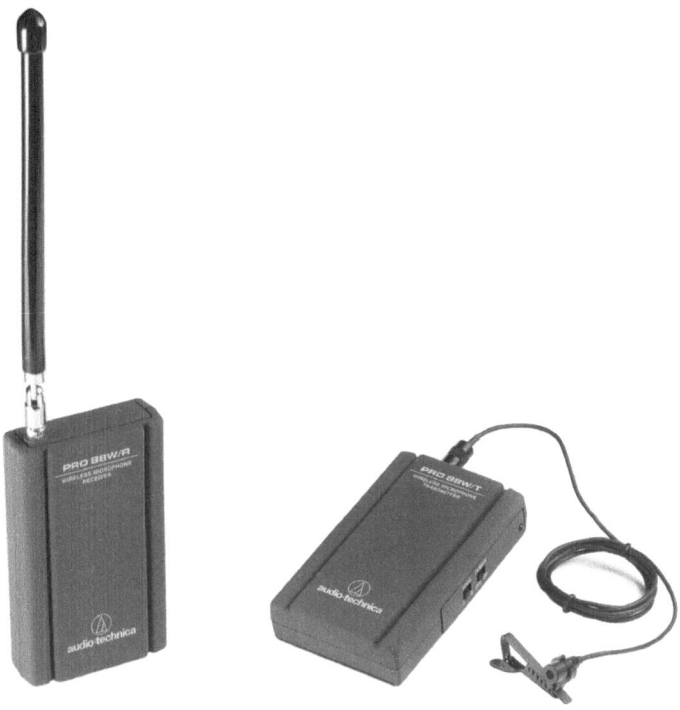

**Condenser Microphones:** Condenser mics are very sensitive to handling noises, and are usually held in a shock mount that helps reduce unwanted noise from vibration that could be transmitted through a mic stand or boom pole to the microphone. Below is an Auray DUSM-1 Universal Microphone Shock Mount that can be attached to a mic stand or boom pole.

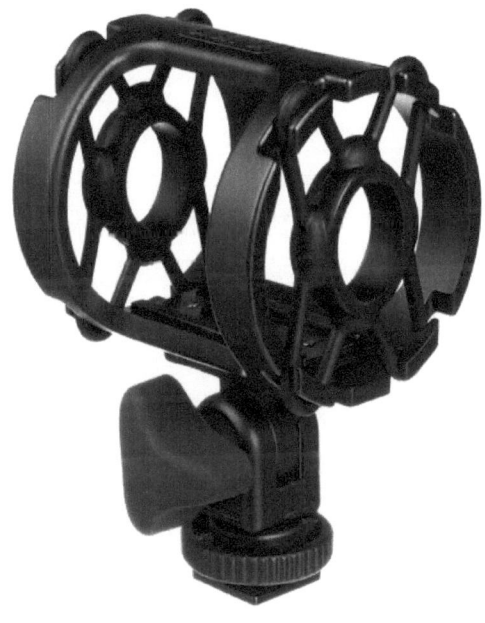

The most commonly used microphones used in video and film production are the cardioids, especially the hyper-cardioid, and the shot-gun.  Both are mounted on a boom pole and held either above pointing down, or below pointing up, at the subject's mouth.  Below is a photo titled "Tournage de film" by PRA (2007) showing a boom operator in action.

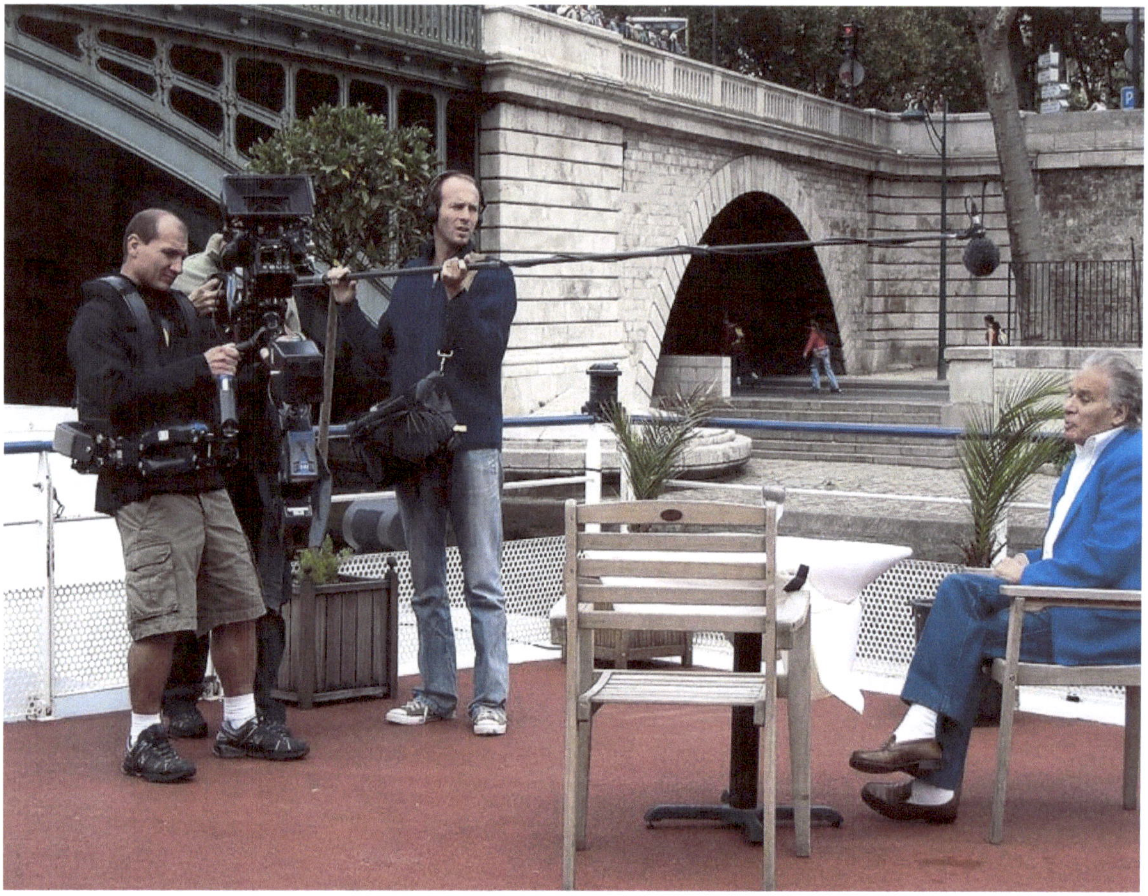

Two moderately priced professional mics I recommend are the Rode NTG-2 Shotgun Microphone that can powered by a battery or phantom power.  It requires XLR connectors and a separate shock mount.

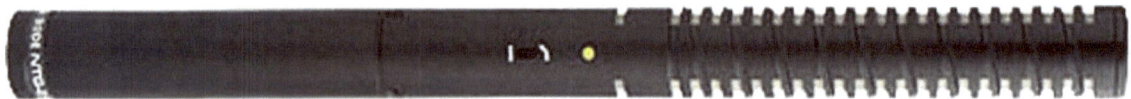

The other is the Oktava MK-012 Microphone kit which comes with a body and screw-on Omni, Cardioid, and Hypercardioid Capsules

It requires a shock mount and phantom power and uses XLR connectors and cables.

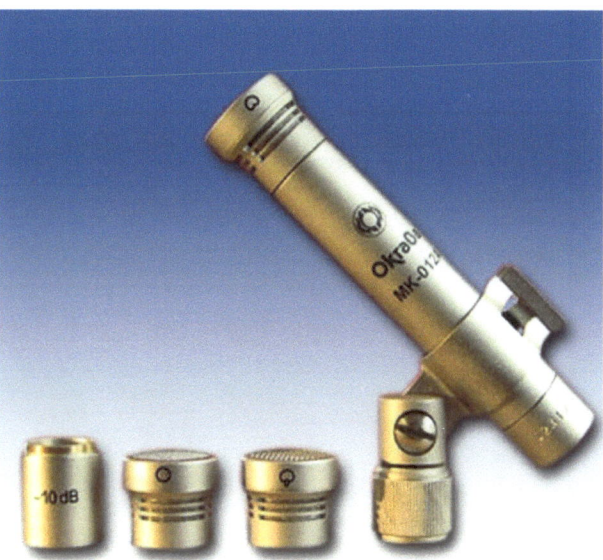

If you're recording outdoors, there are additional items that you'll need for your mic, such as boom pole, foam windscreen, windshield or blimp and other accessories.

**Three Tips:**

1. When hiding lavalieres be aware of the possibility of clothing noise whenever your subject moves.  Here are two excellent videos about hiding mics to get you started.

https://www.youtube.com/watch?v=_sNve5rNAMI

http://youtu.be/D85HmR825wM

2. Using a foam windscreen with a condenser microphones can help reduce wind noise.  In outdoor applications, you'll need to consider using a blimp or windshield with a cover called a dead cat or windjammer over your microphone to reduce wind noise.

3. Monitoring audio is essential if you want the highest quality sound.  Consider purchasing a pair of professional quality headphones for that purpose.

# 10 PUT YOUR KEYS IN THE FREEZER

It's amazing just how loud a refrigerator can be!  If you don't believe me, connect a set of headphones to a smartphone recording app and listen.  Below is a photo titled Koelkast Open taken by  Michael Gebruiker (1972)

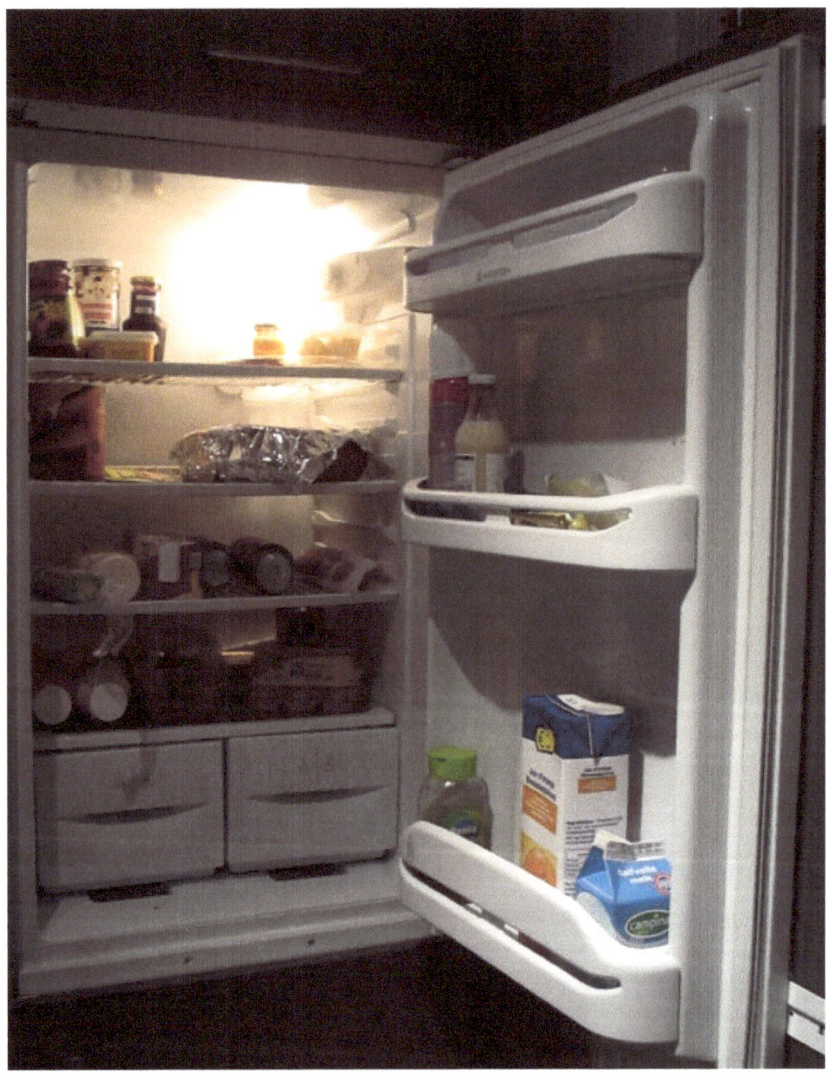

Nothing is more annoying... more of a turn-off...  than a noisy sound track. We hear selectively. A good microphone doesn't.  Put on a pair of headphone and you'll hear every buzz, hum, bleep, bark, fire engine siren, and lawnmower within five blocks.  Don't kid yourself, getting good sound is one of the most important things you can do to improve your movies.

I worked with one beginning director who insisted on filming on the roof of a city parking garage surrounded on all sides by other buildings, each with its own roof top ventilation system. The hum of the fans was so loud you could barely hear the actor's dialog. "We'll take the hum out in post," he told me. Little did he know, you can't get rid of noise like that without also ruining the dialog as well, no matter how many filters you apply.

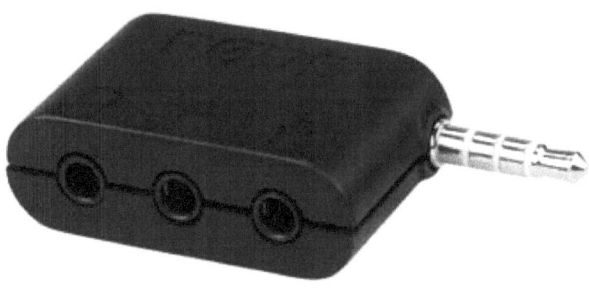

Monitoring the sound you're recording is crucial. One tool I highly recommend is a nifty little gadget called, The Rode SC6 Dual TRRS Input and Headphone Output connector for Smartphones, that will allow you to plug in both a microphone and headphones at the same time. It has two TRRS inputs and one stereo headphone output. It connects to any TRRS device, such as your smartphone, and allows you to use one or two microphones with TRRS connectors while providing a headphone jack for monitoring your recording session and playback. (Note that the two microphone inputs will be recorded to the one mono channel)

**Three Tips about what to do:**

1. Scout out your locations before you shoot. Pay special attention to any potential sound issues you might need to deal with. If it's too noisy, use a different location or plan on re-recording the dialog ("dubbing") in the studio separately.

2. Shut off the refrigerator, air conditioner, answering machine, cell phones, fluorescent lights, or any other equipment that can make noise.

3. Put your keys in the freezer when you shut off the refrigerator. Later, after director calls, *"it's a wrap"*, and everyone is rushing to pack-up and split, you can't leave until you retrieve your keys and turn the refrigerator back on, so the food won't spoil.

## 11. PUT YOU'RE HANDS TOGETHER — The double sound system

Recording quality sound is crucial.  Fifty percent of your movie is the sound and not the picture. Nothing will ruin a movie viewing experience quicker than bad sound.  If you can't hear the dialog, or you hear extraneous noises like an airplane or a barking dog, those distracting sounds will stop most viewers from enjoying your movie.

There is a difference between a how a camera records pictures and how a microphone records sound.  The camera can isolate the subject within the picture frame, eliminating everything else that happens to be outside of it, even if it's inches away.  You can film a close-up of a love scene and all the camera will record is the lovers.  The camera does not see the ten lighting stands scattered around the set, or the crew silently standing just out of frame.  With a camera you have complete control of isolating the image from its surroundings.  Below is a photo titled "They Shot a Movie Once" taken by Hobvias Sudoneighm (2007)  that illustrates the chaos of a movie set.

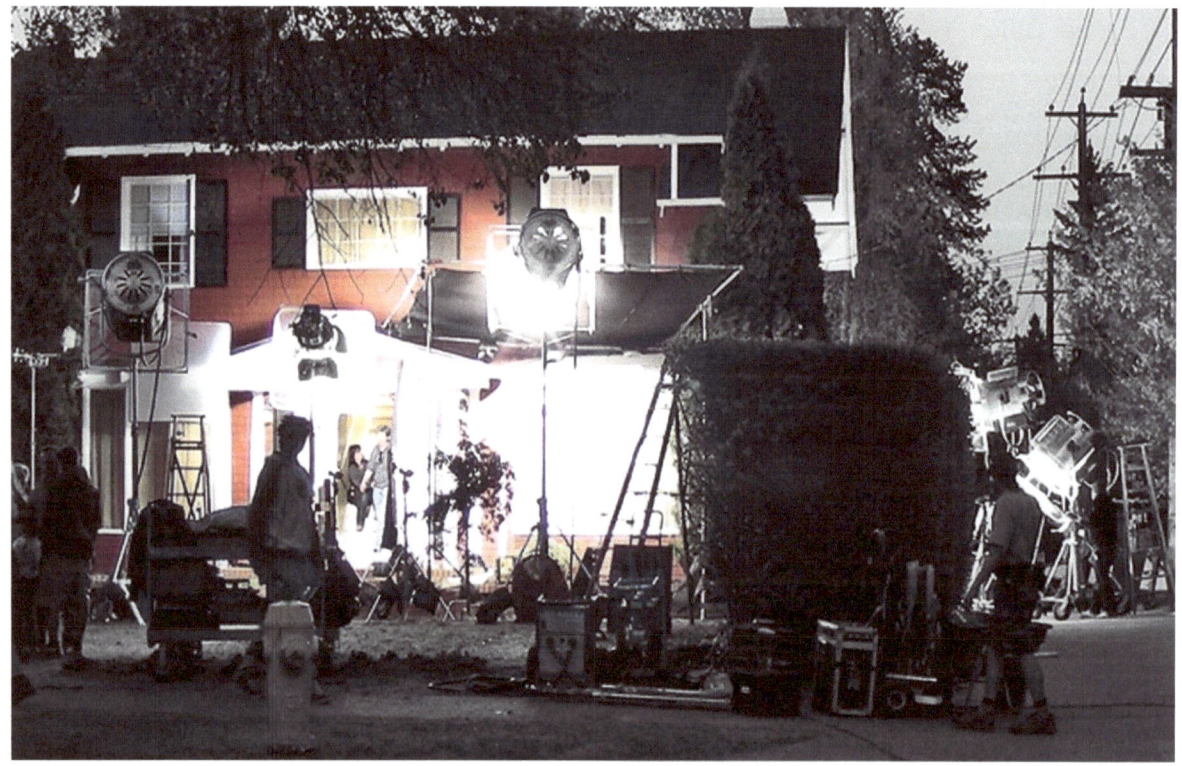

A microphone doesn't work that way. It can't isolate the subject from the background, it hears everything! Not even shotgun microphones can eliminate background noise. Let me say that again, because too many people don't get it — Your microphone hears everything.

Not only that, but the further your subject is from your phone's mic, the less able it is to capture good sound. You can't zoom-in with a microphone, like you can with a camera. The mic needs to be as close to the subject as possible. The further away the mic is from the subject, the lower the quality of the sound recorded, and the greater the chance of contaminating the recording with unwanted ambient sounds.

**Bottom-Line: Get your mic close as you can to your subject!** *Warning technical explanation ahead.* Sound observes the *inverse-square law,* which states that the volume of a sound source is inversely proportional to the square of the distance that the sound travels from it source. Sound recorded by a microphone placed two feet away from a sound source is four times softer. Three feet away it's nine times softer.

The further away the mic is from the sound source, the high the recording level needed, and the greater its ability to record unwanted sounds at that higher level. Get as close as you can to your subject with your mic.

In the previous chapters we've discussed how to connect a microphone and a pair of headphones to your smartphone or tablet so you can monitor and record audio at the same time.

In addition to the Rode SC6 or an adapter with a headphone jack, I would recommend purchasing a few 12 ft extension cables for your microphones. *(For more information about audio cables see the chapter on Getting the Sound In).*

**The Double Sound System:** One technique that Hollywood uses to get clear clean sound is the *double sound system.* In the *double sound system,* the microphone and its recording device are physically separate from the camera. The sound separately from the picture and joined together later in the editing process.

Here's how it works: A clapper, two sticks, your hands, or a Movie Clapper app you can load onto you phone or tablet can be used to make a clapping sound, which is captured by both the camera and the audio recorder simultaneously. This enables the editor to synchronize the sound and picture back together in the editing process.

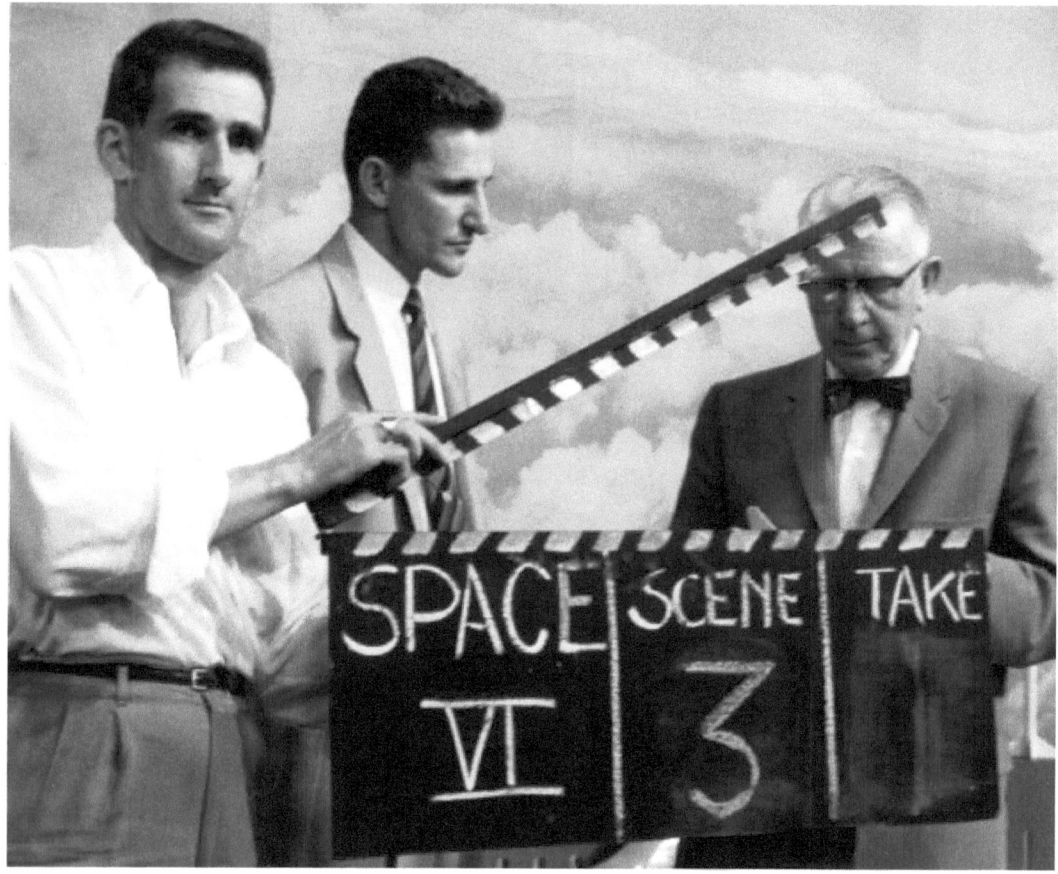

The clapping device needs to be recorded by both the camera and audio recorder at the beginning of each take.   Here's how it's done in Hollywood:

1. The cameraman and sound recordist start recording both sound and video.

2. The camera man announces, "Rolling  camera". And the sound recordist says, "Rolling sound".

3. Now, an assistant steps into the shot, holding the clapper, a pair of sticks, or his hands up in front of the camera.  Recorded by the camera, the clapper shows the specific scene, shot, and take.

4. The assistant then announces, "the scene #, shot #, and take number for the sound recording and then brings the clappers together, making a sharp slapping sound.

5. The assistant steps out of the scene and the director says, "action."

6. At the end of a take both camera and recorder are stopped.  The whole process is repeated for each new take.

7. The sound and picture are synchronized in the editing process by lining up the frame

showing the clapper closing and the sharp single spike in the soundtrack's wave form, shown below.

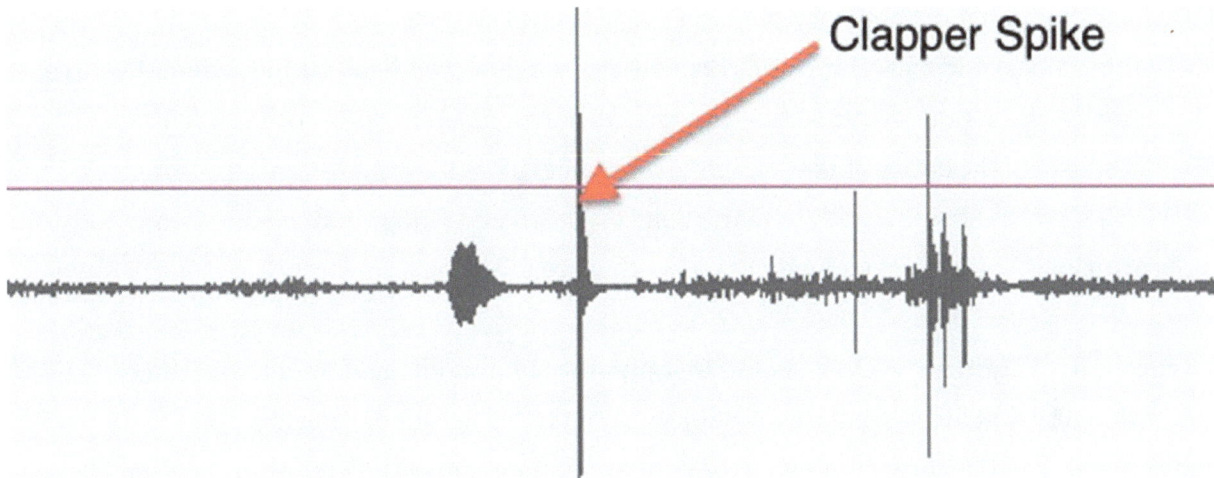

If you'll be using the double sound system for recording, get someone besides the camera-man to record and monitor the sound. You'll need someone with a set of headphones who can carefully listen to the quality of the sound being recorded. Getting volunteers is easier than you'd think. You'd be surprised at how easy it is to solicit volunteers to help you make your movie.

# 12. LIGHTING

Understanding how to light a scene is one of the most powerful tools you have at your disposal. Lighting effects what the audience sees and feels. It is a key aspect visual story telling. There are both technical and a psychological considerations in how you light for the different genres like; comedy, drama, suspense, selfies, interviews, horror, and shooting with a green screen. First let's discuss the basics of how to light, and then explore how to utilize it in our movies.

Whether you're shooting with a smartphone or a high end Hollywood movie camera, the basic principals and type of equipment for lighting are the same.

**Three Point Lighting** — Light is used to sculpt the subject, giving it weight and three dimensionality that helps separate the subject from the background. One, two, and three point lighting, refers to the number of lights used to illuminate a subject. Three point lighting has been used in movies since the beginning of film. The instruments used have changed over time, but the basic principals remain the same. Below is a diagram showing the relationship between the key, fill, back light, and camera in a three point lighting scheme.

**Key light** — serves as the main lighting source, and is usually greater in intensity than the other two sources. The intensity, angle and direction, and color of the key establishes the character of the lighting design. Indoors the key is usually a tungsten, LED, or fluorescent lighting fixture (also called a lighting instrument). Outdoors the sun often is the key light. Metallic or white reflectors are sometime used to direct the light for fill and back light.

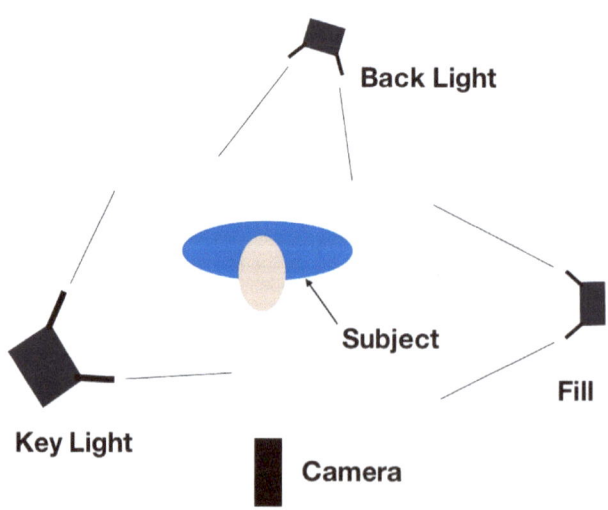

**Fill light** – illuminates the subject from the side opposite the key light and is used to fill in the shadow side of the subject. Many times a white or metal reflector is used instead of another lighting fixture to bounce the key light back onto the subject, allowing a softer lighting effect. The amount of fill varies depending on how great a contrast ratio the filmmaker desires in the scene. The lower the intensity of the fill relative to the key, the greater is the contrast ratio. Sitcoms and comedies typically used a high key 1.5:1 or 2:1 contrast ratio as opposed to drama that might use a 4:1 or higher ratio. The advantage of using high key lighting scheme, in a sitcom or comedy, is that it doesn't require adjustment between scenes. The disadvantage is the loss of expression. Below is still from the comedy TV series All in the Family (1971-1979) notice the high 2:1 contrast ratio.

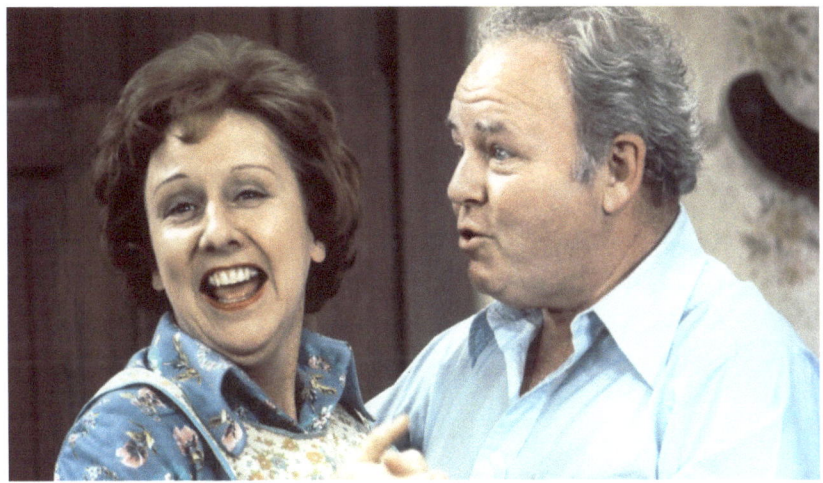

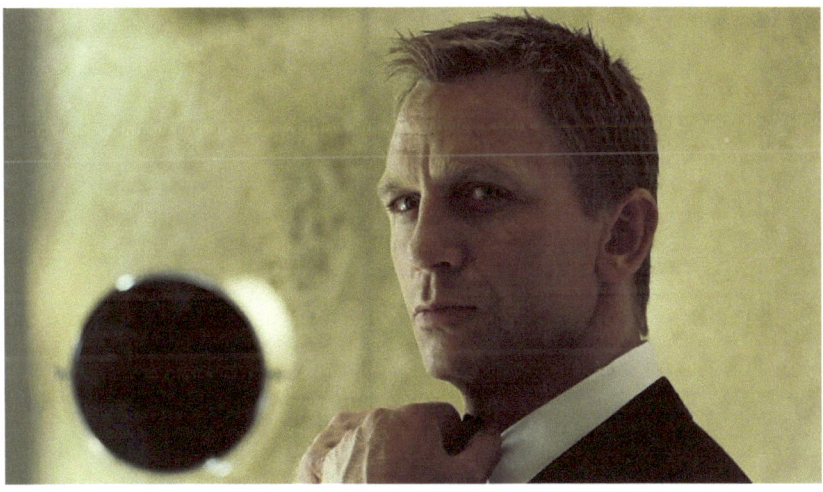

*The photo from the (2006) Bond movie Casino Royale. Notice the low 8:1 Contrast Ratio.*

**Back light** (a.k.a. rim, hair, or shoulder light) – shines on the subject from behind, often on the opposite side of the key,  it helps to define and separate the subject from the background as in this photo of Marlene Dietrict.

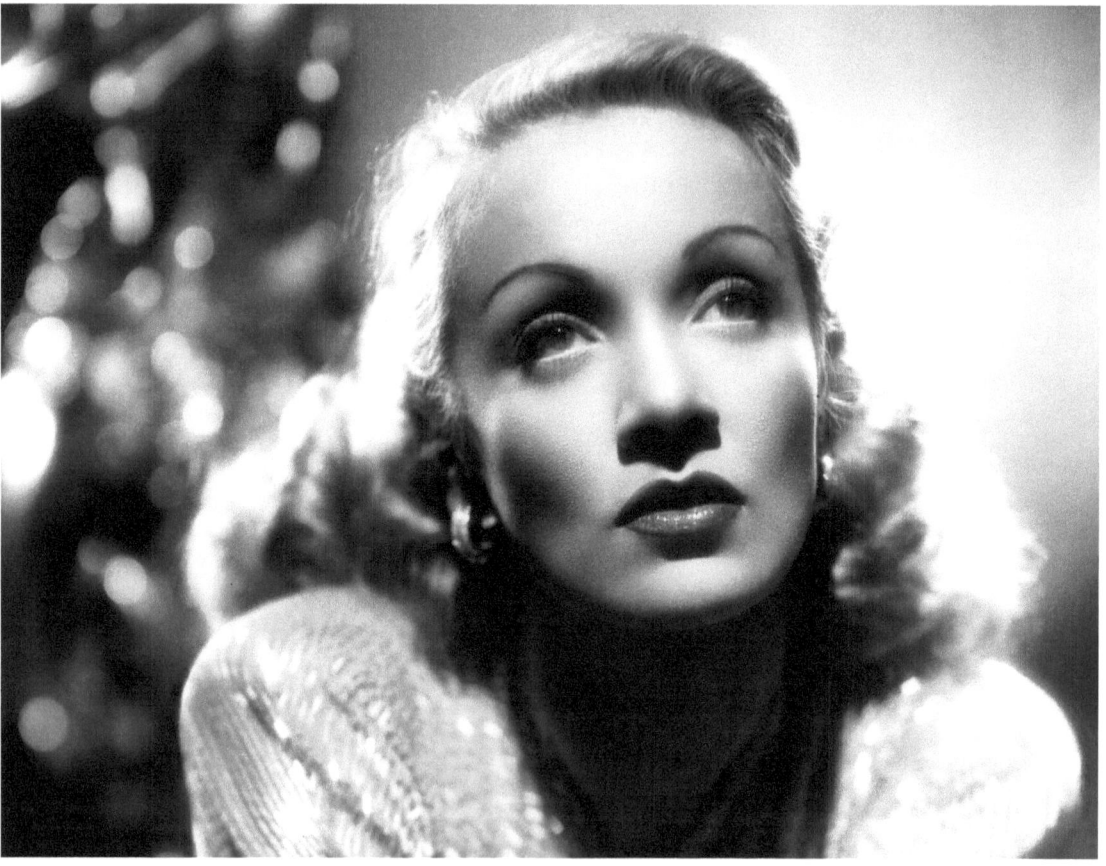

**Lighting Instruments:**  What do table lamps, work lights, spot lights, paper lanterns, DYI movie lighting fixtures, and professional video tungsten, fluorescent, and LEDs  lights have in common?  They're all used as lighting fixtures in the movies.

The control of light, especially spill, is a big issue when using low cost lighting instruments like table lamps or shoot through umbrellas.  Light can go everywhere, especially where you don't want it.  That's why professional lights incorporate barn doors or grids to control the direction that the light shines.  Another alternative is to use a light fixture like the Bayco Brood light or other type of enclosed light source that focuses the light in one direction.  As you can see from the examples below, there are many ways to light a subject or set.

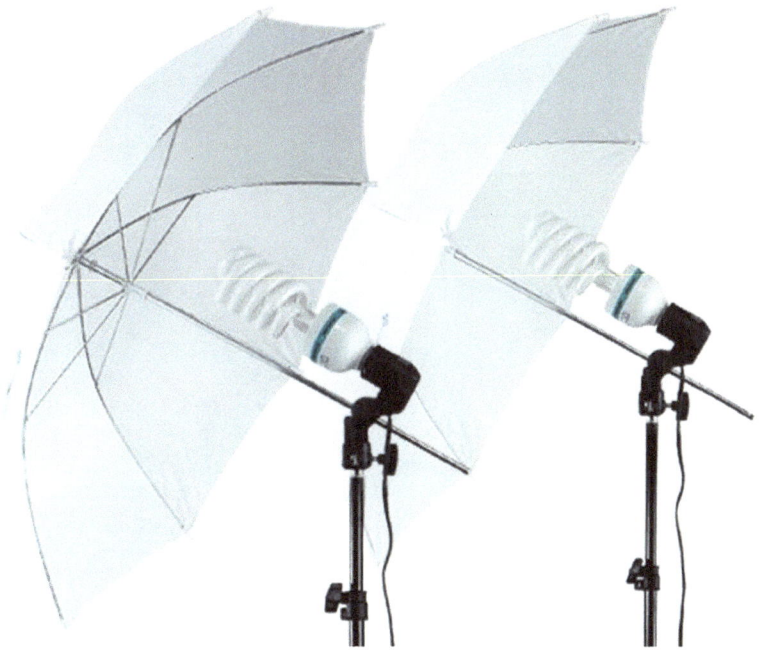

*LimoStudio Shoot Through Umbrella Lights*

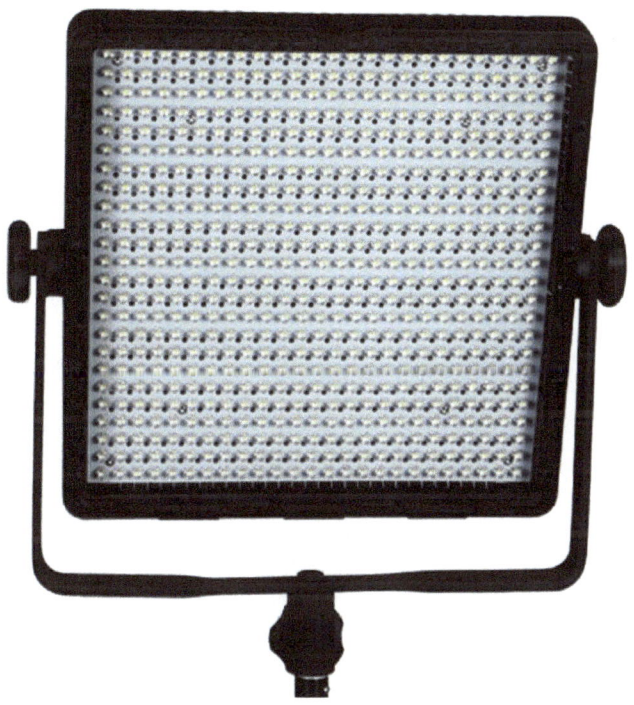

*ePhoto 600 LED Studio Video Light Dimmable lights*

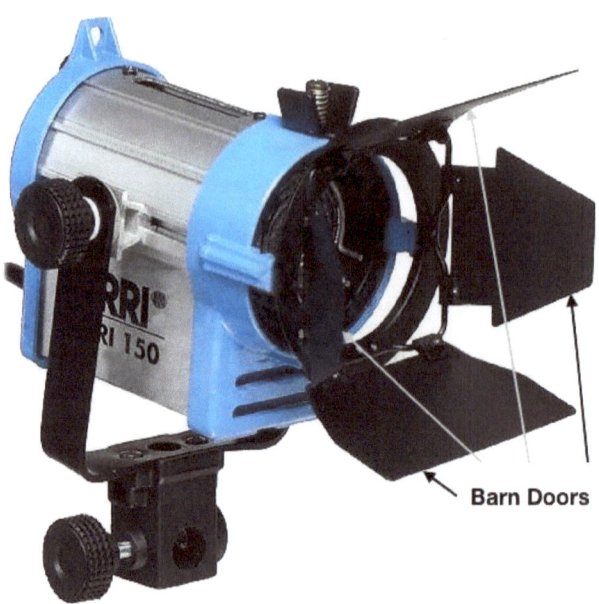

*Arri Tungsten Fresnel with barn doors*

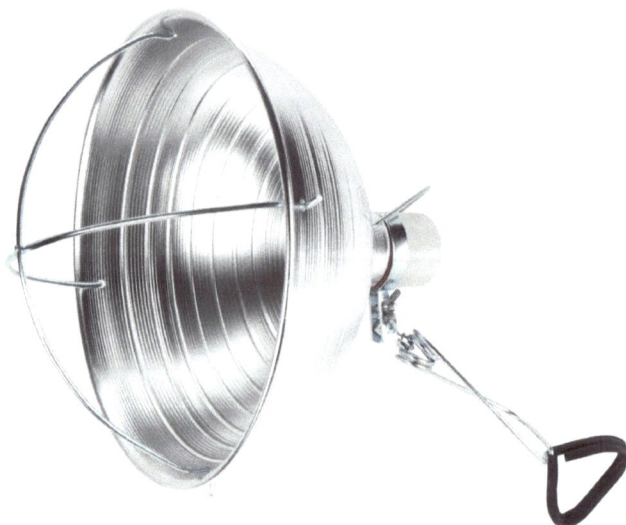

*Bayco 10-1/2" Brooder Clamp light with porcelain ceramic socket*

**Hard and soft lighting** — one of the characteristics of light is how hard or soft it is. By hard light we mean light that is direct and casts hard shadows, like sunlight on a clear day. It is unforgiving, defining shapes with a harsh definition between light and shade. Notice how the hard the light sculpts the features of the faces in the still from the movie The Maltese Falcon (1941)

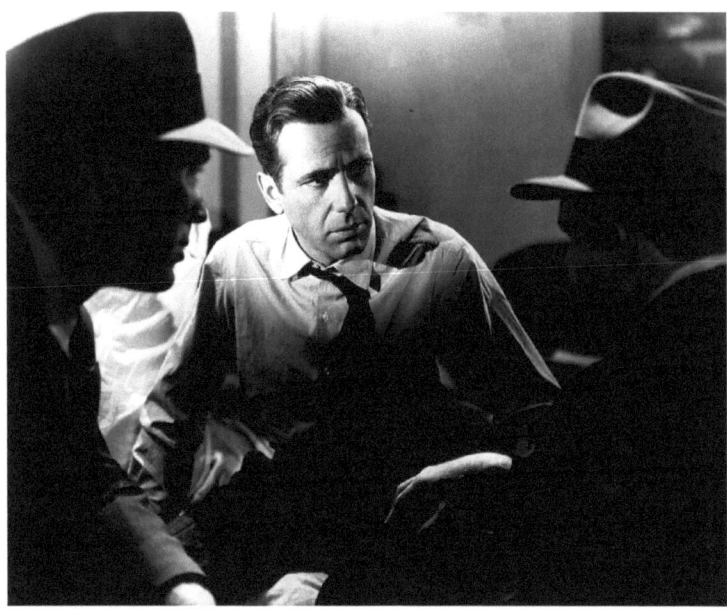

If hard light can reveal every wrinkle, blemish, and imperfection, then soft light can be praised for its ability to soften, transform, and forgive.   Soft light eliminates or reduces shadows by diffusing and scattering the light.  Soft light is the quality of light on an overcast day where there are no cast shadows.

**Diffusion** - You can soften light by shining it through a material that is translucent.  Call diffusion, it can be made from tracing paper, a white bed sheet, or a shower curtain.  Soft boxes, like the Neewer Soft box shown below, come with diffusion on their face to soften the light.

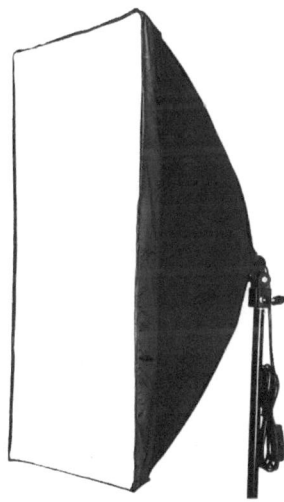

16" to 20" Paper lanterns like the one shown below when combined with compact fluorescent light (CFL) are another simple and inexpensive way to creating soft light, as is shining light through a sheet or shower curtain placed in front of a lighting fixture.

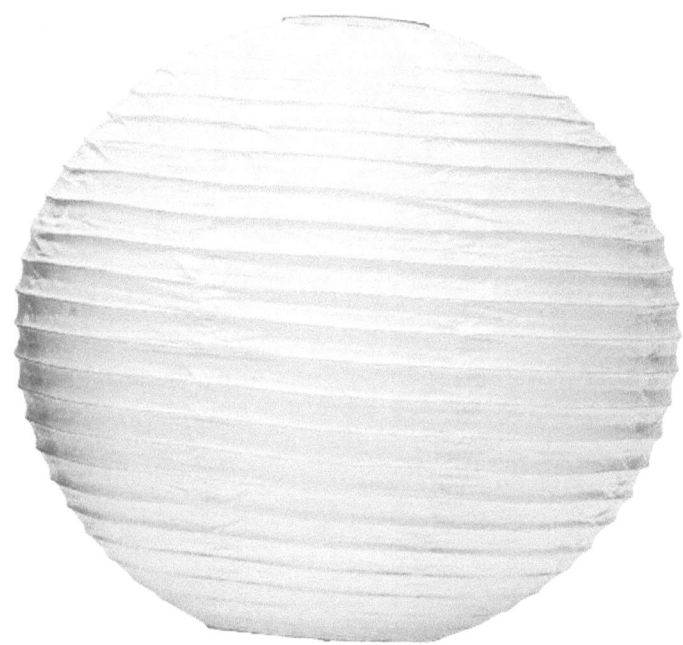

**Using Contrasting Areas of Light:** Many cinematographers refer to lighting a set as painting with light. Using light to control the intensity of illumination within a scene allows us to control the mood, composition, depth, and point of interest. Through lighting we can control where the audience looks and what they see. For example, using contrasting areas of light against dark is an excellent technique for focusing your audiences attention on a specific subject. In the still from the movie Once Upon a Time in the West (1968) below, the placement of light on Claudia Cardinale's face and hair, helps define the composition and the subjects place in the foreground against the darker background. The lighting scheme also reflects her feelings of frustration and resolve.

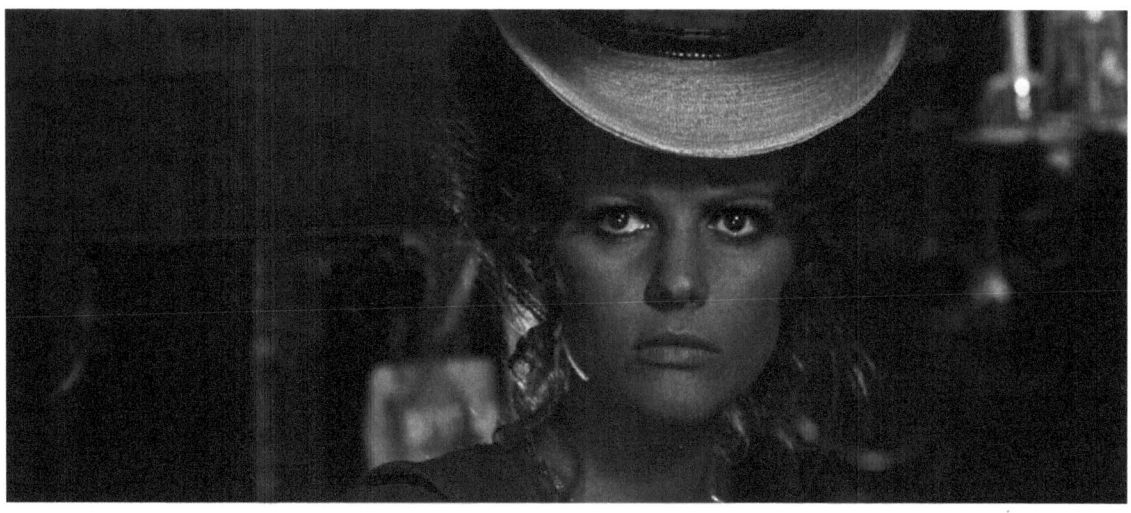

Using a dark silhouetted figure against a light background is another expressive use of contrasting lighting. In the movie American Beauty (1999), cinematographer Conrad Hall has silhouetted Carolyn Burnham (played by Annette Bening) against a bright background. Barely visible in the dark, Hall reveals Carolyn's feelings of desperation.

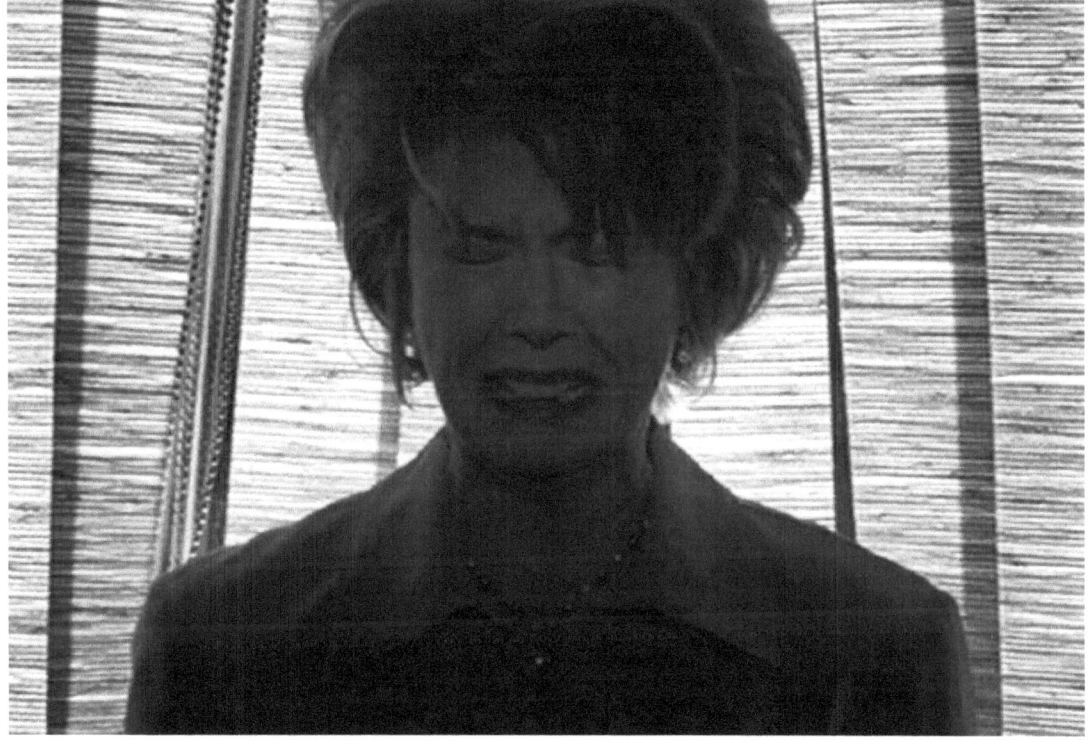

Below we see a wonderful example of how Gregg Toland, the cinematographer for Citizen Kane (1941) uses light to create mood, using areas of light and dark to push and pull the subjects forward or back in space, creating some amazing images.

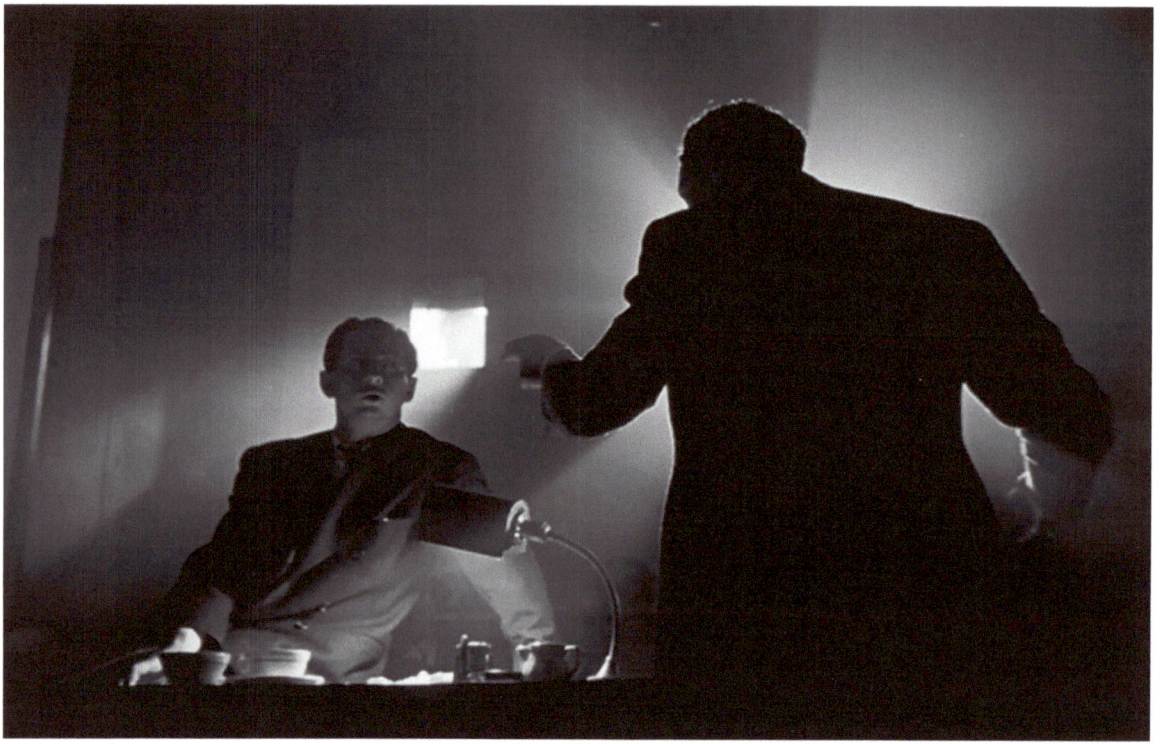

**Three Tips:**

1. One way to see the contrast ratio on subject, without using a light meter, is to squint your eyes as you look at a subject. Squinting allows you to see the subtle changes in values on a face or other object, especially in low contrast ratio situations.

2. Here is a low tech way to determine how hard or soft is your light source. Hold up two fingers between the light source and the palm of your other hand, so that the light casts a shadow cast on your palm. By doing so you'll be able to tell the degree of softness of the cast shadow. The softer the light the less shadow is visible.

3. There is so much information about lighting on YouTube and the internet. Here is a great tutorial on portrait lighting. http://digital-photography-school.com/6-portrait-lighting-patterns-every-photographer-should-know/

# 13. THINK IN SHOTS

Individual shots are the basic building blocks of film. A shot is a series of individual picture frames that run, uninterrupted, from the moment the camera starts until it stops. In Editing, a shot is the footage between two edits. Shots are like individual bones in your body. Each bone contributes to making up a hand, arm, leg, or torso whose function is greater and more subtle that its constituent parts. Shots work in the same way, it's how they are combined together that gives them their power.

Coming from a fine arts painting background, I use to think of each shot as a separate entity. Is it beautiful? Does it have expressive power? Can it stand on its own? I don't think that way anymore. Now when I think of shots, my first thought is how are they going to be edited together. That's primary. Are they going to tell the story I want to tell.

When edited together are they going to help or hinder the shot that comes before and after. Yes, beauty, expression, composition, and lighting are all major considerations and concerns, but only after I'm convinced that what I'm shooting is going to tell the story I want. You could say I've gone from thinking like an artist, to thinking in stories. I still have my artist eye, but now it's tempered by the storyteller.

**How long should a shot be?** As a general rule, no longer than 10 seconds. You'd be amazed at how sophisticated and impatient your audience is. They've clocked thousands of hours watching TV and movies. They have no patients for slow cutting. So, while there occasionally will be times for longer shots, like in a dialog sequence, keep the 10-second limit in mind. Instead of relying on longer shots, stop shooting, then move the camera to a different angle, different subject, or different point-of-view.

**Shot List.** Rather than writing a script, I prefer making a shot list. It's simple to do, and I find, it's a more immediate process for visualizing a story or sequence. A shot list allows you pre-visualizing the organization of your story and what the camera is going to see, shot by shot. It allows you to indicate location, character action, dialog, camera framing (shot size), camera angle, and camera movement, if any. You DO NOT NEED TO WRITE A SCRIPT to put a shot list together. You just need an idea.

Let's take a look at a travelogue video my friend and drum teacher Tracy Rose made.

One day after my lesson, Tracy who is an avid bike rider, showed me a video he'd made of a recent trip he took through Eastern Oregon. It was great. He obviously had a simple plan for what he wanted to shoot, which was:

• Include himself and his friend in the video, including close-ups of both of them joking and enjoying the trip. Doing this changed the video from being just pictures of pretty scenery to the story of two guys having a great time biking through Oregon.

• The video starts with an establishing shot of Tracy, starting his trip. We see the road, trees, mountains, and a sign telling us that this trail is called "Journey Through Time".

• We see not only the scenery and road, but Tracy and his friend looking at it as they ride. The scenery now becomes what they are looking at and reacting too. And we as the audience get to participate in their adventure.

• He alternates back and forth between shots of himself and his friend and the scenery.

• He makes this interesting by varying the size of the images and the camera angles so each shot is different than the one that came before or after it.

• He has captured lots of the wild life, which included a great shot of an eagle flying

• Tracy used an interesting technique to include himself in the video. He'd set up the camera on a tripod so it framed the scenery and the road, then started the camera rolling while he biked out of the frame, then turned around and rode past the camera and out of the scene again. Very simple, but very effective. Later he edited that footage down so it only showed him riding into and out of the shot.

Appreciating the value of music, Tracy added uplifting music to the video, which helps reinforce the idea of the beautiful scenery and two guys enjoying the great outdoors.
*Click here to watch Tracy's movie.  https://www.youtube.com/watch?v=jChGT2ESv1c*

Next time you're going to shoot, take a few minutes, and make a list, *(even one word descriptions will work).* Now you have a plan.

**Three tips:**

1. Time the length of each shot in an action sequence from a favorite movie or TV show. You'll be amazed at how short they are.

2. Do the same for a simple dialog sequence, where two people don't do anything except talk. Even here, notice how the editor is constantly cutting from one type of shot to another. Back

and forth, from a single medium close-up, to a two shot (side view), to an over-the-shoulder shot, to its reverse — the cutting doesn't stop until the scene ends.

3.  Make a shot list for a video travelogue of your neighborhood. Include yourself in it. Don't shoot anything longer than ten seconds.

# 14. MOVE THE CAMERA AND YOU MOVE THE AUDIENCE

Did you know that when you move the camera, your audience experiences that movement as if as if it were happening to them.   Watching movies, especially ones with lots of camera movement, is a visceral experience.  Moving the camera through space is not an abstract idea or concept, it's very powerful because it's so real.  For example, a crane shot can allow your audience to literally fly like Peter Pan, soaring and diving through space.  No wonder we're all hooked on watching movies.  Who doesn't want to fly?

Let's take a look at a simple camera move and talk about how it's similar to our everyday experience. Let's say you want to photograph a tall object like a tree, a building, or a mountain with your smartphone.  One way would be to rotate the phone and shoot vertically, which I don't recommend because almost all professional movies are shot horizontally — in sync with our side-by-side binocular vision.

The second, is to step back far enough from the subject and have it fill the frame.  The problem with this option is that you end up with a tiny image of a big object... and nothing that communicates its scale or size.

The most effective way to show a tall object is the same way you would see it in reality, tilting your head up vertically so you can take in the whole object from bottom to top, thereby showing its height.  In movie jargon, this is called a *tilt-up*.

**Here's how you do it.**

1.  Using a tripod mount, like the Ivation Tripod Adaptor, mount your Smartphone horizontally on the tripod.  You could shoot this hand held, but in general, you'll get better, rock steady, results using a tripod.  *(See the Make It Steady Chapter for a list of mounts, cases, and other accessories)*

2.  Decide on whether your going to tilt-up from the base, or tilt-down from the top.

3.  Open your video camera app and adjust the focus and light levels for your subject, and lock these setting so they won't change while shooting.  (See your app's manual for how to do this)

4. Angle the camera to the starting position; press record, and let camera record (roll) for a second or two, before and after your camera move. This adds a *beginning head* and *ending tail* to your footage, which will make it easier to edit later.

5. Then just tilt your camera up or down. It's that easy. Here's a 10-Second Tip about Tilt-ups. https://vimeo.com/99264354

Tilting-up the camera duplicates how we change our perspective to take in tall objects in real life. And, it is a very powerful tool we can use as storytellers.

**Why does this work:** In real life when you tilt your head up so that you can take in the object, three things happen:

1. You physically move your head or at least your eyes.

2. You invest a certain amount of time to observe the whole image

3. Almost unconsciously you perceive a series of images—one after the other—as your attention moves up the object. While at any given moment a specific image fills your field of view, with each passing second, new images replace the old ones. But psychologically, the experience is seamless—and you're not even aware of the changes.

In the movies this works almost the same way:

1. The camera becomes the audience's eyes, tilting up to take in the whole image — that's the visual.

2. The audience's brain retains all the sections of the object in our memory, splicing the images together to make a vertical panoramic view – that's the temporal.

3. The brain, experiencing the visual and temporal sensation of movement, fills in the physical sensation based memory, and we experience the whole as if it is really happening to us.

In addition to the tilt-up, key camera moves are:

- **Tilt** — Vertical movement of the camera angle, pointing the camera up or down.
- **Dolly** — The camera is mounted on platform that travels on tracks for very smooth movement.
- **Follow** — The camera follows the subject as they walk, either in front of or behind.
- **Pan** — Horizontal movement, left or right
- **Pedestal** — Moving the camera vertically, up or down, the camera's angle remains horizontal. For example you would use a pedestal shot to follow a subject as the sat down, or

stood up.

- **Track or Track** — Same as the dolly shot
- **Zoom** — A change in the lens focal length. The camera is stationary, but it gives the illusion of a moving the camera
- **Crane** — The camera is mounted on a crane that can do any or all of the following: be raised, lowered, panned, tilted, and follow either individually or all at the same time.

We've all experienced the out-of-control, slightly off balance, feeling you have when the camera wildly circles, round and round, two lovers as they embrace. Or, when you watch the background slide across the screen as we follow a character in our movie with a tracking shot. A tracking shot is a shot that moves parallel to our are subject as they drive, walk, or run though a scene. We experience the camera move as if we are actually following along side our subject.

I love camera moves, but like anything, they can be over done. And, because moving the camera is so powerful, I believe, it needs to be used sparingly. There needs to be a reason or motivation for its movement.

## FOUR TIPS:

1. Using a specific camera move, like a tilt-up, experiment with changing the move's speed from very fast to very slow. You'll be surprised at how many different emotions can be expressed and felt with the same move, done at different speeds. There isn't a "right speed." It's a matter of what works in the movie. That's why cinematography is an art, not a science.

2. Shoot a short chase scene two ways. One, using *Follow shots*, and one with *tracking (dolly) shots*. When edited together, which creates the most excitement? The most suspense? What happens when you combine both together in the same scene?

3. Experiment using moves from unexpected angles or positions, for example like a worms-eye or birds-eye view dolly shot. These kinds of shots can be fun and add a lot of character and excitement to your movie.

4. Whenever you record, get in the habit of leaving some head and tail room to your footage, to facilitate editing later.

## 15. DEVELOPING YOUR STORY — Start at the End

When writing your story — Start at the End.

# TheEnd

I was part of a team competing in a 48 Hour Film contest, where you had 48 hours to write, shoot, and edit a 5 to 7 minute film, in a genre which was randomly assigned to you at the start of the 48 hour time period. We got suspense. There were 12 people on our team, but we weren't involved in the creation of the script, that was the responsibility of the director and the producer. The crew got the film completed and submitted on time, but we didn't win because it didn't have an ending. The director had ideas for some scenes, including dialog, but they never coalesced into a complete story with a beginning, middle, and end.

Determined to make his film work, the director later added more scenes in an attempt to explain the reason for the actor's actions and motivation, but because it was now an afterthought, the action and the dialog sequences didn't make sense. The photography and acting were great. But, by not defining the ending (or the plot), the director couldn't structure the scenes so that they got him to where he needed to go. It's like leaving on a trip and not knowing where you'll end up. Your trip becomes more of a joy ride, than a journey to get to a specific place. There is nothing wrong with filmic joy riding, unless you want to make a coherent movie.

My point here is that once the story's ending is established, even if it changes later, it allows you, the film's creator, to structure all the scenes from beginning to end in such a way that they have a cumulative effect. Each shot or scene builds on the one that came before and after it. That way you know exactly where you're taking your audience

Knowing the end allows you to create a shot list, storyboards, or a script. Sometimes you'll need a script, especially if your movie has lots of dialog, and action. Other times, just a shot list or storyboards will do. The shot list can be a simple list of :

- The characters and the action of scene
- The time of day and location
- Dialog (if any)
- The type of shot, camera angle, and lens choice.

• B-Roll — Photos, details of some subject or object, reaction shots from another participant, a bystander, or an audience bobbing their heads up and down to music, applauding, laughing, drinking, dancing... etc.)

As an example let's put a shot list together for Bill and Nancy's 25th Anniversary party so you have an idea of how this is done. Starting at the end, our video culminates with the couple taking to the dance floor to dance to their favorite song, moments later friends and family join in. Now that we know where we'll be ending up, let's create a shot list for the event.

Since getting ready for the party might be a pretty boring sequence, let's spice it up by using what's called *parallel editing or cross cutting* to alternate between two activities that are happening simultaneously. Many of these shots when edited together will be only few seconds long.

1. Close-up of Nancy looking in the mirror putting on lipstick.

2. Close-up a deviled eggs being arranged on a platter, and then being carried off to another room.

3. Medium shot from inside a closet behind some shirts looking out. Bill slides some of the shirts aside, chooses one and removes it.

4. Close-up of dining room table full of food and wine, the wine glasses are being arranged on the table. Below is a picture titled Good Company by Joe Lodge (2011)

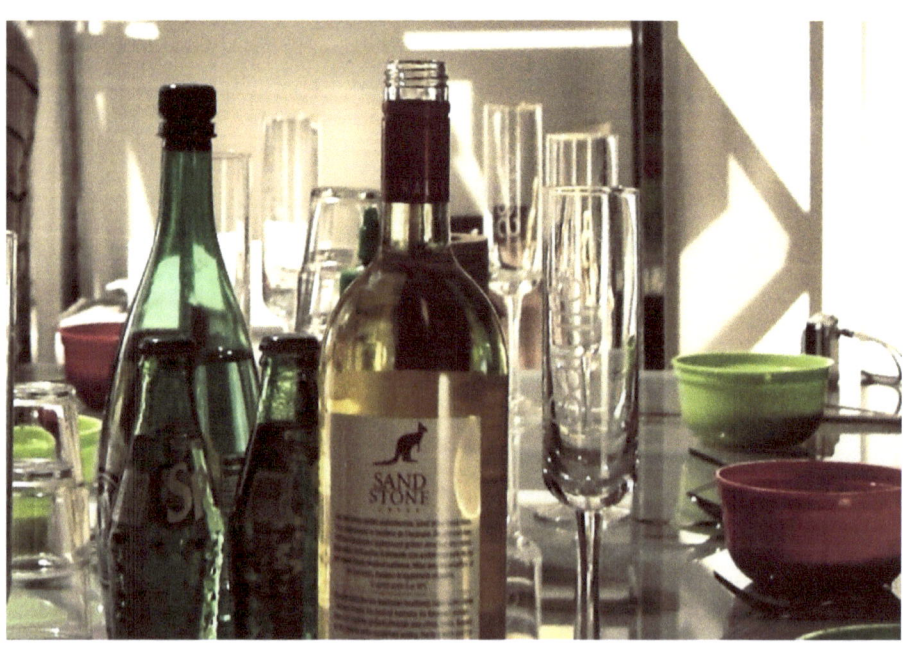

5.  Medium Close-up of Nancy (seen from behind) sitting at dressing table, Nancy reaches in to an open jewelry box and takes out a bracelet and puts it on and say, "ready."

6.  Medium Close-up table from above.  We see a hand enter the frame, take a glass and pour some wine.  The camera tilts-up to reveal Bill and a room full of guests behind him, smiling he turns and joins his friends.

7.  We then have a series of 2 to 5 second shots of friends wishing the couple happy anniversary.

8.  We then dissolve to a 30-second photo montage with either titles, voice over narration, or just music of the Bill and Nancy's wedding, honeymoon, first house, birth of their children, major vacations and events.

9.  Then back to Bill and Nancy surrounded by friends applauding.  They take to the dance floor as their favorite song plays, we watch them for a moment or two and then their friends join them on the dance floor, we fade to black.  The end.


Sometimes you'll need a script, especially if your movie has lots of dialogue and action. How to write a script is a topic unto itself and more than we can cover in this book.  I recommend the following excellent resources on that subject.

- *Screenplay* by Syd Fields
- *Essentials of Screenwriting* by Richard Walters
- *Lew Hunter's Screenwriting 434* by Lew Hunter
- *The Anatomy of Story* by John Truby
- *Million-Dollar Screenwriting: The Mini-Movie Method* by Chris Soth.

# 16 LITTLE DID THEY KNOW — Creating Suspense

Alfred Hitchcock is considered the master of suspense. When asked about his movies he spoke about the difference between surprise and suspense. Imagine he said, "two men sitting at a table in a café talking. They talk for a long time, say two minutes. Suddenly there is an explosion. A bomb hidden under the table explodes. That's surprise."

Now, let's look at the same scene again with one change. This time we show the audience the bomb under the table, which is set to explode in two minutes, just as the scene begins. The men don't know about the bomb. The longer the men sit at the table talking, the more anxious the audience gets. The camera keeps cutting to a close-up of the bomb's clock ticking down to zero. The viewer is thinking, "For goodness sake, stop talking and get out of there". The tension builds and builds. And finally, at the very last second the police chief interrupts the men and disarms the bomb. That's what I call *Little Did They Know* or suspense.

Hitchcock warned movie maker about the audience's negative reaction to blowing up a twelve year old boy and a bus full of people in his thriller Sabotage. He admitted it was a mistake, and advised against doing it.

You can also use *Little Did They Know* in reverse by showing the audience something that the hero of the story is doing, without any previous explanation of what it means. Thereby letting the movie reveal what is going on, as it plays out for the audience. Using the following shot list, lets see what *Little Did They Know* looks like in reverse:

1. Our movie opens with a medium close-up of a man sitting at a work bench, seen from behind, loading bullets into a rifle clip.

2. Wide shot: He picks up the rifle and clip and leaves the room.

3. A medium shot of a car, seen from behind: The door slams and the car backs out of the driveway, filling the frame as it comes towards the camera.

4. Low angle wide shot: The car approaches the camera and stops, filling the frame in a medium shot. The door opens, but because of the low angle, we only see two feet get out, walk past the camera, as it pans around following the man, who is walking up a gravel path.

5. Close-up: We see a side view of The man lying on the ground, rifle raised. He hesitates, checking the alignment of his telephoto site, then repositions the rifle, aims, and fires five shots.

6. Medium Close-up: Another man picks up a pair of binoculars and looks through them.

7. Medium wide shot: The man on the ground is looking through the rifle site, grimaces and

says, "damn".

8. Close-up: The man's POV (Point of View): a paper target with only two holes in it, none of which are anywhere near the bulls eye. Cut to:

9. Medium close-up of the instructor and student on the ground saying, "Yeah... Keep trying, you'll get it.

In the example above, we've kept the audience in suspense about who this man is and what he's planning to do with the rifle.

**Three Tips for how to create suspense:**

1. THE SECRET: Show the audience something that the hero doesn't know. Or the reverse: show the audience something they don't understand, which is to be discovered, later, as the movie plays. The longer you can stretch the mystery out the better.

2. THE ACTION: Show the hero going about doing his thing.

3. THE DISCOVERY: Show the hero's reaction as he, or the audience, discover the secret.

You can create suspense about almost anything, from a birthday to a product introduction. It just requires a little forethought and imagination. It's fun and is much more interesting for both the filmmaker and the audience.

# 17. VIDEO CPR — Understanding Point-of-View

There is one concept in visual story telling that, once you understand how it works, will expand your film awareness and make everything you do much, much richer. It is one of the foundations upon which all good visual story telling is based.

It has three parts. I call them C, P, and R, or CPR. My CPR has nothing to do with Cardiopulmonary Resuscitation, but it will give your movies new life. With CPR, we need to think in terms of combining three different shots together to make a filmic statement. It's very much like using a noun and a verb to build the basics of a sentence, in order to express a complete thought. Listed below are the three different types of shots we need to construct our sentence:

*1. SHOT C (stands for the word to see or look):* we see the hero move his head or eyes to look at something or someone.

*2. SHOT P (is a Point-of-view shot):* we see the hero's Point-of-View (POV) of what she is looking at.

*3. SHOT R (is a reaction shot):* we see the reaction on the hero's face to what she has just seen.

Look at any movie and you'll find hundreds of CPR's. For example in Alfred Hitchcock's movie Rear Window, Jimmy Stewart, who is the hero, is confined to his apartment in a wheel chair because of a broken leg. To pass the time, he spends the whole movie looking out his window, watching his neighbors. Which, knowing Hitchcock, is going to get him in trouble.

Hitchcock's Rear Window (1954) is nothing but a continuous series of CPR shots, repeated over and over again. In the three still from the movie below we watch:

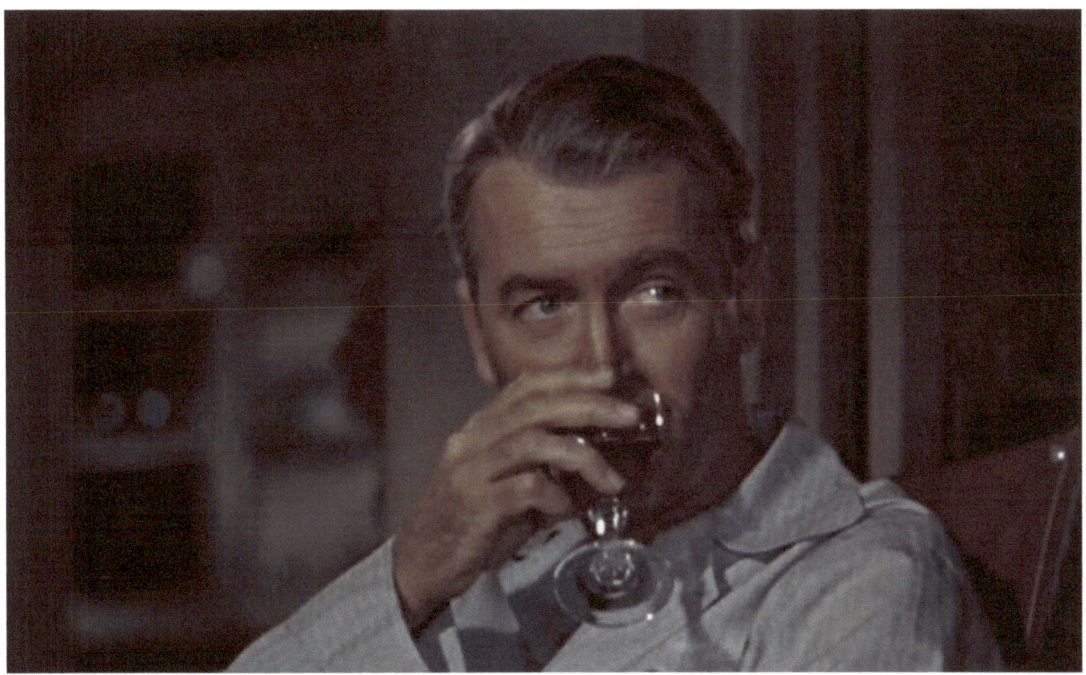

Stewart looks, that's **C** .

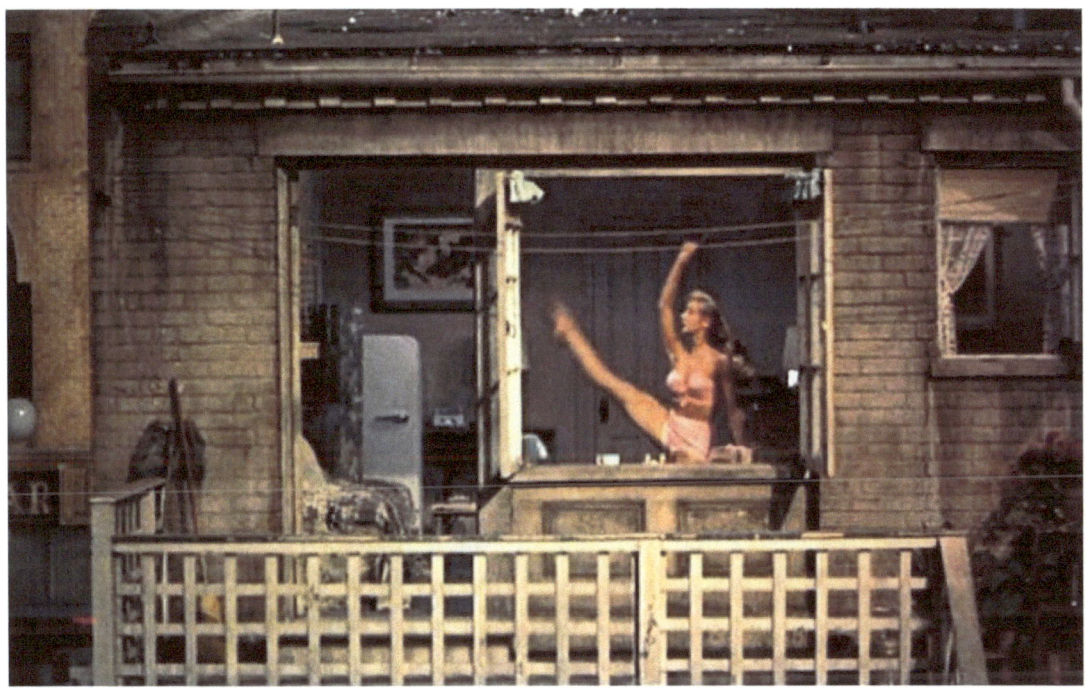

Then we see what he's looking at, *his point-of-view*, that's **P**.

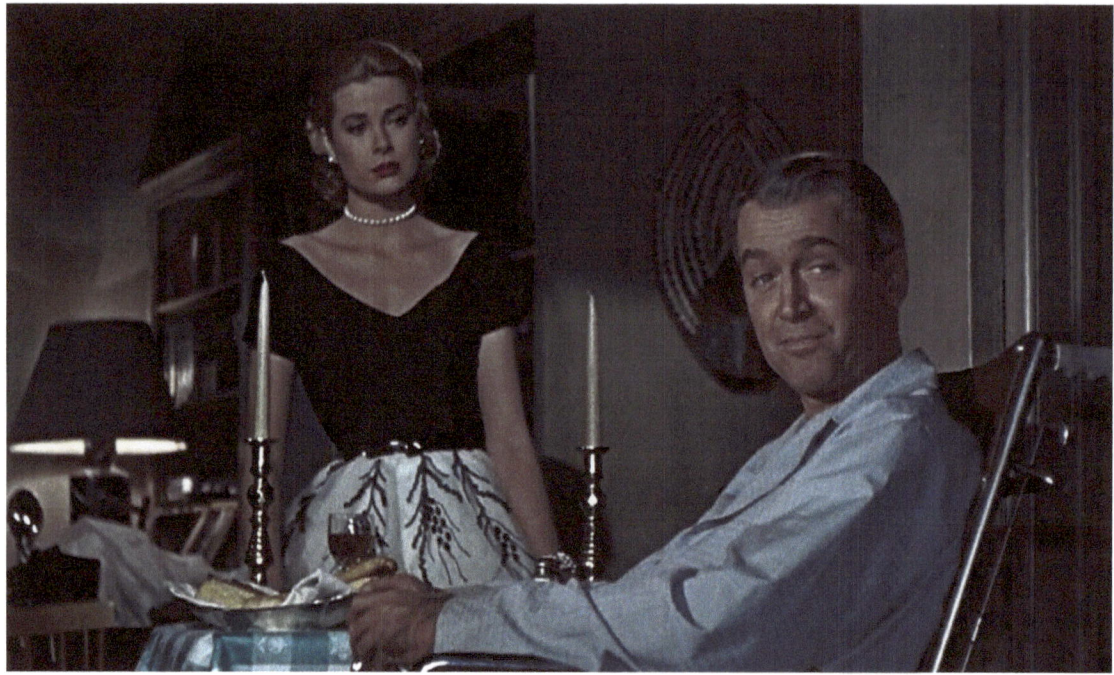

And then we return to see Stewart's and Grace Kelly's *reaction* to what he's seen, that's **R**

CPRs are a very powerful tool we can easily incorporate into our filmic vocabulary. Using CPR sequences, you can capture emotions, show excitement, create mystery, reveal thoughts, show a secret, and much, more.

So you're asking yourself, "That's great for you, but how can I, the novice, use this?" OK, let's talk about making a movie of your child's birthday using CPR's. Let's say she's eight years old. With a little planning before the party, we've created a shot list to illustrate how you might do this:

- ***C***: we see your child looking out the window.
- ***P***: we see a car pulling up and your daughter's friend gets out and waves.
- ***R***: a close-up of your child smiling and running to the door.
- The two children meet at the door and run into the living room...
- ***C***: your child is sitting at the center of the table with her friends, she turns and looks towards the kitchen.
- ***P***: we see your wife smiling as she carries the birthday cake into the room.
- ***R***: we see your child and her friends all making an Oooh! faces.

With what you now know you can go on and finish the video, shooting CPR's about — opening presents — capture a child grabbing one of the presents — show the kids playing in the yard — watch the party breaking up — and even a shot of you seeing your child asleep on the couch... you carry her up to bed... you close the door, and smile, as the ending. How's that for a birthday movie, you'll watch over and over again, year after year.

I think you can see how powerful this concept is for creating an exciting and dynamic story. Use this for any subject.

## Three tips:

1. CPRs don't have to be just about what the hero or star of your story sees and reacts too. It's about what anybody sees. Incorporating outside reactions like this into your video adds depth to whatever is happening. In a business related video CPRs are a great way of showing customer endorsement, not by telling, but by showing your customer's reaction and appreciation for your product or service.

2. CPRs aren't just for kids and people. Animal's reactions are another form of expression you should consider.

3. Sometimes it works to do the filming all by yourself. And, sometimes you just can't be everywhere, like at a birthday party. Almost everyone has a smartphone. Recruit other parents or friends to help you. Explaining the story and shots you're trying to get, and planning who will shoot what, will guarantee your success. You can tag team how your shooting, looking for special moments, then having one of you shooting "C" and "R" shots and the other capturing the "POV's.

# 18. VIDEO SCRABBLE — The power of editing

Don't be intimidated by movie editing. It's simple... and powerful. It has the ability to shape your audience's experience, thoughts, and emotions, simply by how you select, trim, and arrange your shots.

Alfred Hitchcock when talking about storytelling and editing said,

*"What I'm concerned with is the manner of telling the story and how you put your scenes together, and in consequence create an emotion in an audience... Let me give you an example... We take a close-up of [a] man and cut to what he sees. And what do we show? A woman nursing a baby. You cut back to [his] face reaction and he smiles. Now what is he? He's a benevolent, nice gentleman. Take away the middle piece of film (the mother and the baby) and substitute a girl in a bikini. Now he's a dirty old man. That's what I mean by the purity of montage [editing] and the control of film."*

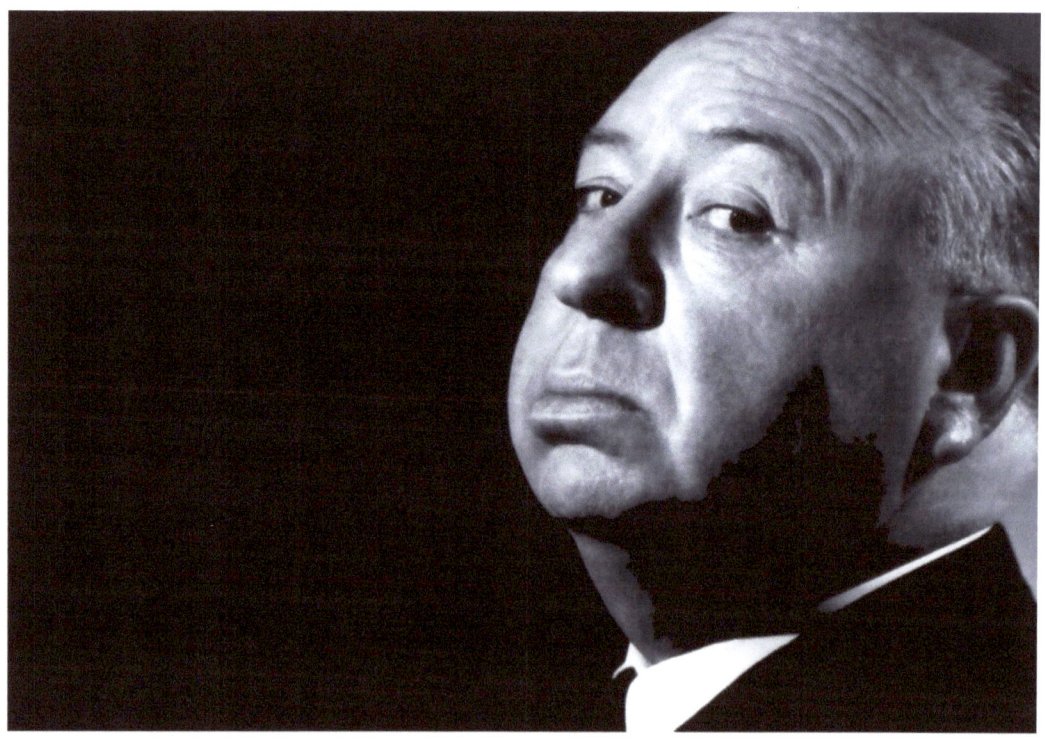

Photo of Alfred Hitchcock Presents (2010) by Insomnia Cured Here.

Think of shots as words you use to create sentences. How you edit your shots together allows you to quickly assemble an image sequences that describe how or what your hero is thinking or feeling. It can express ideas, create suspense (*see Little Did They Know)*, fear, love, and establish relationships between things. Scramble them up and rearrange them in a different way, and you create a whole new meaning. Here's an example of two sentences using the same words, but having different meanings, images can be used the same way:

*Woman, without her man, is helpless.*
*Woman! Without her, man is helpless.*

But there is more... When you're editing a film, you're manipulating time and space to create a new reality. What shots you use when editing your movie may or may not have any relationship to reality. It's deception... make believe that allows you to tell your story. When the pieces are put together, the edit appears to be happening, right now, in front of your audience.

Here's an example of how this works: We'll use three shots, each filmed at different locations and on different days. Editing them together, we see a woman holding a bouquet of flowers walking from screen left to right. Cut to, a man walking from screen right to left. Cut to, the man and woman meeting in front of a church. They embrace, holding hands as they go up the stairs and into the church.

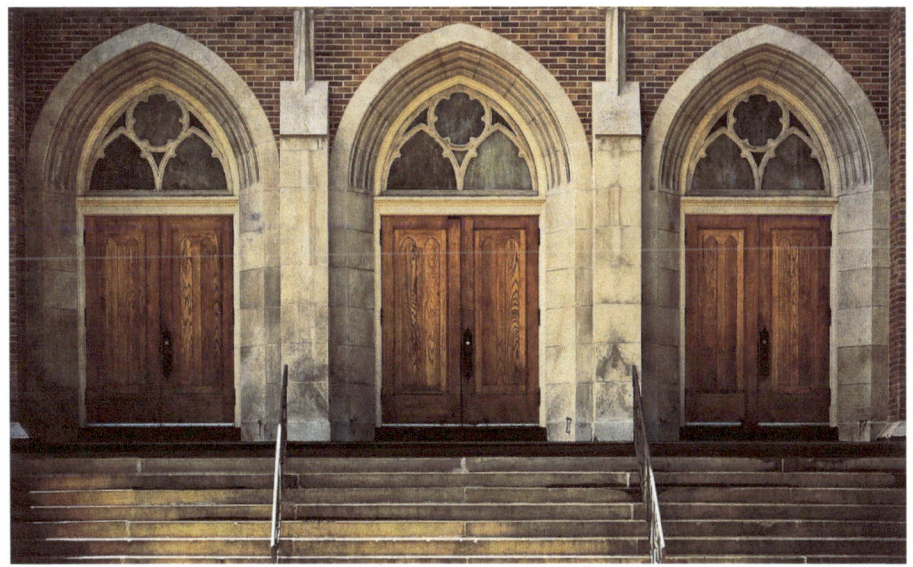

*Let's See What's Behind Door #3 by GFPeck (2009*

What your audience experiences when viewing this sequence is a man and woman walking to church from different parts of town, they meet, go up the stairs, and enter the church to get married.

Hollywood movies are made the same way. Nothing is filmed is sequence or in the same location. It's only when the film is edited together, that this new reality is created. You can use this same process to film a birthday, vacation, anniversary, business video, product introduction, or your next Hollywood blockbuster. It just takes a little planning.

Another technique used frequently by Hollywood editors is the compression, or elimination, of time or events. For example: We watch a movie of Tom leaving his apartment.... Then cut to Tom exiting the elevator at work. We as the audience, didn't need to see Tom in his car, inching along the freeway, or standing in line waiting for a crowded subway car, unless it's important to our story. Don't be afraid to take out the boring bits. The more you can do this the better. Your audience will thank you for it.

If you know how to use a word processor — to cut, paste, and move words around — you should have no problem using film editing software. In the latter case, instead of manipulating words, you'll be dealing with visuals (shots). You'll cut out shots you don't need or trim shots, and move shots around, all with the click of a mouse.

**Smart Device Editing Software Apps**  I recommend  using the following editing apps:

- iMovie
- Pinnacle Studio 2.0 for iOS devices
- KineMaster Pro for Android
- Movie Edit Touch for Windows.

**Computer Editing Software Apps**  If you plan on editing on a computer I recommend:

- iMovie for Macs
- Final Cut Pro X for Macs
- Adobe Premier for Windows or Mac
- CyberLink PowerDirector 13 Deluxe for Windows

**Three Tips:**

1. Think in terms of a beginning, middle, and end. Always know the end before you begin. Always! Coming up with how something ends is the hardest part of the process. Don't start without it. It affects both the beginning and the middle. When you don't have an ending, it's too easy to lose your way in the middle and not know how to resolve it.

2. Don't be afraid to play. Duplicate a sequence and try changing the order of shots in the new one. In the Hitchcock example above, we saw how replacing the shot of mother and child with a girl in a bikini, changes the audiences perception of who this man is, from a nice gentleman to a lecher. You can create suspense, surprise, dislike, or love, simply by changing the arrangement of your shots.

3. To create an environment that never existed, try combining unrelated shots together. Don't be afraid to use shots taken at different times or places in your story. Especially, if they are of great interest or quality. The viewer will never know, where you got them from, unless you tell them. I wouldn't.

# 19. MOVIE TIME AND MOVIE SPACE

In the movies everything is condensed down to its essence, and is seen, or observed, from multiple points-of-view. To understand this better let's differentiate between what we experience in our day to day lives, let's call that *Real Time and Real Space*, and contrast that with what we create in movies, through a process of construction known as Editing, which takes little pieces of film and puts them together to create *Movie Time and Movie Space*.

My experience of *real time* events are, that they are mostly off and on affairs, either they happen instantaneously, or they are drawn out over time. They are observed from one primary point of view, mine. That's *real time and real space*. In between, there are long boring pauses or, other activities that fill up the time, while the event is occurring. For example: I'm traveling from San Francisco to New York. I've already been at the airport for 45 minutes, going through security, checking my bags, buying a soft drink... waiting. And oh yes if I'm lucky, another half-hour in the car getting to the airport. That's *real time and real space*. As a movie, to show all this would be pretty BORING.

The movies are different. Here's a shot list of how my trip to New York might be filmed and edited together:

1. High Establishing shot: of a residential San Francisco street, we hear the bell of a cable car as it passes by.

2. Medium shot: Suitcase in hand, I leave my apartment closing the door and walk out of the shot.

3. Close up pan: of a jets landing gear as it touches down on a runway.

4. Medium Shot cab interior: I get into a cab and close the door.

5. Close-up: of the back of the cab it pulls away from the curb and the camera, joining other traffic on a busy New York street.

In less that ten to fifteen seconds I've traveled from San Francisco to New York. We've also changed our point-of-view from the 3rd person — the establishing shot, to the 2nd person —my leaving the house, back to the 3rd person — the jet landing, to the 1st person — my getting into the cab, to the 3rd person — the busy New York street. My English teacher would never allow me to change my point-of-view like this. But, that's *Movie Time* and *Movie Space*. We've kept all the good interesting bits and gotten rid of everything else.

Think about it. In real life we see everything from one perspective and time frame. In the movies we have super powers over time and space. We can observe the action from anywhere and any point-of-view. We can be up on an roof watching a scene from above; then right next to our hero to see what the hero is looking at; and then step back and watch him react from a different angle.

By the same token, we don't as filmmakers, have to be stuck with one location for a whole scene or sequence. As we've discussed before, there is no reason you can't film different parts of a sequence at different picturesque locations, and edit them together, so that it seems as if the scene occurred in one place. That's what they do in Hollywood.

For example, we're filming a chase scene in which we'll use four different locations:

1. Location #1,*(a small office near you)* The hero running out of a private office is being pursued by two men.

2. Location #2, *(a large insurance companies offices, somewhere down town. This is shot on Sunday when no one is using the office)* High angle shot of our hero races in between and around rows of desks in a large room full of cubicles and busy workers. Moments later we see who he's being chased by.

3. Location #2  A medium close-up, our hero turns looking back at his pursuers and then to the left.

4. Location #2 *(but this could be at any location)* A close up an red illuminated Exit sign.

5. Location #2  Low angle shot of our hero running towards and past the camera.

6. Location #3, *(the stairwell of the local campus parking garage)* High Angle full shot, A stairway landing. The door bangs against the wall as our hero flics through the door and down the stairs.

7. Location #3, *(Same as shot 6)* The camera holds on the empty landing for two beats, then, the pursuers bursting through the same door and stop on the landing, listening, trying to decide whether to go up or down. They mistakenly go up.

8. Location #4, *( The exterior of an office building in a different part of town)* Medium shot of a building's exterior on a busy city street at rush hour. A door opens and our hero emerges, pauses then turns and joins the foot traffic.

9. Location #4, High Angle Wide shot, we watch as he hurries down the street disappearing in the throng of pedestrians hurrying home from work.

10. Location #4, Medium Close-up. Two men appear through the same door, searching, but not finding their quarry in the mass of humanity, they stand there wondering what to do next.

Each shot was filmed in a different location and on a different day. But, that doesn't matter, because you, as the director/editor with shot list in hand, have the power to edit these shots so they will seamlessly flow together. The audience will never know. That's *movie time* and *movie space*.

The great Russian movie director and author V.I. Pudovkin said, *"To show something as everyone sees it is to have accomplished nothing"*.

Movies are different from our everyday experience. Pudovkin also felt that, editing is the foundation of film. And, by editing he meant combining individual shots together so that their sum was greater than their parts. Remember, you create new meaning every time you combine shots together.

## Here are three tips:

1. Think of making all your videos with all the boring bits taken out. For example: As soon as there is a break in the action or story, go to the next important scene. Don't bother with transitions or showing how you got there, just go there. Think of time as elastic. You'll be surprised at how well this works.

2. Explore shooting a scene from different angles. (High, low, from behind). Don't be afraid to experiment. Be the fly on the wall or the ant watching the giants above. Make the world you're creating unique.

3. Try shooting a scene using different locations and combining them together. Remember the background is an important character in your movie, make every effort to incorporate interesting locations into your shooting plan.

# 20. AVOID THE MIDDLE — The rule of thirds

You don't need a degree in art or photography to create great looking images. Simply use the *Rule of thirds*. It takes the guesswork out of composing pictures and it's powerful, because you can use it for just about any subject or situation. And, it works!

The *"Rule of thirds" is* a technique many cinematographers use when composing pictures. Begin by dividing the picture frame into three equal horizontal and vertical thirds like the grid of a tic-tac-toe game.

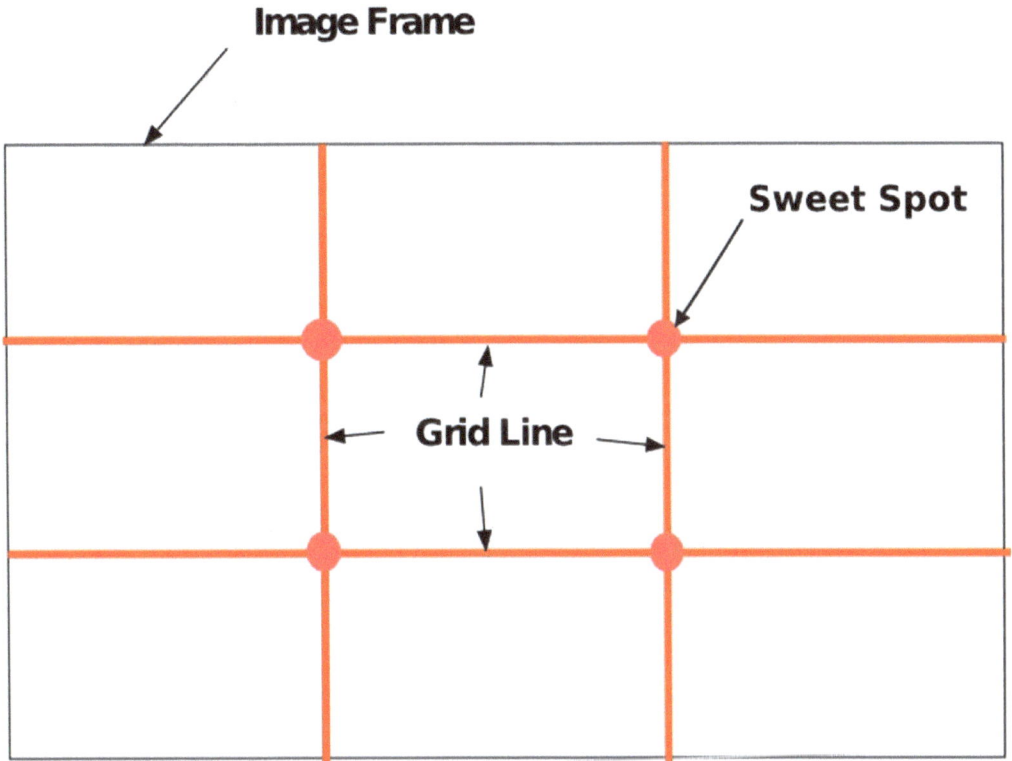

Now compose your pictures on or near the grid lines by aligning your subject on either the horizontal and/or vertical lines. The *Rule of Thirds* works for composing pictures of action sequences, products, food, portraits, landscapes, group shots, just about anything.

A powerful variation on this concept is to align your subject on the point of intersection of a horizontal and vertical grid line. I call these four intersection points on the grid *sweet spots*. Using *sweet spots* allows you to create very dynamic compositions.

Most smart devices and camera apps come with the capability to display a thirds *Grid* on your phone's screen. You'll find the *Grid* display either in your app's settings, or in your phone's camera setting section. For example: the *Photo & Camera* settings on my iPhone 5S has a *"Grid"* setting that I can turn on or off for my camera. See the screen shot below. If you don't have a grid selection on your phone, it's not hard to picture imaginary grid lines on your camera's viewfinder.

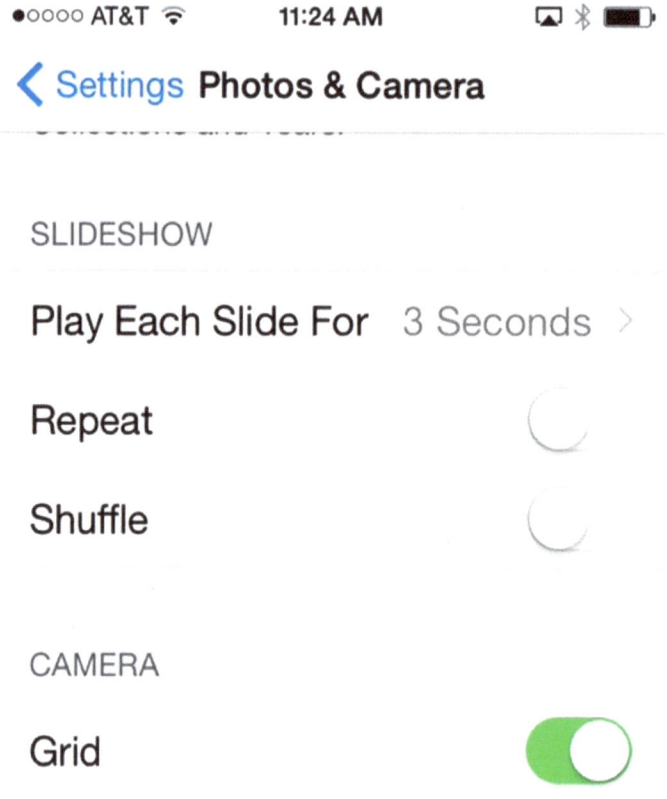

To use the *Rule of Thirds* for composing landscapes, align the picture's *horizon line* with either the top or bottom horizontal grid lines. In the photo titled Idyllically Landscape in Chonzuo below by Kedibeder (2010) the image's horizon line is aligned with the top horizontal grid line. One third of the image is sky, two thirds are mountains and valleys.

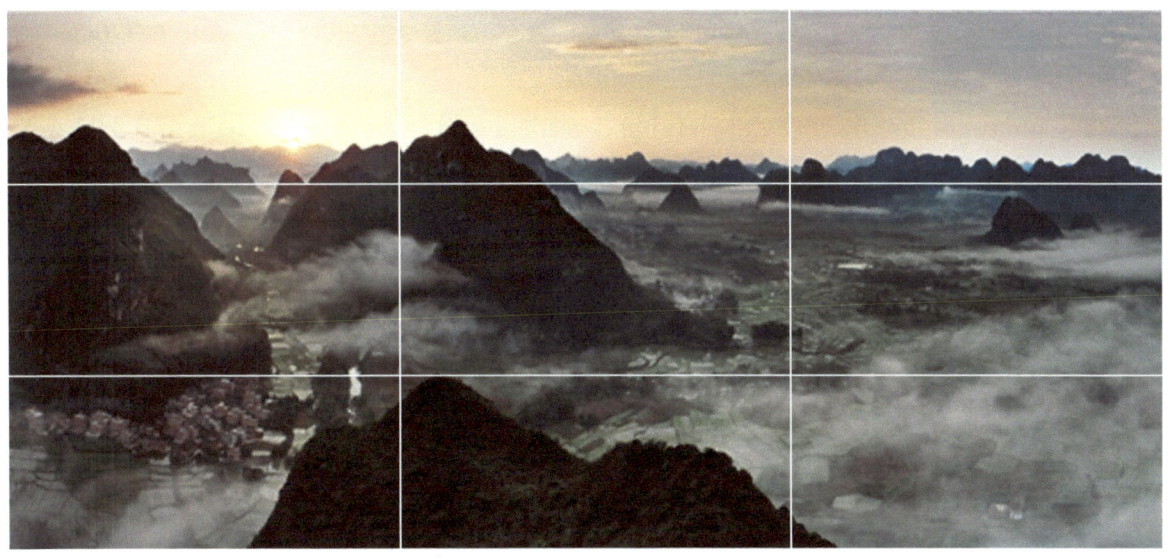

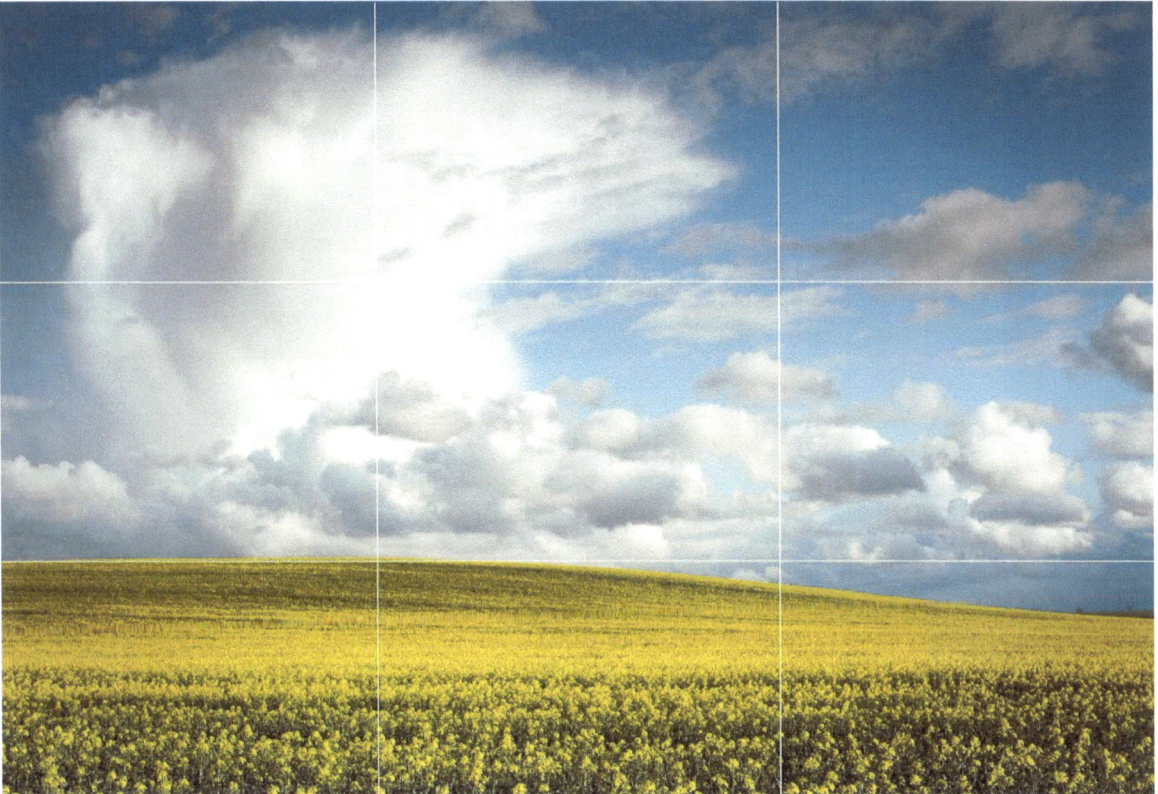

In the photo above titled, Landscape outside Barnwell – Jamesthe1st (2012)  the image's horizon line is aligned with the bottom horizontal grid line.  One third of the image is flowers, two thirds are sky.

There are no hard and fast rules for using the *rule of thirds* to compose pictures. Only suggestions. For example, in the photo below, titled Yellow Mountain Landscape by Chi King (2006) the photographer has used the left hand vertical grid to arrange the light and dark areas within the frame. By using the *grid's sweet spot*, where both the horizontal and vertical lines intersect, the photographer has created a very dynamic composition.

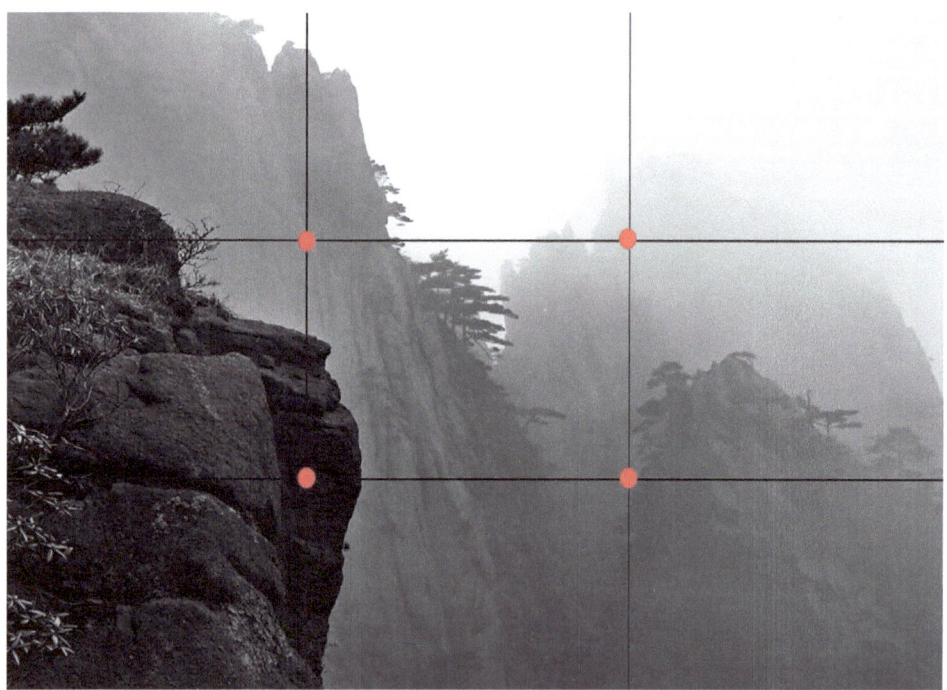

**Three Tips:**

1. Shoot lots of pictures. Stills images are fine for now. Shoot anything and everything. The idea is to develop an understanding of how to quickly compose a picture. The more you do, the better you'll get. Have fun. Study each when you're done, delete all except the best few. I suggest that you don't show them to anyone... these are just for you to learn with.

2. Shoot even more, framing your subject using one of the four *"sweet spots"*.

3. Try composing your shots two ways: One, using just the grid lines; and the other, working with one of the four sweet spots on your grid.

In the next chapter titled, *Head Room, Nose Room, and Dead Space,* we'll explore how to compose pictures of people using the *Rule of Thirds* and much more.

# 21. HEAD ROOM, NOSE ROOM, AND DEAD SPACE — Composing pictures of people

Composing pictures of human subjects using the *rule of thirds* is more involved than composing pictures of landscapes or objects. With a human subject we're concerned not only with the placement of the person within the image, but also the space around the subject so it can breathe within the boundaries of the picture frame, and it doesn't feel cramped or crowded. The three concepts of subject placement we need to be aware of when using the *rule of thirds* are: *head room, nose room, and dead space.*

In most photography the eyes are considered the most expressive aspect of the face. It is said, that the eyes are the mirror of the soul. One way to use the *rule of thirds* is to align the subject's eyes with the top horizontal *grid line*. And, by placing your subjects eyes, on a *grid line* your image becomes more pleasing, natural, and balanced. This works for almost every shot from an extreme close-up, to full shot. It even works for animals.

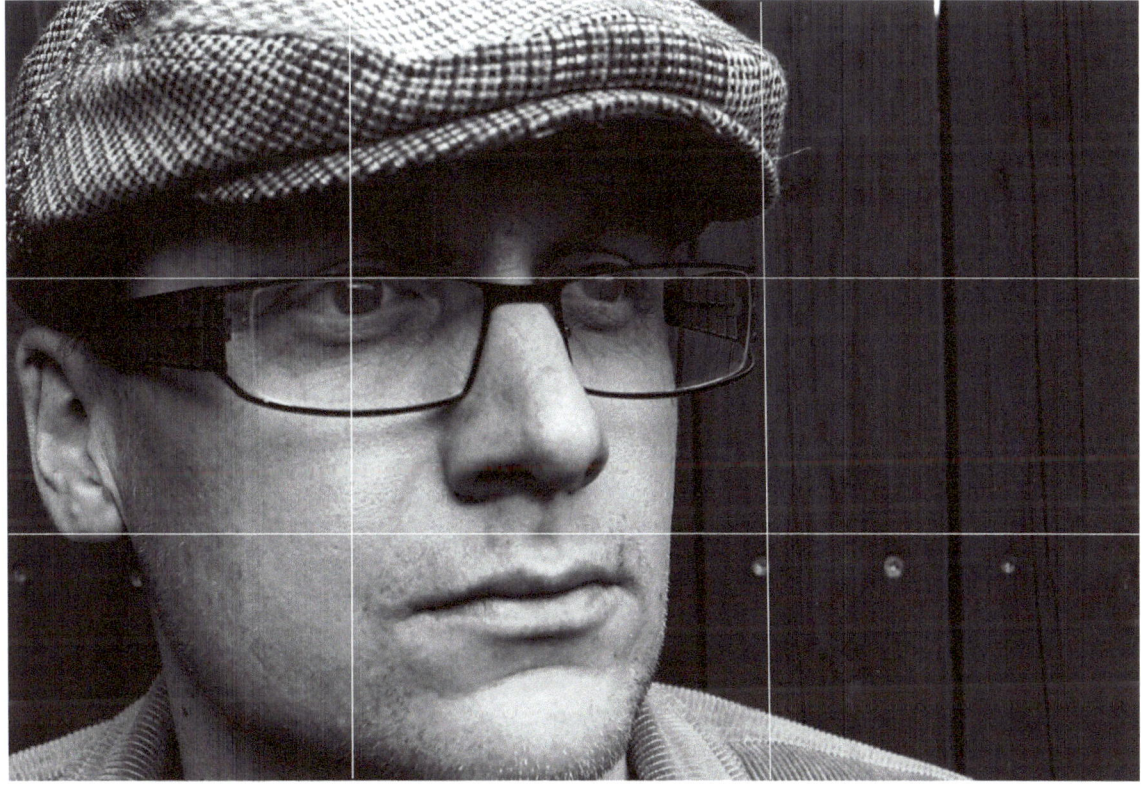

In the Self-portrait by Pavel P. (2012) above, we can see that the eyes are aligned with the top horizontal grid line and the figure is located over to the left hand side of the image giving the figure lots of room to breathe within the frame. Allowing extra space within the frame for the subject to breathe and not to feel crowded is called *Nose Room*.

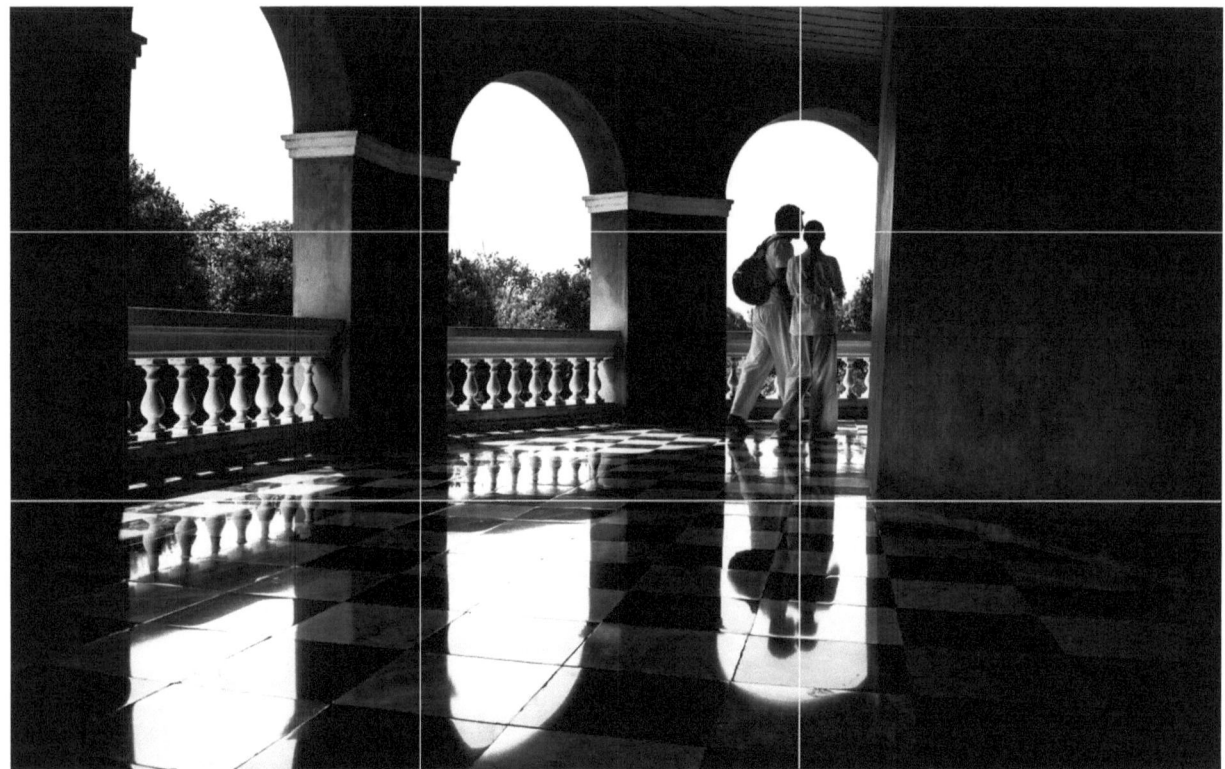

The Couple by Mrhayata (2006) seen above is a *Full Shot* (the whole figure is seen within the frame). Even here we can see that the couple's eyes are aligned with the top horizontal grid-line. Notice the need for Head Room in this picture, which allows the figures to breathe within the picture frame.

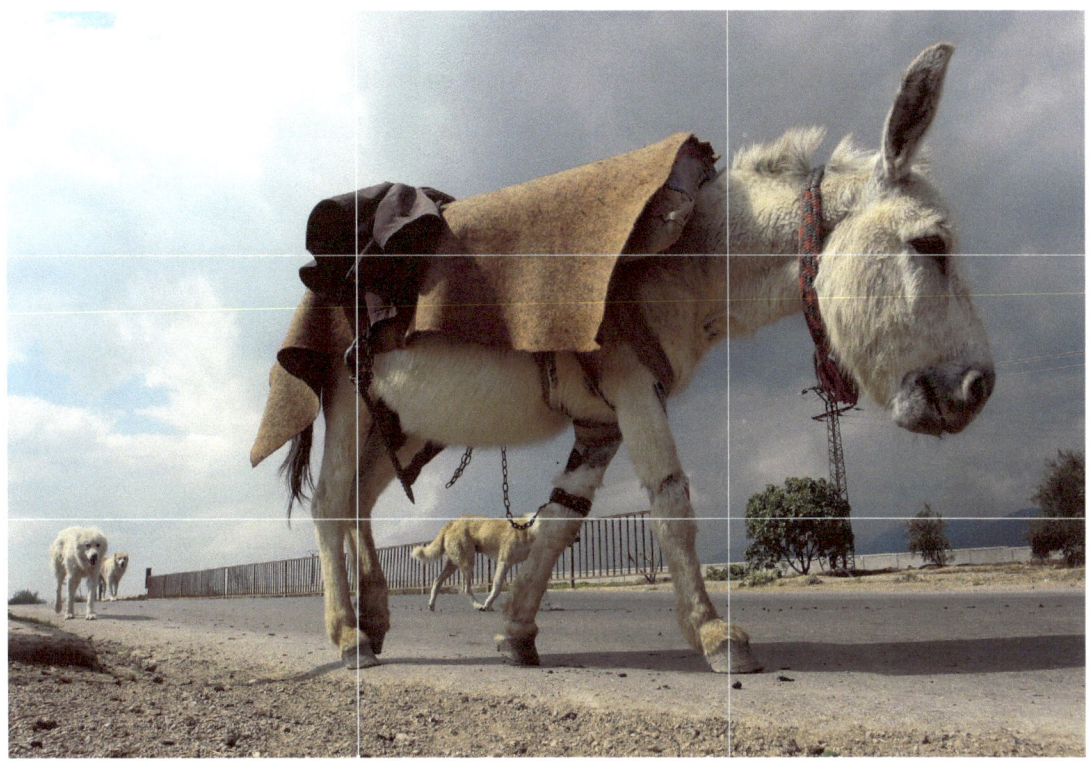

Shepherds' Donkey – James Gordon (2008) below is another *Full Shot*. Notice the donkey's eyes are aligned with the horizontal grid-line.

**Head room** is the amount of space left around the top of a subject's head so that the subject doesn't appear crowded in the picture frame. The amount of *head room* varies with each type of shot. For example: there is no need for *head room* in the extreme close-up of the Frontman below because the top of the head in not visible in the frame. *Head room* is necessary in both photos of the Couple and Shepherds' Donkey, which allows the figures to breathe within the picture frame. Even the donkey's ears need head room.

**Dead Space:** On the other hand, any space above a subject that does not add anything to your composition is considered *dead space*. Especially if what is in the background is not an important part of the story in your picture. Using the *rule of thirds* to compose your pictures will help you immensely in getting the correct amount of *head room* and reducing *dead space*.

**Nose room** refers to the amount of blank space left in front of the subject in the direction they are facing, so that they are not cramped within the frame.

The Frontman by  John O'Nolan  (2010) is an *Extreme close-up,* where only part of the face is visible in the picture frame.  Notice is this picture the face is aligned with *sweet spot* at the intersection of the top horizontal and right hand grid lines.  This unusual placement, and the amount of Nose Room, gives this image a very dynamic quality without cramping the image in the frame.

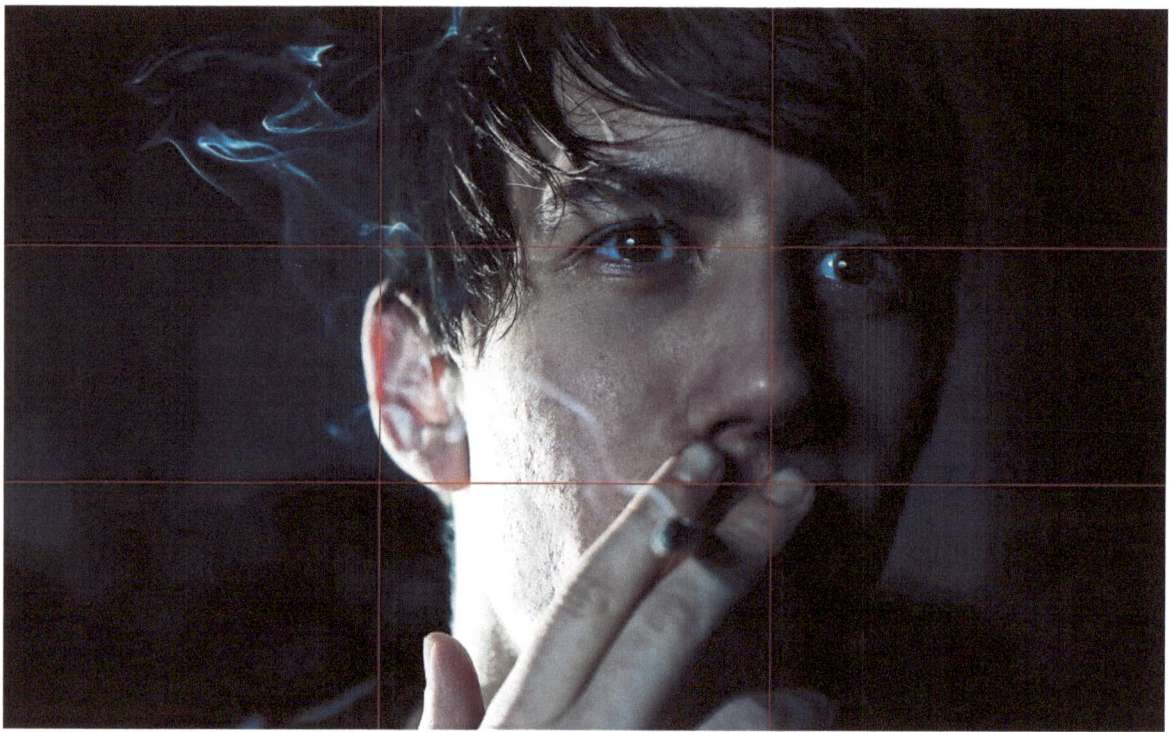

**Three Tips:**

1. Practice keeping the correct amount of *head room* when shooting a subject moving from foreground to background, or visa versa.  You'll find that you'll tilt the camera up as the subjects face fills more or the frame (close-up), and down for the wider shots, as the subjects moves further away from the camera.  A tripod is very helpful for keeping your subject framed while shooting.  *(Though I don't recommend using the digital zoom on your smartphone, this technique works the same way when zooming in or out.)*

2. Practice keeping the correct amount of *nose room* in the picture frame while your subject moves across the set.  Filming a subject as they move requires practice and experience.   You'll want to anticipate their moves...  not react to them.  A good way to practice this is to have a

friend pace back and forth across a room, pausing now and then, while you film. Keep your eyes on the subjects shoulders and which way they are facing, that will give you a clue as to which direction the subject is going to move next, even before their head does.

3. Experiment with *nose room*. For example, what happens when you change the framing and don't leave enough *nose room* in the frame. Take a look at the cropped version of the *"The Frontman"* below. In the original (above), the subject has plenty of headroom: the image, conveys the idea that he is relaxed, nonchalant, watching the world go by, and doesn't feel crowded within the frame. Not so in the lower version. We've cropped the image and eliminated all the *nose room*, the subject now communicates a feeling of being off balance, anxious, and claustrophobic. Experiment and see how many different ideas or emotions you can express simply by changing the amount of *nose room* or *head room* in your images.

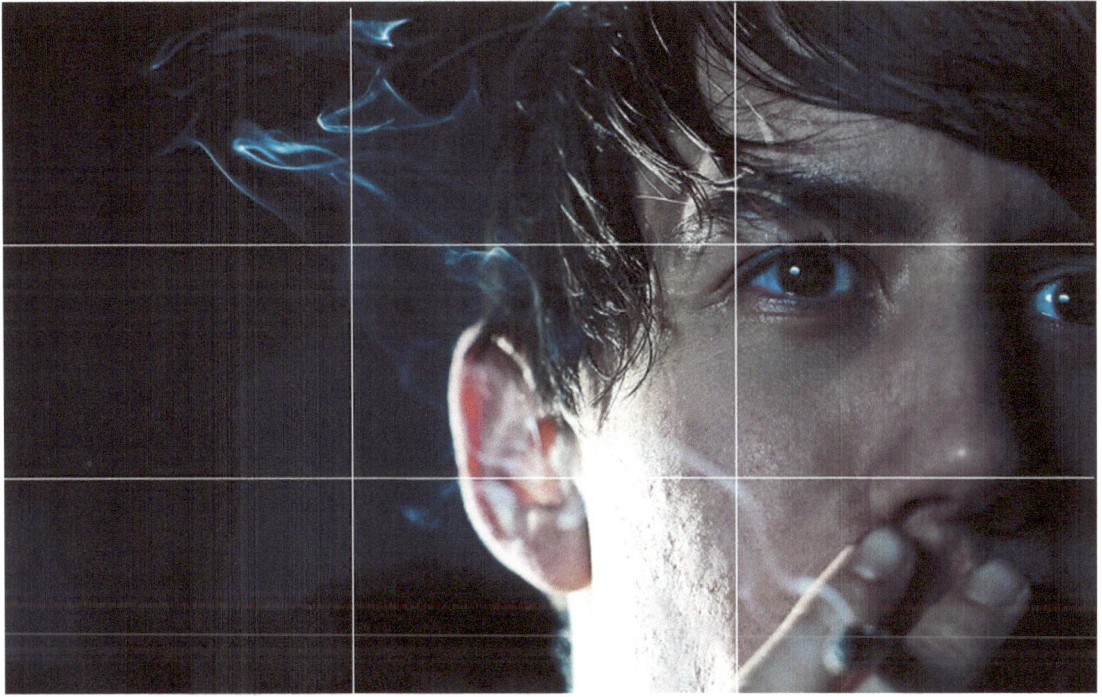

Cropped version of The Frontman by John O'Nolan (2010) illustrating the expressive power of an image when you change the amount of nose room. Notice that the eyes are still aligned with the top horizontal grid line.

**Bonus tip:** Here is a quick and easy way to do *what-ifs* with your compositions. Use your finger to crop out an element within the picture frame, before making any changes.

For example: Take a look at the photos of the Couple and the Shepherds' Donkey above. You can non-destructively recompose the image by holding up your index finger horizontally, in front of the photograph, so that it cuts off most of the space above the Couple and the Donkeys' heads... use this tip to test your compositions before you make any changes.

# 22. UNDERSTANDING CAMERA ANGLES

The camera determines what the audience sees. Changing the audience's point-of-view by changing the camera's angle is a powerful tool we can use to control what our audience experiences and feels.

Let's take a step back for a moment and clarify the difference between camera angle and a lens's field-of-view (also defined as a lens's angle-of-view). A camera's angle is defined by how the position of the camera changes vertically, either looking up, down, or from *eye-level*. Camera lenses are defined by their field-of-view from wide angle to telephoto, thereby indicating how much of the scene the lens sees, and not the camera's physical location in space. For example, a high angle shot could be done with either a wide-angle or telephoto lens.

The camera angle can change many times as a scene progresses, each from a different point-of-view, which can represent either the changing mood of the character, or the changing point-of-view of the audience, such as a change from first person to third person narrative. It can also be done to provide visual variety, like an overhead shot used in a chase scene. The change in angle **does not** have to be great to effect the audience. As a matter of fact, many directors utilize subtle changes in angle to affect the audience without the viewer being aware of it.

Let's take a look at the different camera angles and discuss their emotional and experiential attributes:

**Bird's-eye view**: – A *Bird's-eye-view* is shot from high above looking down on an object or person. It can be almost god like, making whatever is shown appear insignificant and emotionally distant. Below is a photo titled In and Our by Chrisade (2014).

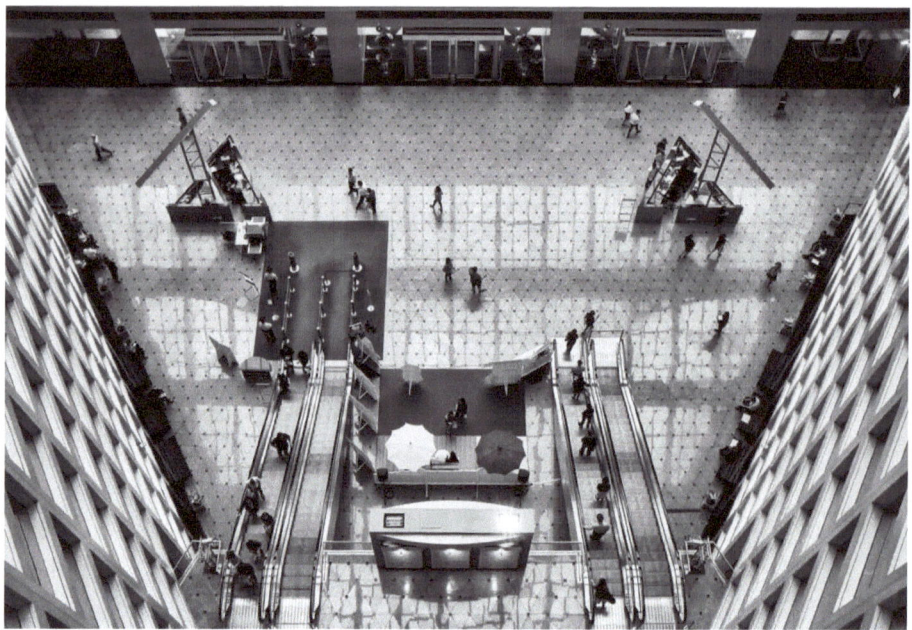

**High Angle:** A *high angle* is a shot taken from above a subjects eye-level. It is used to maintain emotional distance. Increasing the angle of the shot above eye-level changes the degree to which this shot makes an object or person smaller, less significant, weak, or in danger. The high angle framing shown below from the TV series The Good Wife (2009) illustrates Alicia's and Diane's emotional distance from Colin Sweeney, a suspected wife killer, and client accused of murder.

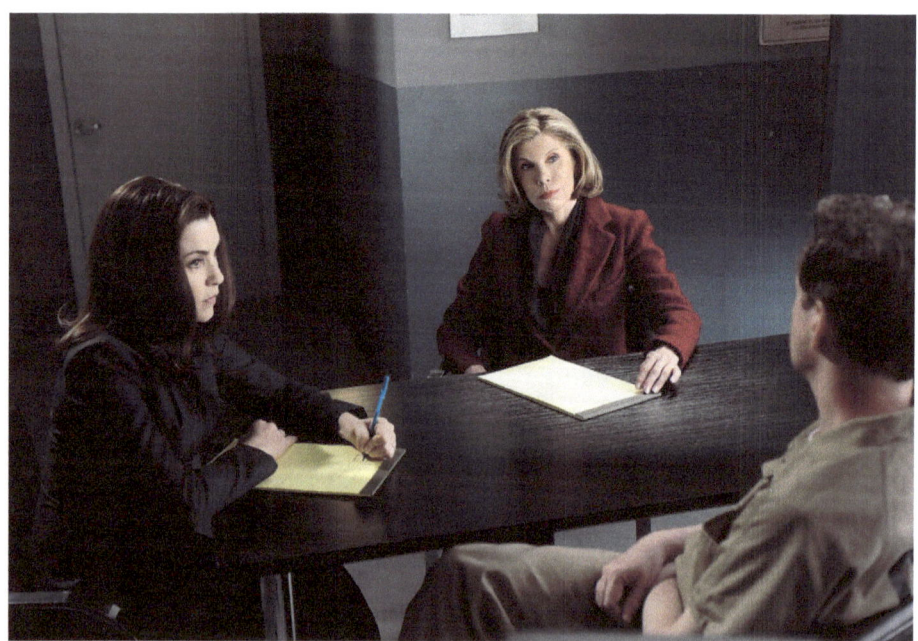

**Eye level:** When the camera is at the same height as the subject it puts the viewer right in the action and on equal footing with the actors. This angle is used frequently in comedies and is often described as being neutral and having no dramatic effect on the viewer. Eye level shots are frequently used in comedies like Frasier because they are considered dramatically neutral. Frasier (TV Series 1993 – 2004)

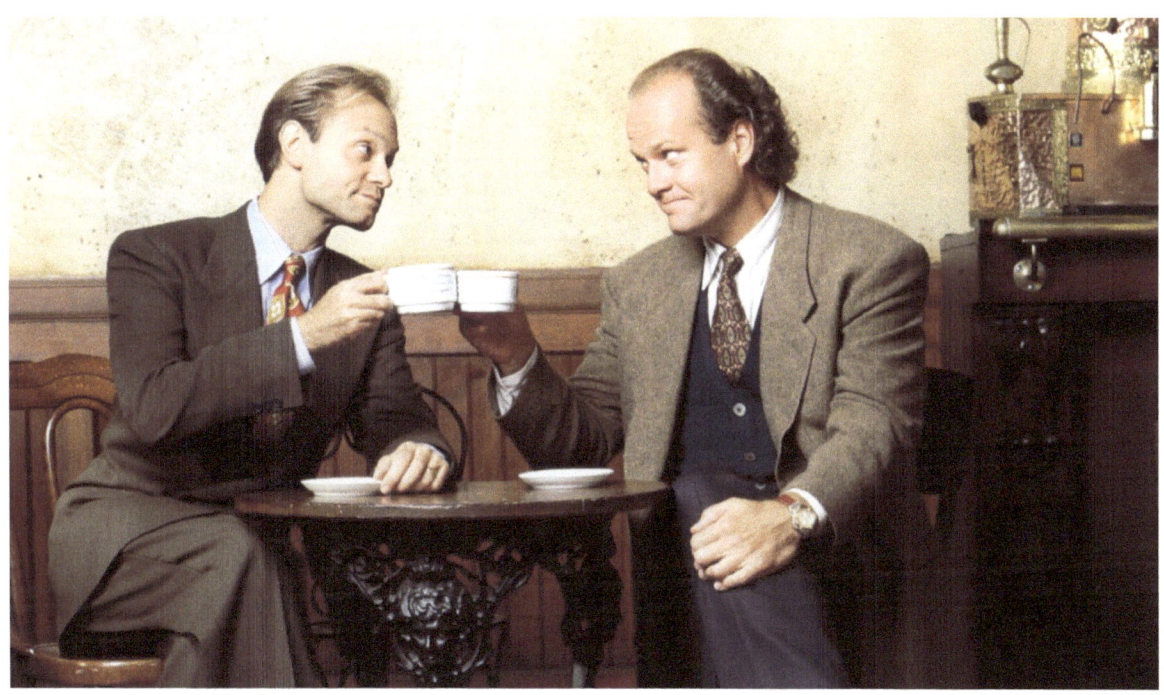

But, this can change when a close-up is used to emphasize a special moment, such as a subjective shot. *(see the chapter, Subjective Shots for more details)* A close-up has the power to focus our attention on an emotion, a thought, or reveal a reaction or point-of-view. The intensity of the emotion is determined by the proximity of the camera to the subject. In the still from the movie Silence of the Lambs (1991), despite the fact of the shot being at eye level, this point-of-view shot of Hannibal Lecter communicates menace and control.

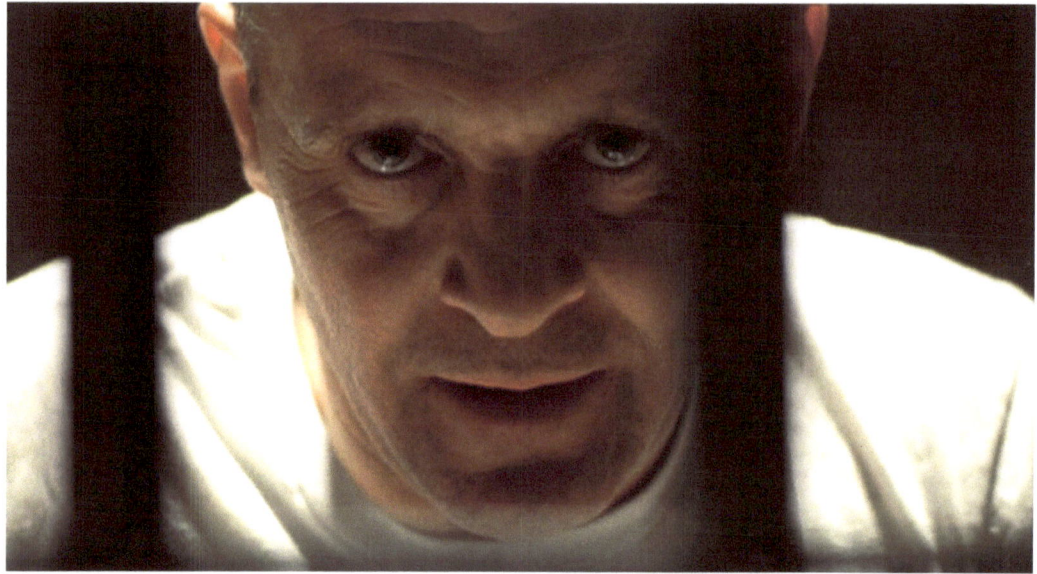

**Low angle:** shot will make the subject look, powerful, dominant, intimidating.  It is also used to make a short actors look taller.  Below is a still from the TV series Breaking Bad (2008-2013). This low angle shot, helps portray Walter and Jessie as being both powerful and intimidating.

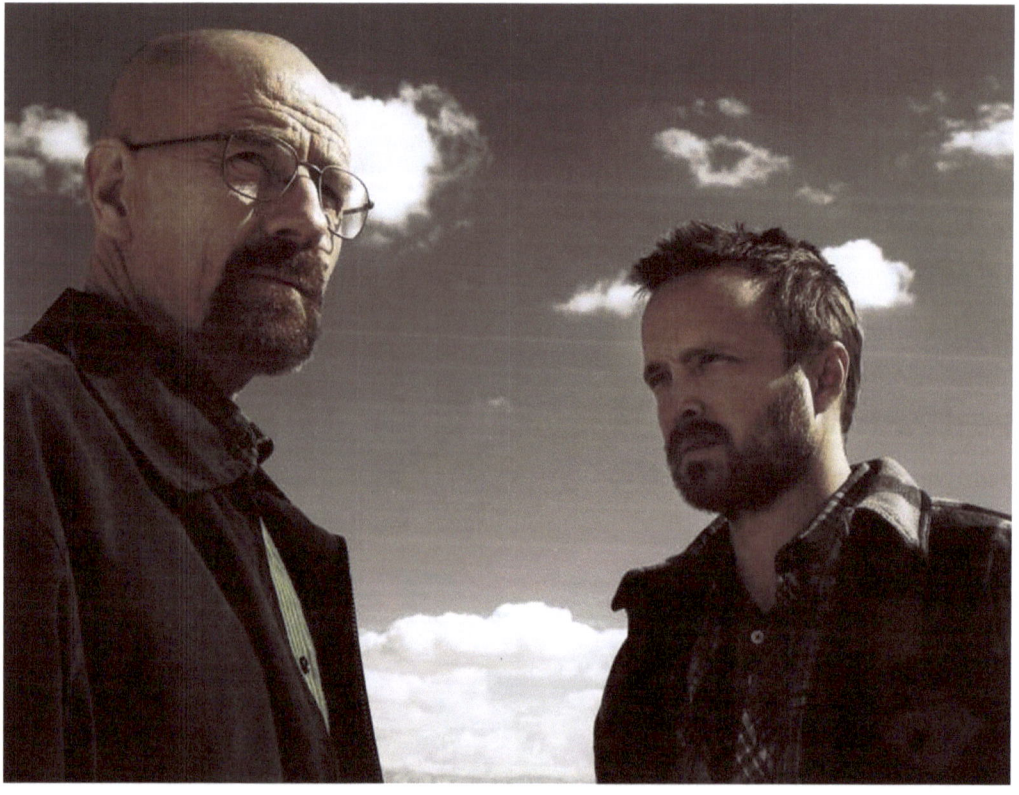

**Worm's-eye view:** Looking up to something. It makes objects look tall, strong, powerful and larger than life. The use of worm's-eye view shots is one of the many wonderful hallmarks of this movie classic, Citizen Kane (1941)

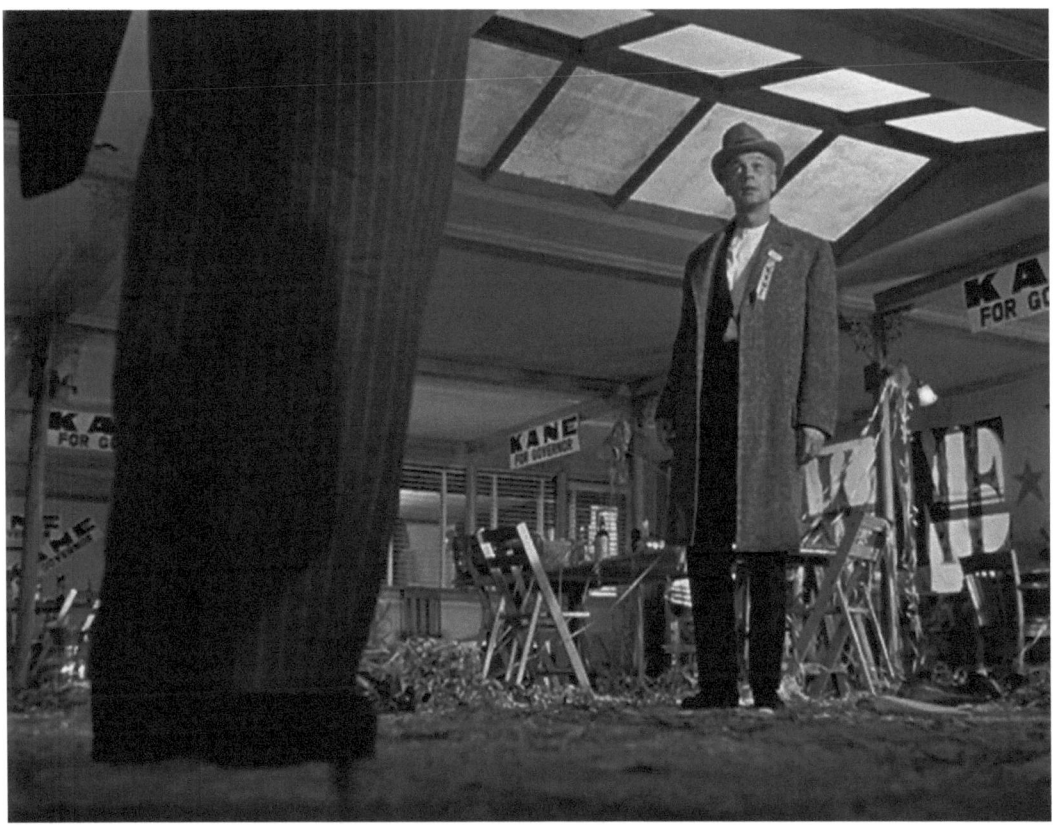

**Dutch Tilt:** The camera is set on a axis that is not horizontal, so that all the vertical lines in the shot are at an angle. Portrays imbalance, off center, something creepy, dream-like, disorientation, instability, unrest, and danger. It is often used as a Point-of-view shot for a subject who is drunk, delirious, or under the influence of some drug. Below we see a still from Spike Lee's movie Do The Right Thing.

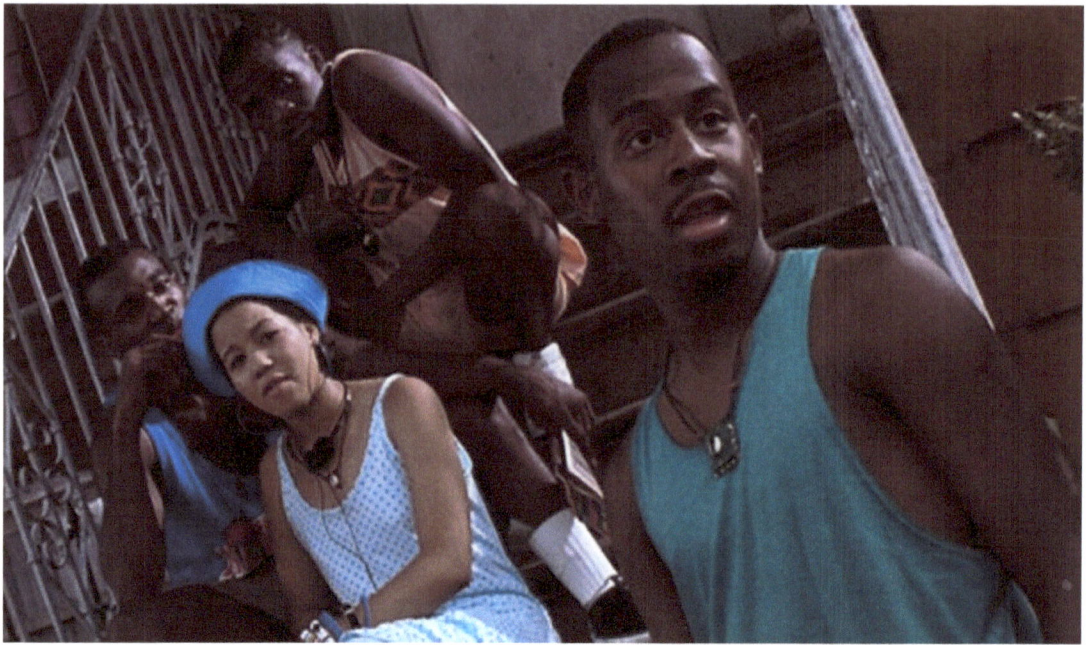

**Three Tips:**

1. Experiment with a variety of camera angles. Take three shots of the same subject and with the same lens: One, where the camera is eight inches above eye level looking down; one eight inches below looking up; and the third at eye level.  How do these three differ from each other?

2. Repeat number one, but this time increase the height or depth of the shot to 18" to 24" above eye level?

3. Experiment with different lens attachments *(fish-eye, telephoto, normal, or wide angle)*. Is there a best lens for each type of camera angle?

# 23.  INTRODUCE THEM TO YOUR WORLD – Using Establishing shots

Establishing shots are used to show your audience where your movie is taking place.  It's an important part of video storytelling and film language.  Many scenes, open with an establishing shot to help the audience get its bearings by establishing relationships between characters, objects, and places as the scene starts.   They can be famous landmarks like the Statue of Liberty, the Eiffel Tower, or the Las Vegas Strip; or a barroom; or leaves falling to the ground, or a field of grass dancing in the wind; or the interior of the New York City library's reading room as seen in the movie Ghostbusters (1984).

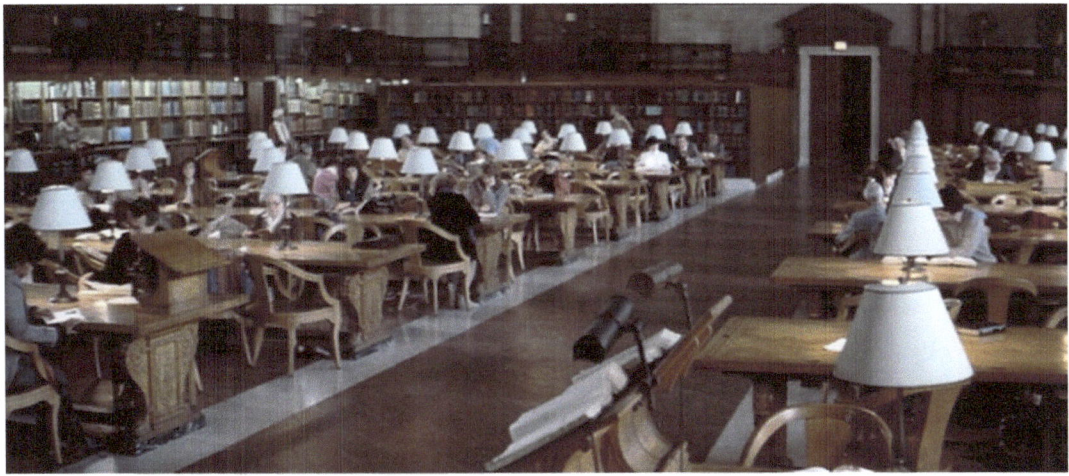

Sometimes, instead of a single establishing shot, you may wish to use a series of shots—a sequence—to give a more complete picture of the location.  For example, if your location is the beach, you might have a long shot, then a shot of waves rolling in, and finally a shot of a crab scurrying along the sand.  It's up to you and what is needed to inform the audience about where they are.  Let's look at two famous Hollywood movie examples, and then we'll discuss how you can do it.

**Woody Allen's Manhattan** opens with a series of black and white shots of Manhattan at night.  This montage sequence of beautiful images and music is designed to convey Woody Allen's feelings about the special magic that is New York City seen at night from the movie Manhattan (1979)

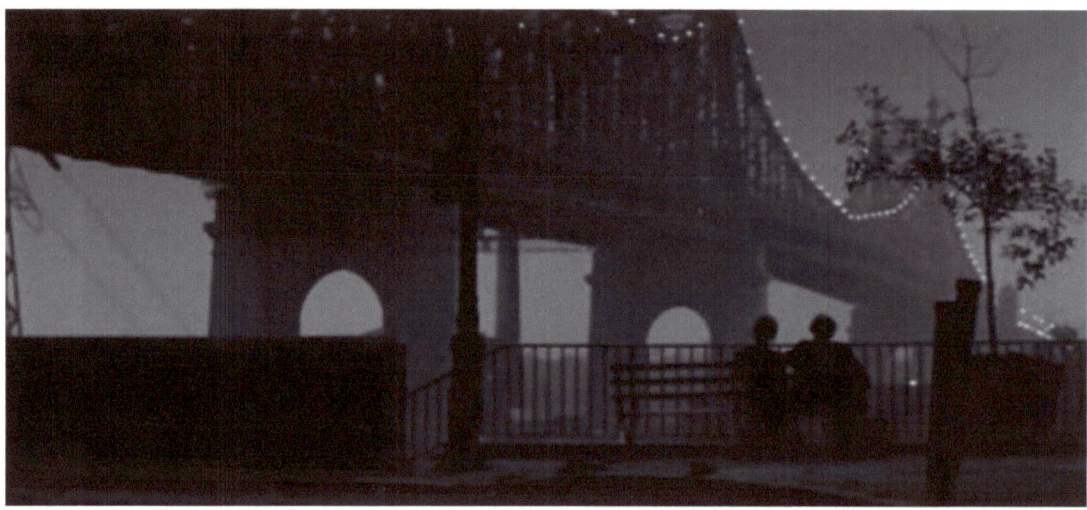

**Frank Darabon's The Shawshank Redemption** (1994) opens with an aerial tour to introduce us to the prison, a location that functions as an important character in the story

Interestingly, Darabon's establishing shot doesn't come until eight and half minutes into the film, after you've met the two main characters — Red played by Morgan Freeman and Andy Dufresne played by Tim Robins. It's one continuous aerial shot. It opens as we see a grey bus driving up the tree lined roadway leading to Shawshank prison. We fly past the bus and over the fortress type façade of the prison offices...

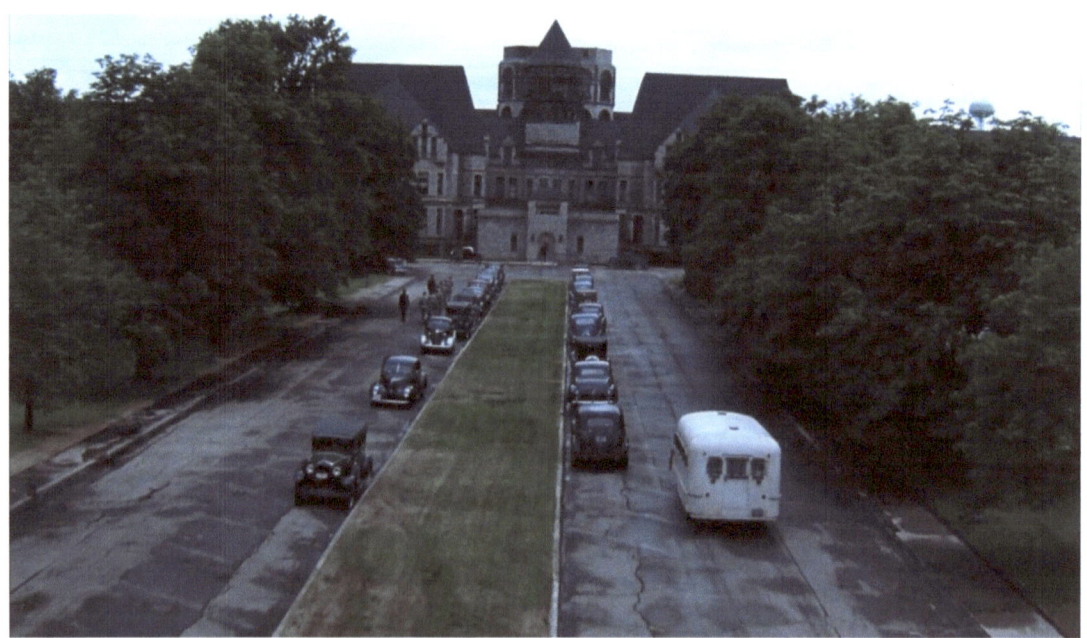

...over the guard's lookout posts, the prison yard and buildings, and circling around the a flag of the State of Maine we watch as the inmates, in the yard, hurriedly walk toward the rear gate where the grey bus and the new prisons are arriving. The shot ends there as we cut to the inside of the bus and a medium wide shot of Andy Dufresne sitting in the back. And we hear Morgan Freeman's narration saying, "Andy came to Shawshank prison in early 1947 for murdering his wife and the fellow she was banging." With that one shot the audience now knows where the rest of the film is going to take place.

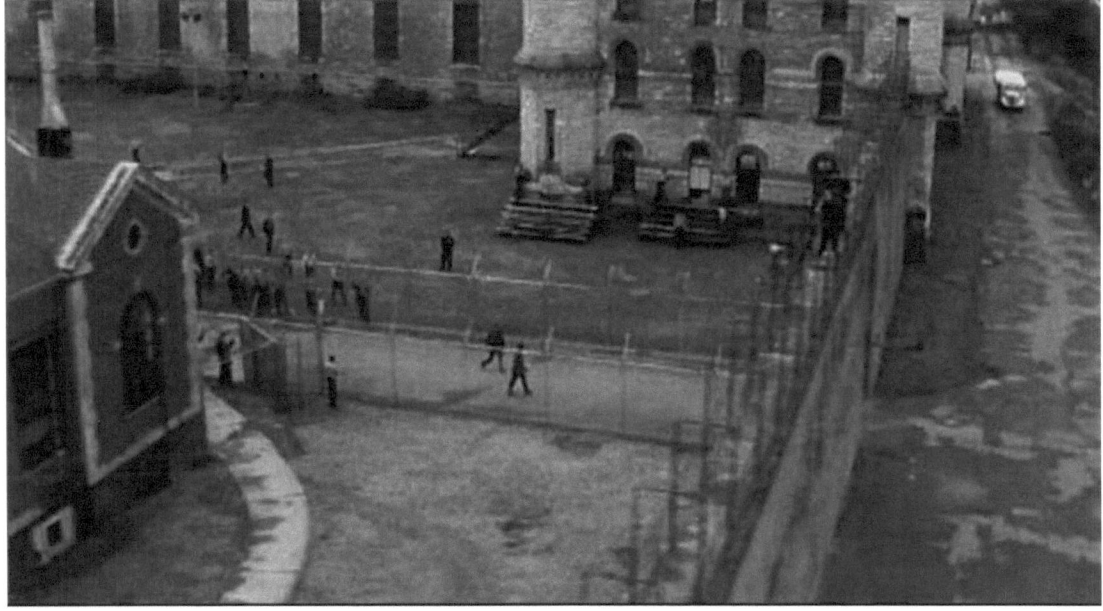

**How can you do it:** In many cases, you'll only need one shot to establish a sense of place. Let's say we're going to film a party at a friends house. We'll use a simple establishing shot of the house and street where the party is taking place as our example. You'd be surprised at how much information you can show with a single establishing shot. Below is a photo by lori L. Stalteri called White House (2011) that would make an excellent establishing shot.

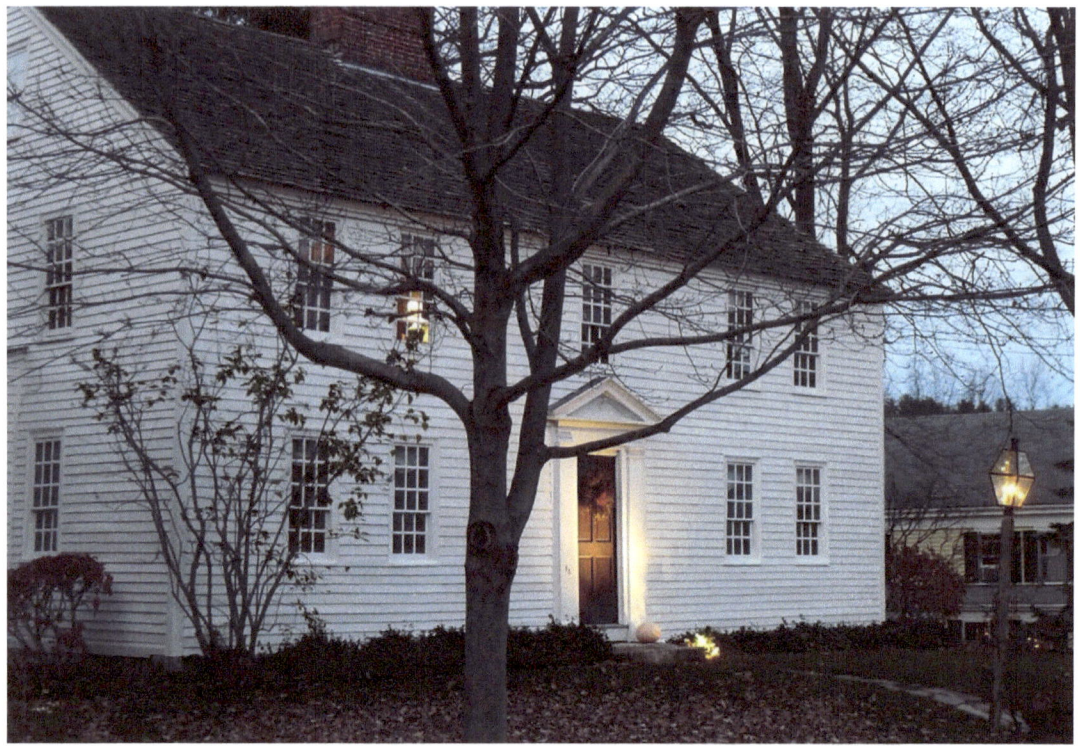

For example: It's easy to show if the party is in the city or the suburbs. Is the lawn and garden well tended or, are there weeds and overflowing garbage cans. Is there an old jalopy parked in the driveway or, a new Mercedes. The street lights come on and you know it's early evening. We know it's fall because we see bare trees and leaves on the ground.

Our minds process images at lightning speed, so your audience has taken in all this information in a second or two, and you can now move on to tell the story. In the example above we have establish location, time of day, season, and economic and social class. It's a story all unto itself.

**Here are three tips on using establishing shots:**

1. Establishing shots can be of any location. Exterior or interior. If your establishing shot is of an interior, is the room tidy, neat, rundown, are their dirty dishes in the sink, or is everything spotless. Think of it as telling us who, where, when, what, and how. The establishing shot in Alfred Hitchcock's movie Rear Window is brilliant example of how to inform the audience about a character's life in just one shot.

2. Depth is good. Think in terms of fore, middle, and background. On exterior shots, showing a branch in the foreground of the frame helps establishes depth and a sense of

environment.   In an interior shot,  have a vase or glass in the foreground, or shoot through the slats in a chair helps to add depth.

3.  Try moving the camera on a dolly or slider for your establishing shot.  This will produce very dynamic images.  *(see Make it Move – Tools for moving the camera for simple tools and techniques for moving the camera.)*

# 24. SHOOTING AT KID LEVEL

Enter the world of children — and get great images from their point of view. One of the wonderful things about film is its ability to transport the viewer to another place, another world. In this case, to experience things as kids do. It means getting down... on the floor... on hands and knees... or belly, with your camera. It's another world down there, one many of us have fond memories of. Below is a photo by Adam Jones titled Children at Nativity Play - La Cumbre - Argentina (2009)

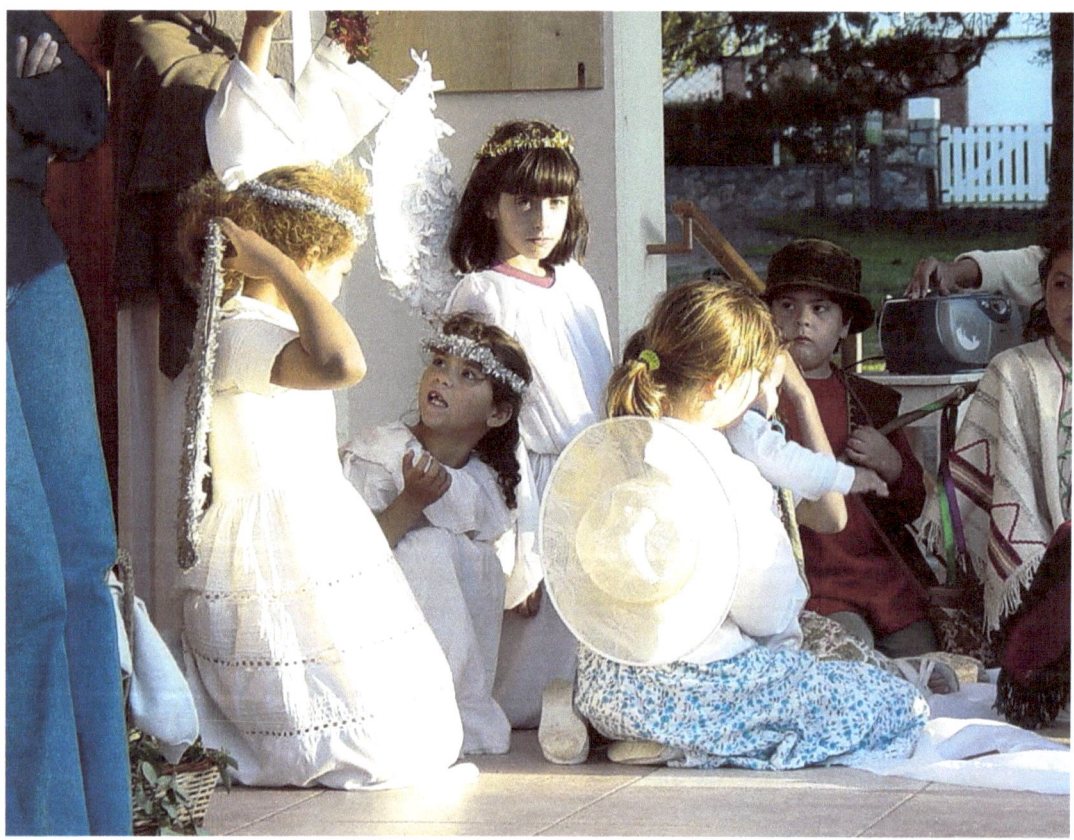

Take a look at the photos and videos you've shot of your kids. If most of them are taken at adult eye level looking down on the subject, you have an opportunity to break new cinematic ground and visually enrich your movies and photographs.

In addition to your movies being a video record of your family, why not make them entertaining as well? How about shooting the adults from the kid's point of view.

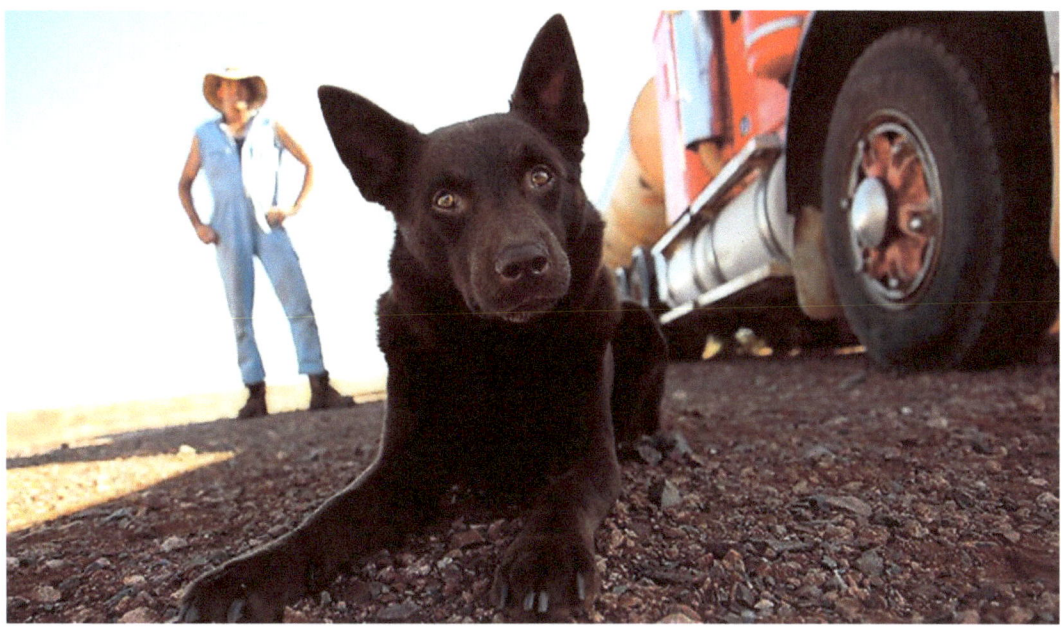

Above is a still from the movie Red Dog (2011) which illustrates how being in the action isn't just for filming kids, but for pets as well. Why not show your audience the world the way your dog or cat sees it. The best way to do that is get low and close to your subject. You'll be surprised at how entertaining it can be.

**Three tips:**

1. To get steady shots from near ground level, use a mini tripod like the GorillaPod shown below.

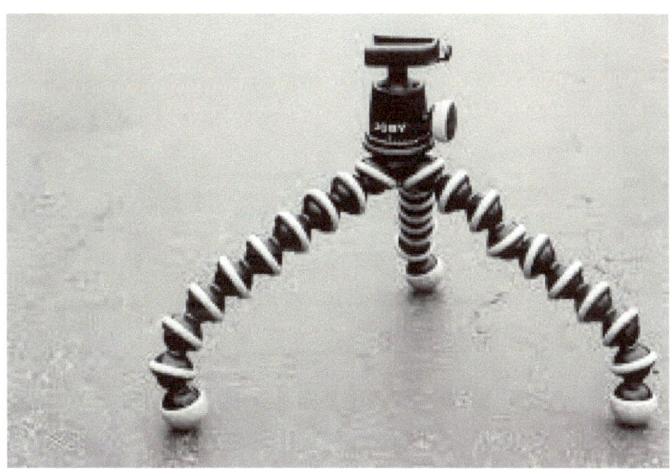

2. There is a psychological element in where you place your camera. Shooting down on characters can make them seem less important, while shooting up can make them seem larger than life.

3. You don't need to have kids or pets in a scene to use a low angle shot to add interest to your movie. It's just a different, more dynamic way of seeing the world. Try it. Happy shooting.

# 25. MASTERING CAMERA ANGLES

Studying Alfred Hitchcock's movies is a great way to learn how to combine different camera angles and shot types to create mood and emotions. Understanding how to utilize these filmmaking techniques can enhance any type of project, whether it's fiction film, a music video, family documentary, business or service ad, or your child's birthday party. In the following analysis of a scene from Psycho, we'll consider three types of shots:

- A *Bird's-eye-view* is shot from high above looking down on an object or person. It is a very unnatural shot, almost god like, making whatever is shown as being insignificant and emotionally distant.

- A *high angle* is a shot taken from above a subjects eye-level, but is not at an extreme angle, like the *bird's-eye view*. It is used to maintain emotional distance. Increasing the angle of the shot above eye-level changes the degree to which this shot makes an object or person smaller, less significant, weak or in danger.

- A *Close-up* is a certain feature or part of a subject that takes up most of the frame. A close-up of a person emphasizes their emotional state. The tighter the close-up the greater the emotion.

Below are the shots Hitchcock used in this sequence:

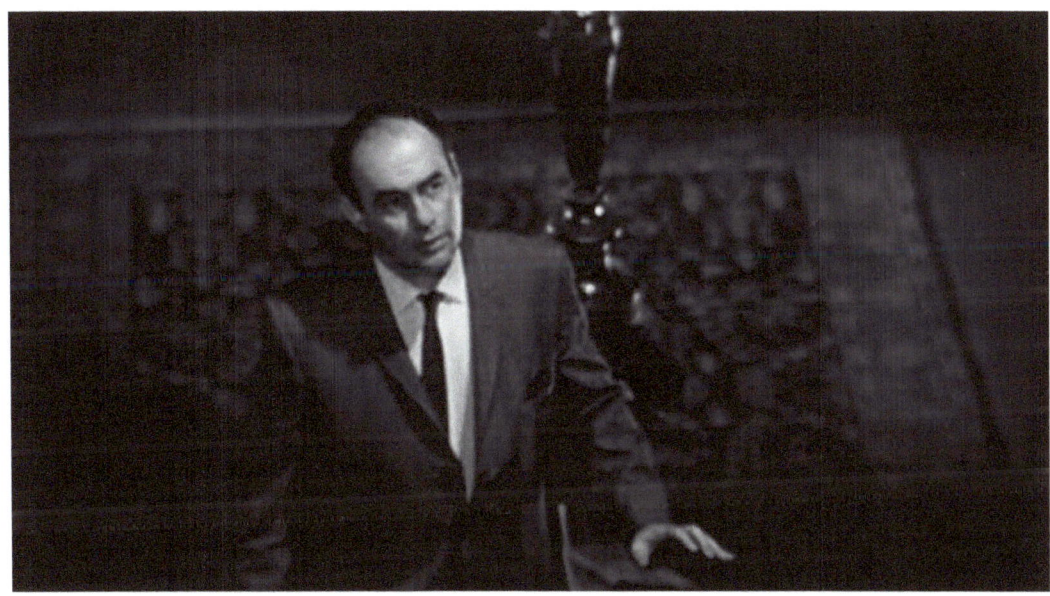

1. Arbogast enters the house and climbs the stairs –High Angle Shot, Psycho (1960)

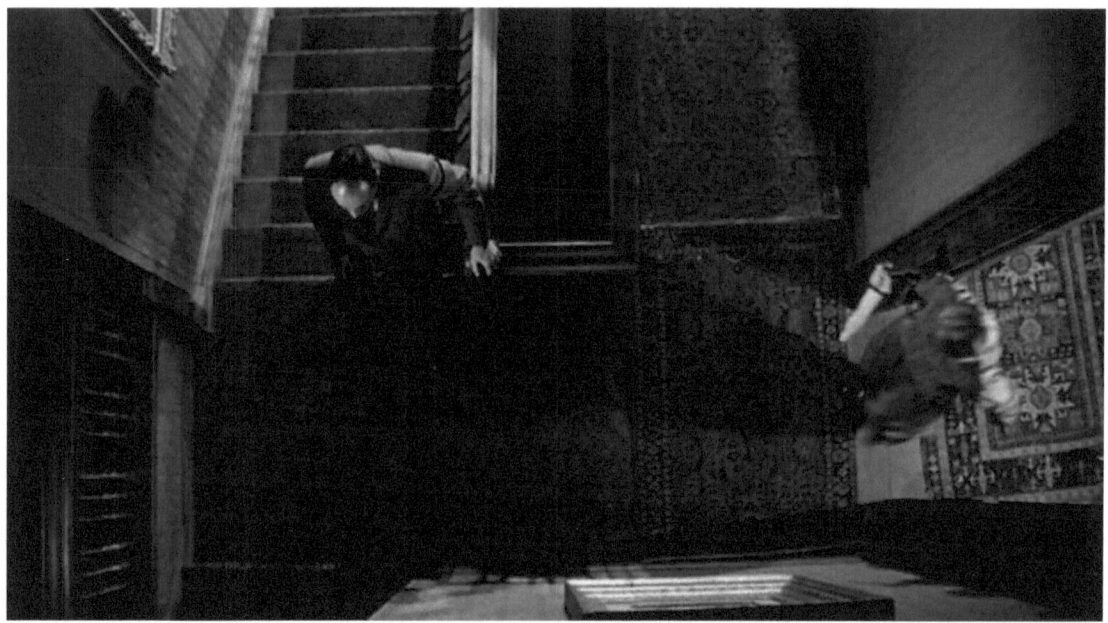

2. Arbogast reaches the top of the stairs — Cut to: Bird's-eye view. A figure emerges from bedroom on the right and raises a knife to stabs Arbogast.

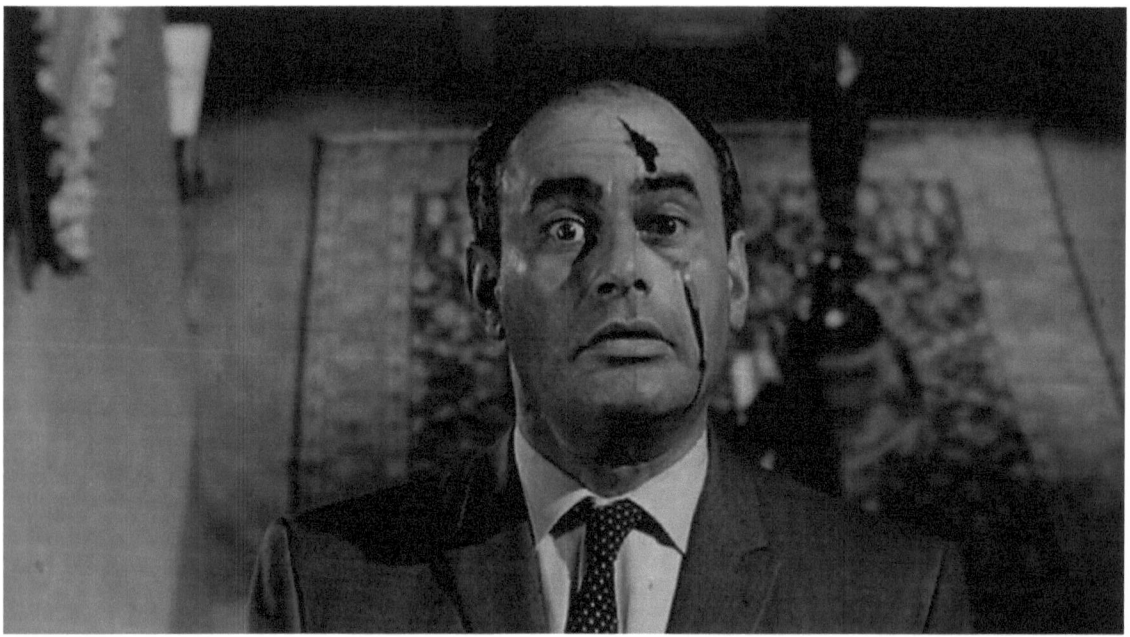

3. Cut to: Close-up of the knife cutting Arbogast, he falls backwards down the stairs.

**Three tips:**

1.  Develop a short scene and create a shot list for it that includes; medium, low or high angle shots, and close-ups. As you put your list together, consider what do you want your audience to experience? And, how are your shot choices going to help you achieve that goal?

2.  Experiment with using different degrees of High Angle shots to express danger, alienation, or helplessness. Notice how the feeling created changes as the shot's angle rises above eyelevel?

3.  The further away the camera is from the subject the more neutral is the emotion. Experiment using the subjects' proximity to the camera to either distance the audience from the action, or put the audience right in the middle of it.

# 26. SUBJECTIVE SHOTS — Who's Point-of-View is it?

There are two chapters in this book where we've discuss point-of-view. One is titled *"Video CPR"*, which talks about how to shoot and edit a scene using the three basic shots which I called "C","P", and "R".

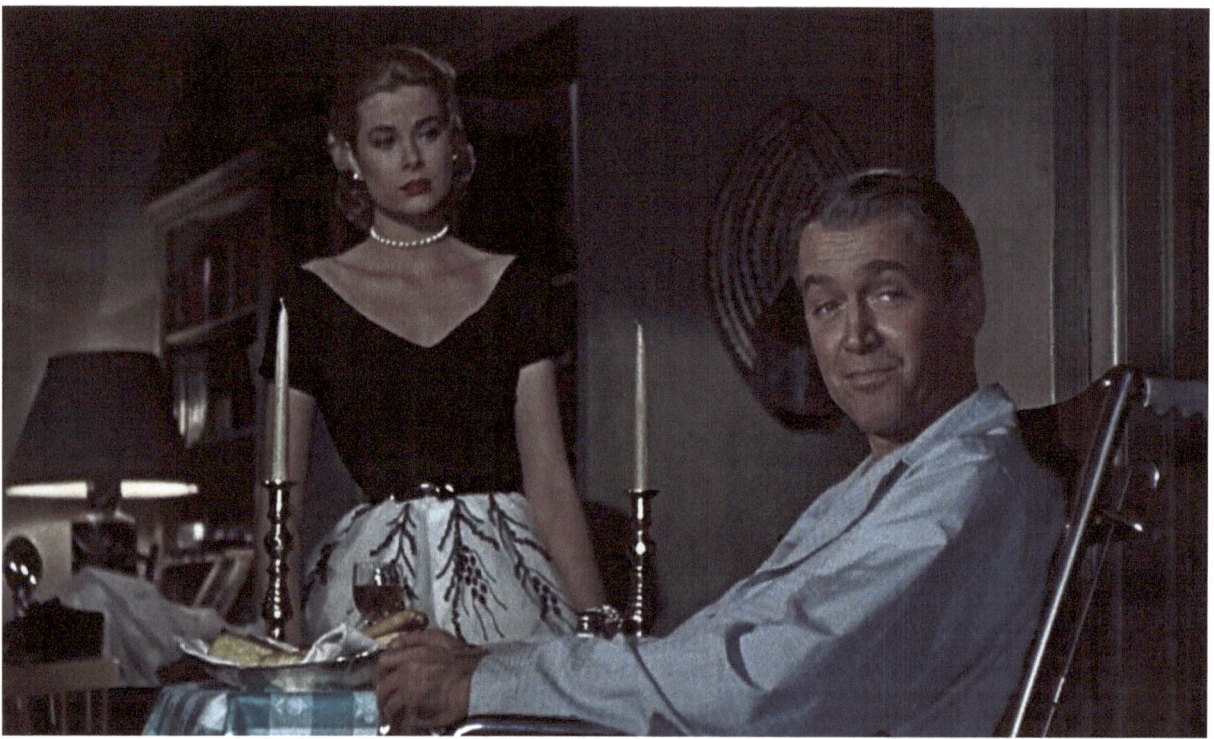

The second point-of-view is *"Shooting at Kid Level"* where we explore lowering the camera to a child's or animal's eye level to show the world from their point of view. This is considered a *subjective shot*.

Both are different. In the CPR sequence, we're seeing what the subject of the scene is looking at. The "C" *(see)* and "R" *(reaction)* shots don't have to be at eye level to work. They can be from any angle or position as long as the camera can see the subject "look" and "react".

In a *Subjective shot* the camera (who's POV is our Hero or lead actor) is usually at the subject's eye-level. We see what they see. By doing this, we place the audience right in the middle of the action, not outside of it. You're telling the story from the first-person's perspective rather than the second or third person omniscient observer. In many movies, at crucial points in the story, the camera will switch to a subjective shot, to emphasis what the hero is experiencing. For example here is a *subjective shot* seen from Indiana Jones' POV of Major Toht from the movie Raiders of the Lost Ark (1981)

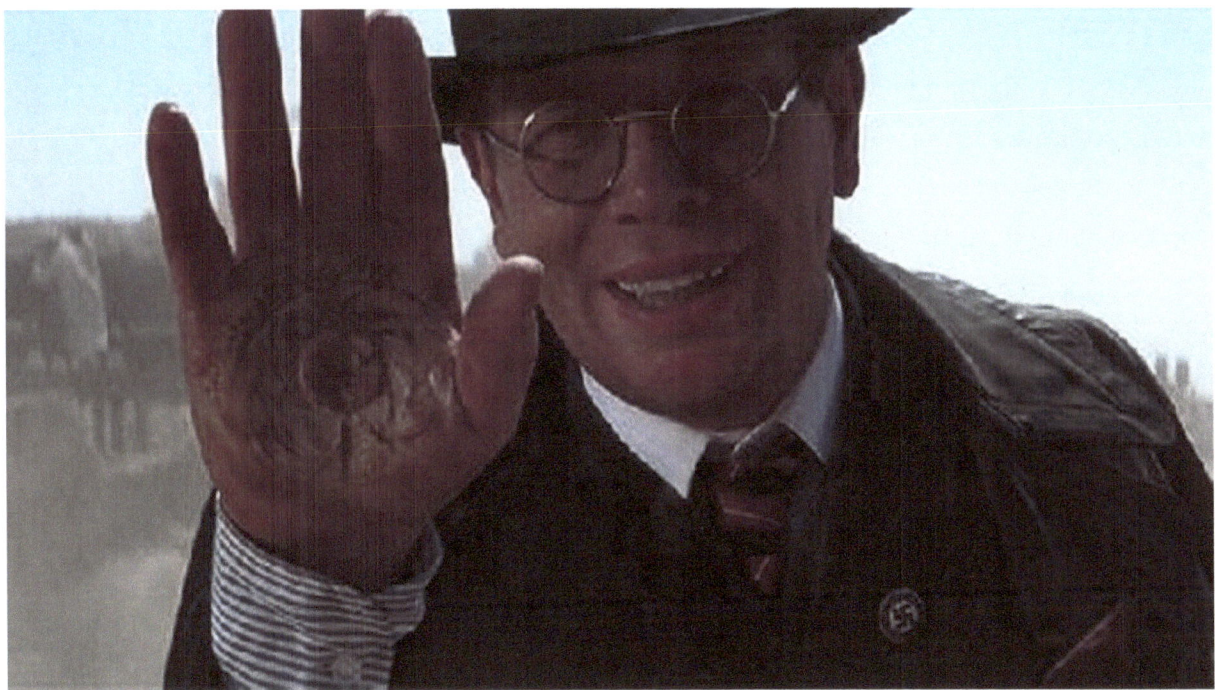

Many times in a movie when a character sits down, the camera booms down with them, so that it is always at the subject's eye level. That way the audience experiences the world, subjectively, just like the subject.

In a dialog sequence we may sometimes take both character's subjective POV. For example: if someone in that scene is standing next to our seated actor, looking down, we can change the position of the camera to show a POV for each actor. The standing actor's POV will be shot from above, looking down. And the reverse shot, the camera will be looking up, representing the seated actor's POV. This also maintains the eye-line between the two actors for continuity.

**Three Tips:**

1. Think of the camera as being the audience's eyes. What you shoot is what the audience sees and feels. If you want the audience in the middle of the action, put the camera there. If you want the audience to be an objective observer, move the camera outside of the action, looking in.

2.  By editing together both the Subjective shot and CPR shots, we allow the audience to see everything the way the subject does.  It allows the audience to be in the action, seeing and feeling everything that our characters do.

3.  By the same token there is no reason you can't combine different types of camera angles with subjective shots.  Sometimes, the more camera angles you combine together, the more interesting it is for your audience.  Telling the story from many different perspectives in a chase or fight scene, can be very effective.  Doing so you go from: the hero's first-person's subjective POV; to the second person's perspective; and to relieve the building tension, completely stepping out of the action by showing the third person omniscient observer POV, and then step back in again.  By doing this you can create a very exciting sequence, with many ups and downs, for your audience.

# 27. THE 180° WORKSPACE — The 180° Rule *(Continuity)*

You're planning to shoot a scene for a new video for your business. We've put together a shot list, found a location, worked out where the actors will stand (the blocking) and how they'll move within the scene. What we need to do next is plan where we'll put the camera so that there will be no break in *continuity,* and the edited shots will fit together smoothly from the beginning to the end of the scene.

We need to be concerned about *continuity* because there is a right and wrong location for the camera, in relationship to the actors, and if you set up your camera in the wrong location, you'll confuse your audience about where they are in space.

We utilize the *line-of-action* to locate our camera. *The line-of-action* is an imaginary line drawn from one actor to the other, that defines the boundary of a half-circular 180° space in which we can safely locate our camera, and not confuse our audience about the location of the actors, the background, and any other objects within the picture frame. (see the diagram below)

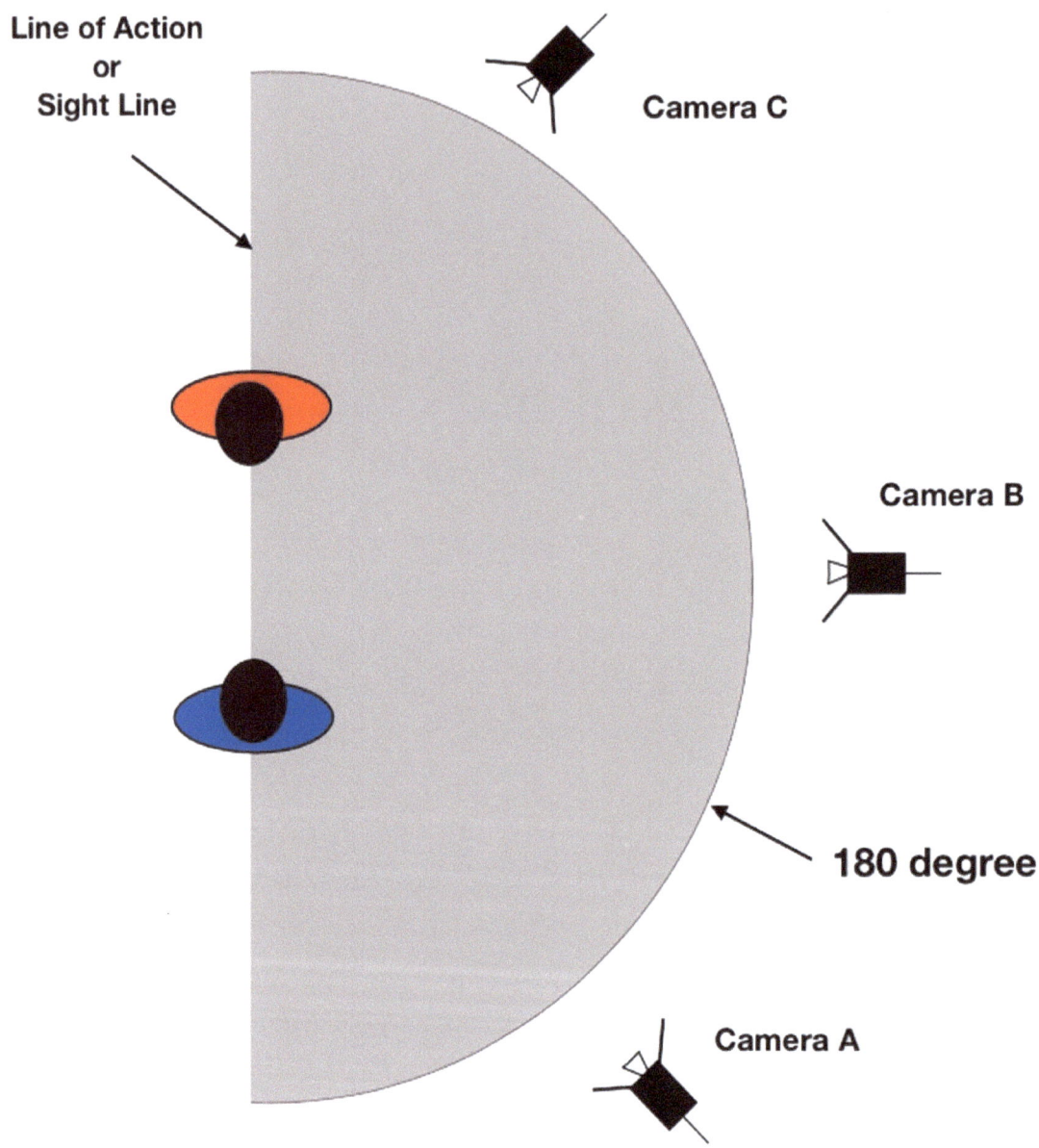

**Line of Action
or
Sight Line**

**Camera C**

**Camera B**

**180 degree**

**Camera A**

When we set-up our cameras anywhere within the 180° half-circle defined by the *Line-of-Action* we can maintain *continuity* of the edited images. That's called the *180-degree rule*. It allows us to use the working space on one side of the *line-of-action*, the grey semi circle in the diagram, to position our cameras anywhere within that area and maintain consistent screen direction and space.

In the diagram above all three cameras are set up on one side of the *line*. Below are the images captured by these cameras. Notice that in all the shots from camera's A, B, and C both men are seen on the same side of the frame in each picture. And, they maintain eye contact with each other. When edited together these images will smoothly flow from one cut to the next.

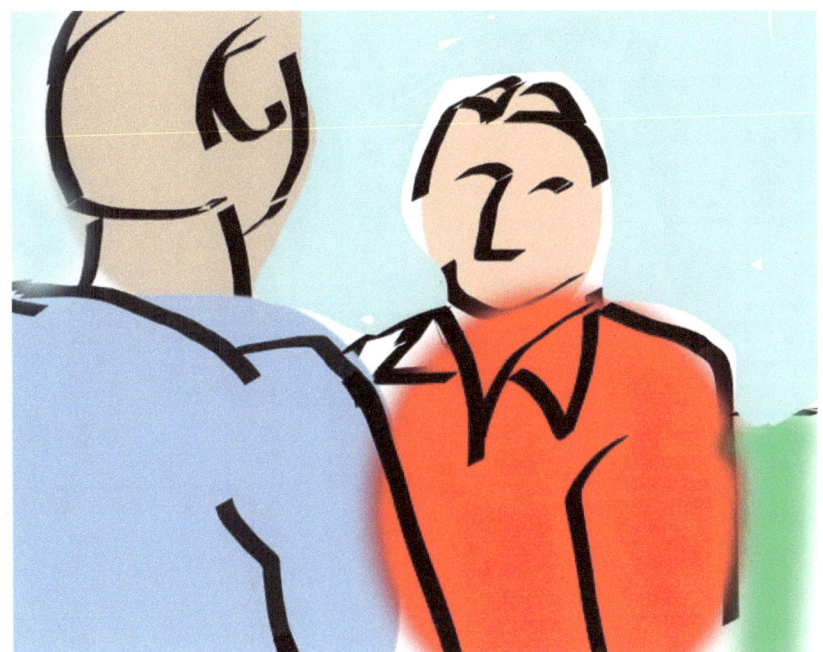

Camera A

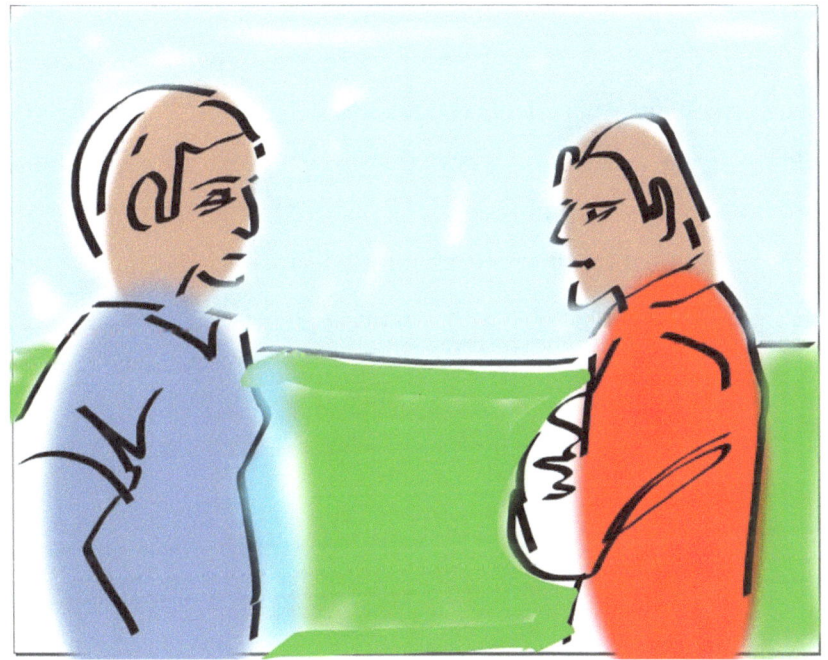

Camera B

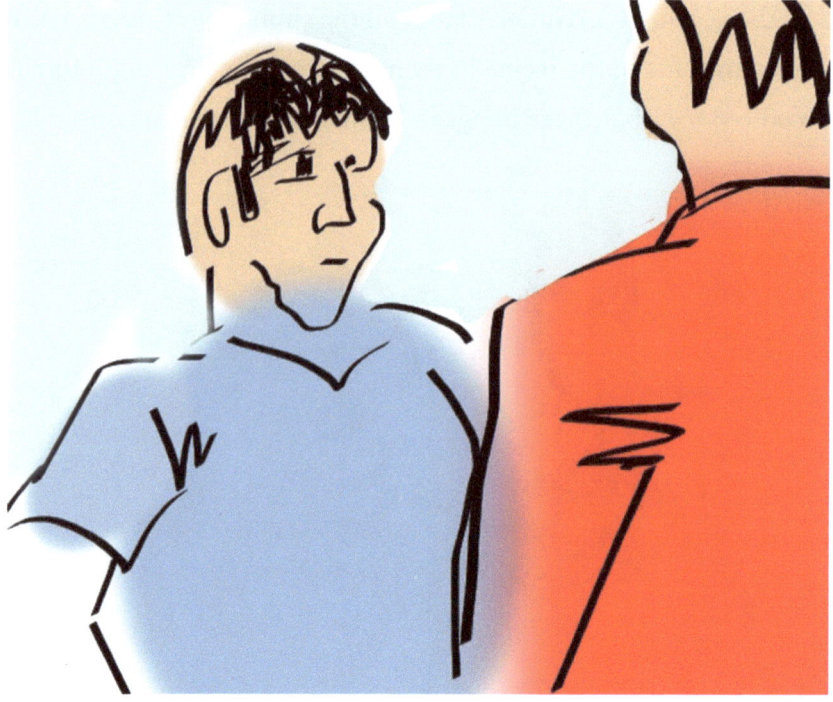

Camera C

The big problem with crossing the line is what happens to your actor's eye line and the background of the scene. A movie's continuity works because the audience understands the geography of the scene.

In the example below, Camera D has crossed the line of action. Comparing the shots from Camera A and D we can see how this effects the actor's eye line and the background of the scene. We now see a building in the background where there wasn't one before. When editing these shots together the actors jump from one side of the picture frame to the other, and the background with the building pops up in one shot and disappears in the next, confusing the audience.

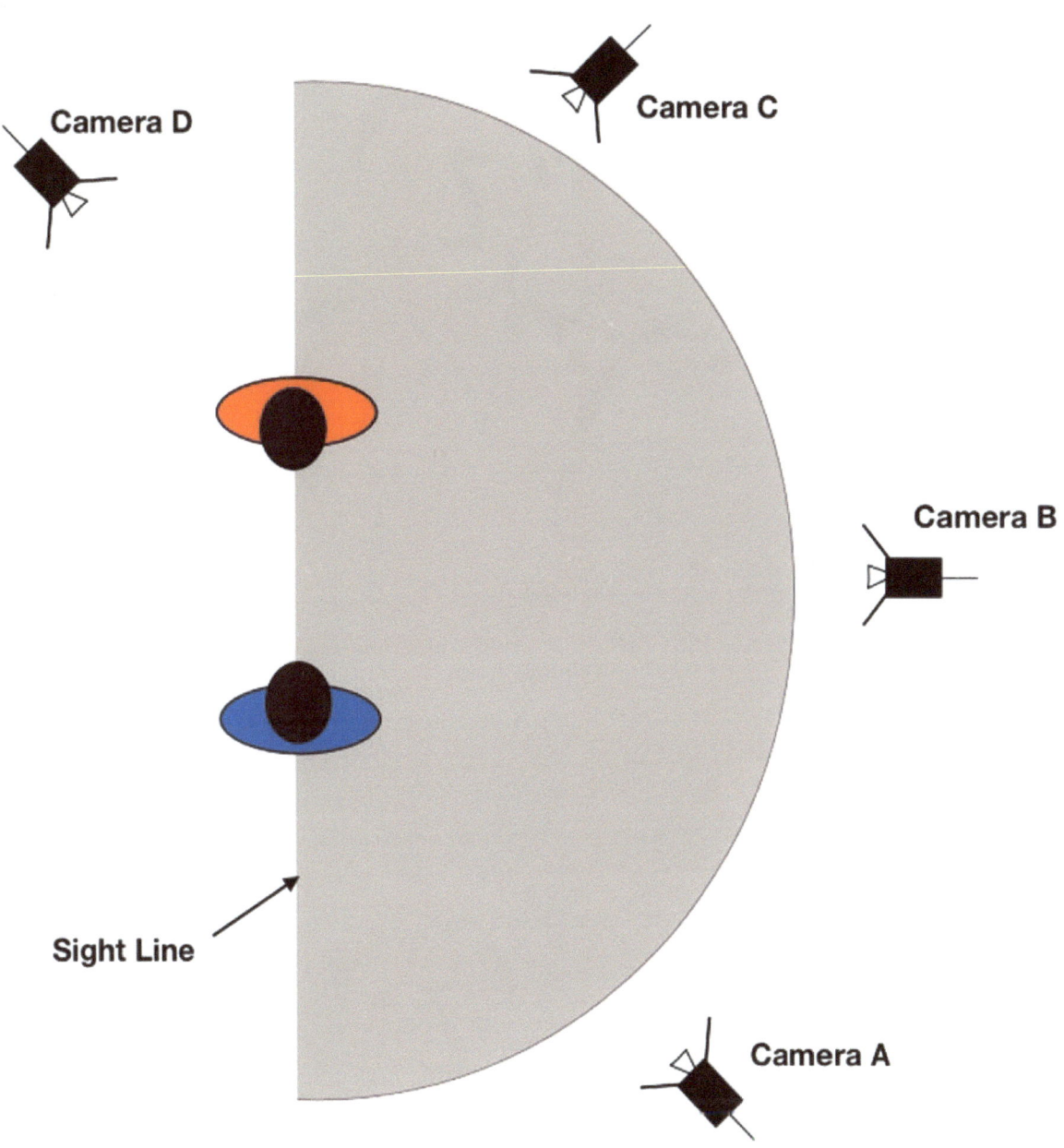

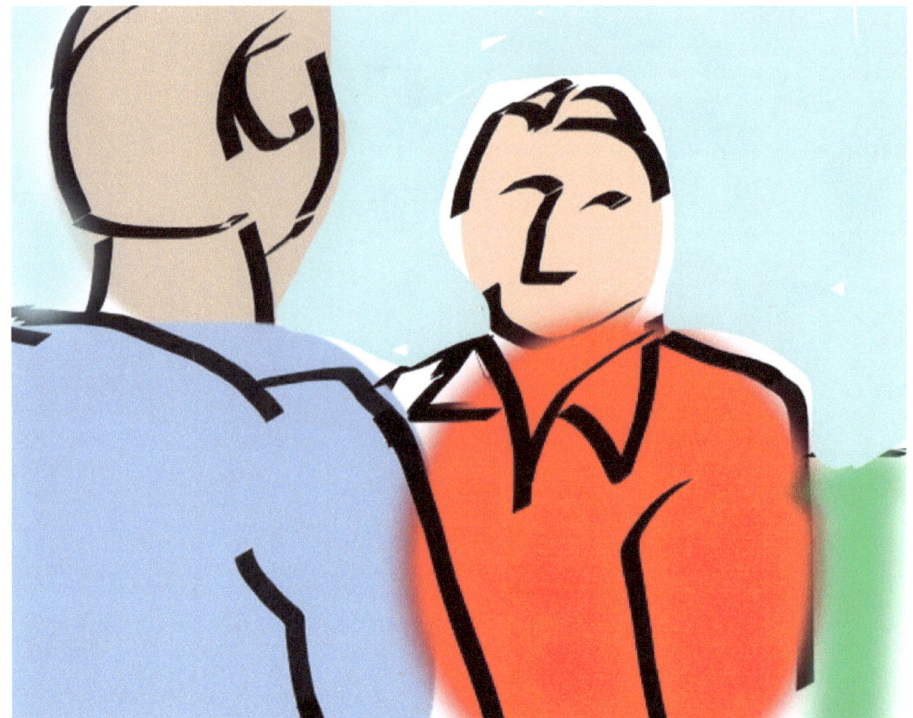

Camera A

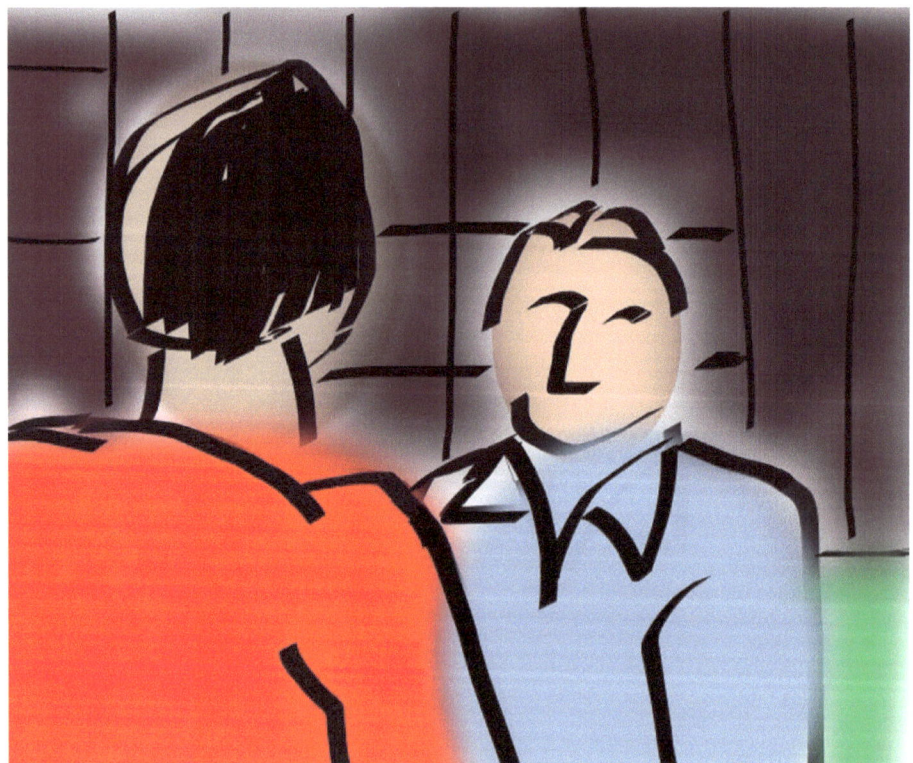

Camera D

The 180° Rule is one of those concepts one needs to understand when filming. The most important thing to remember is to establish the *line-of-action*, and then decide which side of it are you filming on. Once you understand that, then everything else will easily fall in place.

**Three tips.**

1. Experiment with shooting and editing using your actors *line-of-action* to establish the 180-degree workspace. Try different type shots (singles, two shots, over-the-shoulder, and close-ups): shoot from different locations, some on the line-of-action, but not over it, and others within the 180° workspace.

2. When setting up your camera think in triangles. Using three camera positions around your line of action is an excellent strategy for getting all the coverage you need for editing. (see the diagram above)

3. Experiment shooting Point-of-view shots from different locations relative to the actors. What happens when you set up the camera on, or near, the line of action?

What happens when you vary shot size and/or camera position? And, how does that effect continuity? We'll explore that in the next chapter.

# 28. SHOT SIZE, SHOT ANGLE, AND THE
# 30 DEGREE RULE

An important component of cinematic language is understanding how to combine different size shots within a scene. Called the *30 degree rule*, it is a major aspect of *continuity editing* and cinematic language. The *30 degree rule* gives us guidelines for how to assemble different size shots so we can avoid *jump cuts* between shots.

A jump cut is read by the viewer as a gap, or jump, in the smooth flow of time and space in a scene. It occurs when the relative size or angle of a shot hasn't changed enough from the shot that came before it, making the viewer aware of the edit.

To avoid this jump, each new shot needs to either change size by thirty percent, or change the angle of view by 30 degrees from the shot that came before it. *The 30 degree rule* allows us to establish a logical unity of shots in a scene, regardless of their scale or camera angle, as long as they are 30% greater or smaller than the image that preceded it, maintaining continuity.

Let's take a look at some stills from the TV series "The Good Wife" (2013) to see how the director and editor utilized different shot sizes and angles in the opening sequence of Season 5, Episode 14, titled "A Few Words".

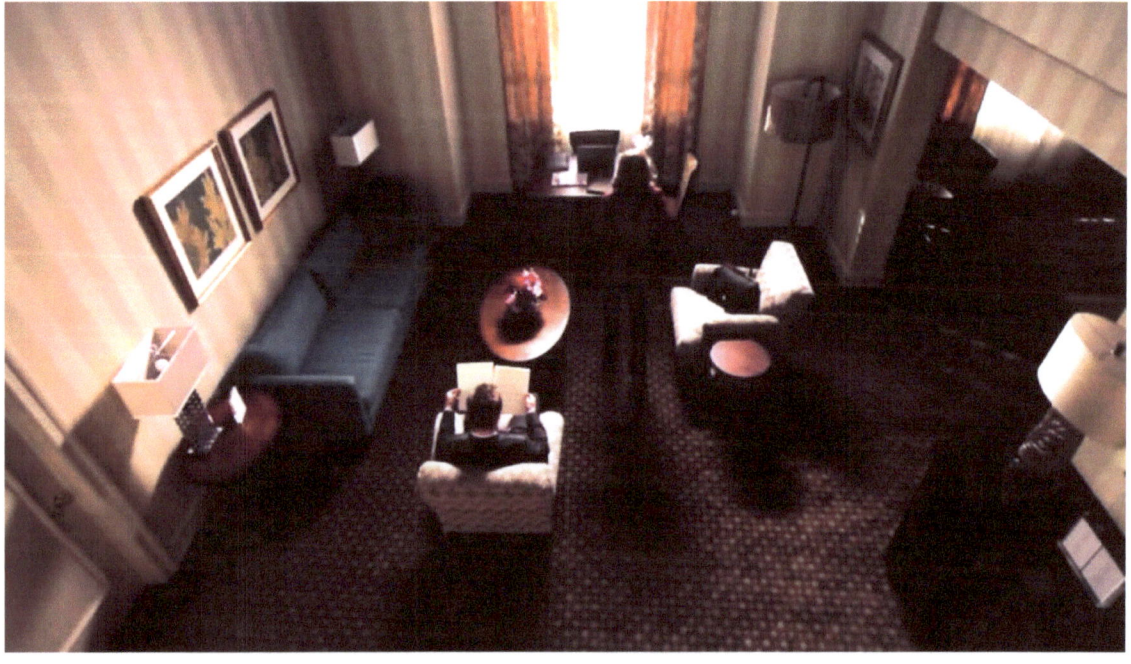

**Shot 1:** Is a birds-eye view of an establishing shot of Alicia and Cary in a hotel room reviewing

Alicia's speech. Alicia paces back and forth as Cary reads. Shot with a 15mm to 20mm *wide angle lens* (equivalent to a smartphone with a 0.45X wide angle lens attachment). Because of it's high angle it creates an unnatural feeling of extreme depth, thereby conveying the tension that both characters are experiencing about the speech.

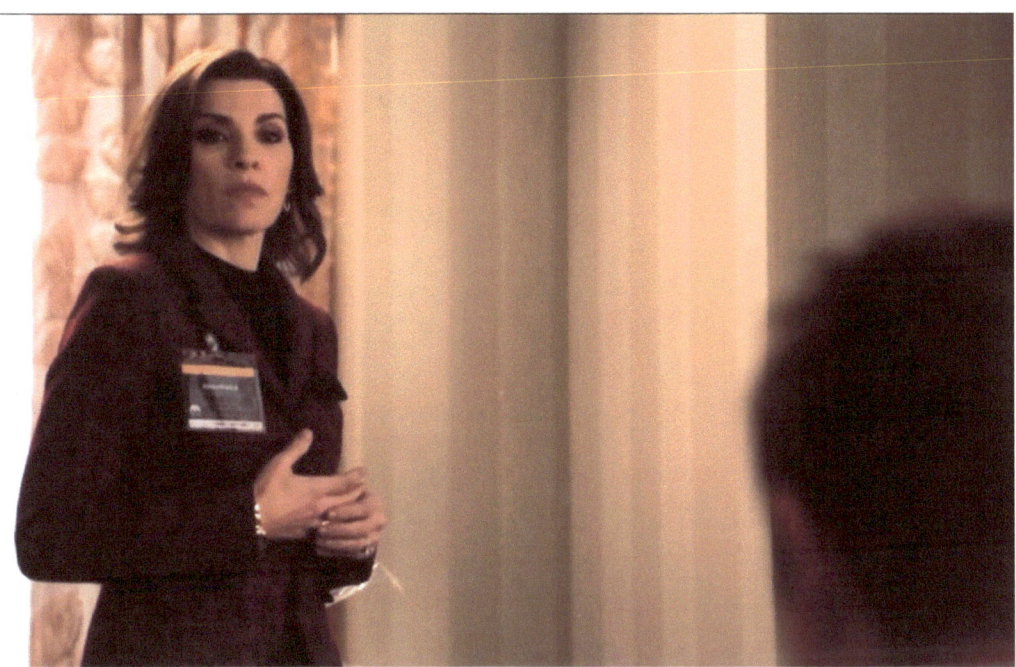

**Shot 2 & 4:** Are *over-the-shoulder (OS)* shots of Alicia talking to Cary. Shot from Cary's POV with a 30mm to 50mm lens, which is the standard lens on most smartphones. By shooting from slightly below, looking up at Alicia, the director emphasizes Alicia's positive status. The standard lens emphasizes the distance between the two characters without undo distortion.

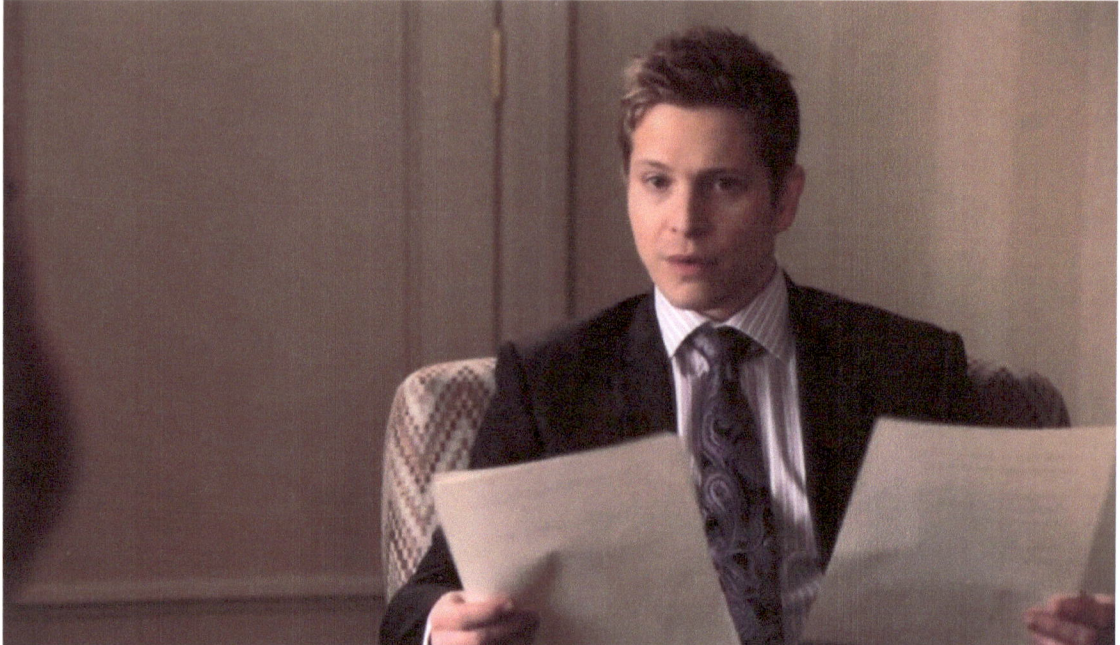

**Shot 3:** Is an over-the-shoulder (OS) shot of Cary with the same normal lens used in shots 2 & 4. It's shot at Cary's eye level, not from Alicia's, thereby giving them both equal status.

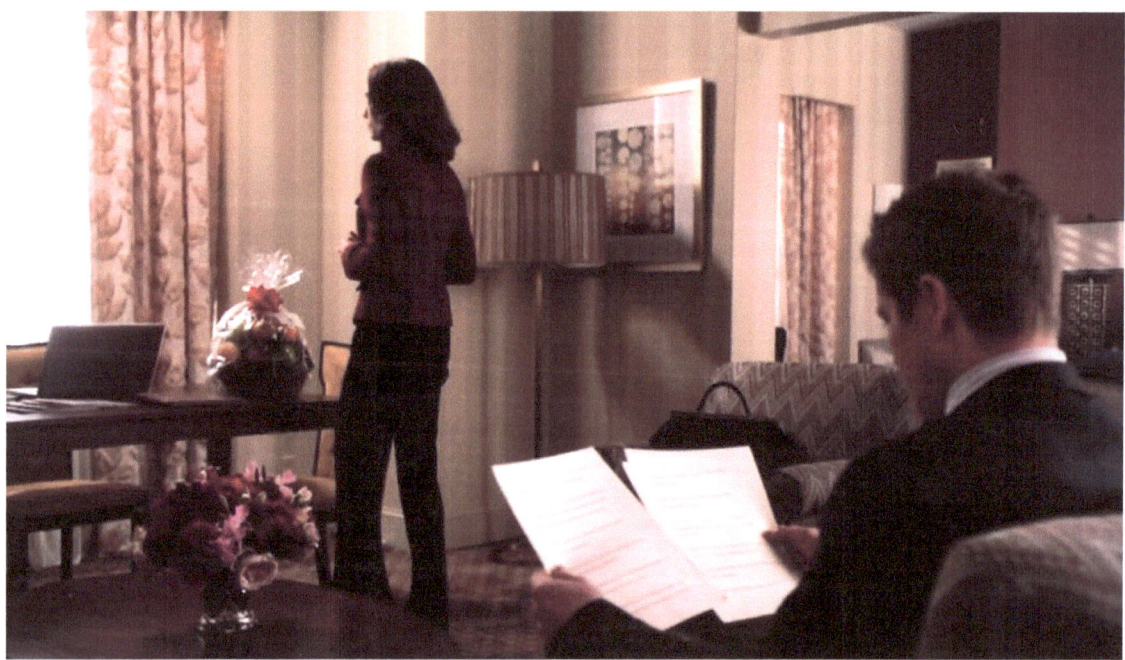

**Shot 5:** Is a full shot of Alicia and Cary, filmed with a 20mm to 30mm lens. The full shot allows us to clearly see Alicia's body language as she fidgets. The camera is shooting from Cary's eye level looking up at Alicia.

The rest of this scene continues as a conversation between Alicia and Cary. It is edited together alternating between the camera setups of shot 2 & 3.

Logically you'd think that these drastic changes in image size would jar us out of the movie. They don't. If anything, they do the opposite... drawing us into the story. Surprisingly, this pretty much describes how we experience the world as we go through our day. We are constantly shifting our gaze from one object to another... from looking at something in the distance... then to the details of an object in front of us... to the person in the next room. Not only do we jump from one image to another, but we create an ongoing story about all this in our minds. All day long we're jumping from one image to another in the same way that a filmmaker changes shot size and camera angle in a scene, only he or she is much more selective about what they show the audience. Like us, the filmmaker is leaving out details that the audience has to fill in for themselves. In a movie, like in life, the audience becomes an active participant in the creation of the story. It becomes our story, at least while it keeps our attention.

## Three Tips:

1. Write a short one minute scenario for yourself, then film it. Experiment shooting each camera setup a number of different ways: For example: One as a profile view in extreme close up; another with the camera down on the floor; a third as a frontal view with the camera located one foot above eyelevel. The idea is to get a variety of shots that you can experiment with as you edit. *(See "The Eyes Have It" and "Understanding Camera Angles" for more details.)*

2. The French new wave Filmmaker Jean-Luc Godard deliberately chose to break the rules in his movie Breathless (1960), using *jump cuts* in a new and novel way of editing a movie together. Below are stills that illustrate one of many jump cuts from Breathless where Godard purposefully uses jump cuts to break the 30 degree rule and create a new visual language in this film.

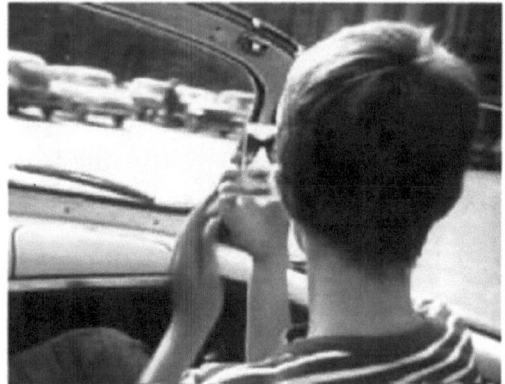 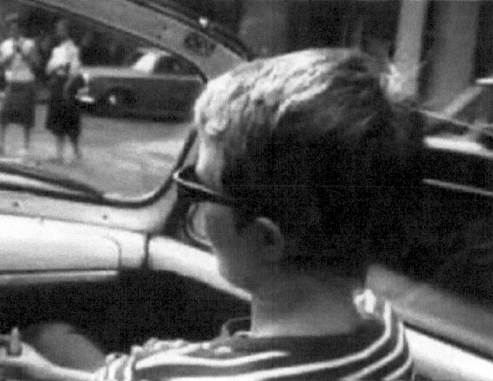

Try editing a scene using mostly jump cuts. It can be quite challenging to create a smooth flowing sequence where the audience doesn't notice any gaps or jumps. Go on... try it... you'll have fun. See the movie *Run Lola Run (1998)* for ideas about how to use jump cuts.

3. Yes, shot size has an emotional component. It is a way pointing out an important detail about a subject. As you think about your scenario, keep this in mind. We'll explore the emotional meaning of shots in more detail in the next few chapters.

# 29. WHERE DO I STAND? — Staging the Actors Part 1

You've got everyone assembled: The actors have learned their lines, your phone's battery is fully charged, and the lights are on their stands waiting to be positioned. Everyone is ready... waiting for you, the director, to tell them where to set up the camera; where to stand; and how to move in the scene. And there you are, without a clue. Intimidating yes... but it doesn't have to be. Let's break it down.

For *continuity* purposes we need to understand two basic things. One, how are the actors arranged relative to each other, and two, where is the *line-of-action* within that arrangement. As we discussed in the chapter about the *180° Rule*, the *line-of-action* is an imaginary line drawn from one actor to another defining where the camera can and can't be placed within the scene without confusing the audience about where they are. (*see The 180° Workspace for more details*)

All *blocking (or staging)*, or where the actors stand in the scene, is based on an understanding of five different *positions* that two actors might assume relative to each other. Regardless of whether they're facing each other or not, the *line-of-action* between them remains the same.

**The Five Actor Positions:** each position establishes its own line-of-action (*see diagram below*)

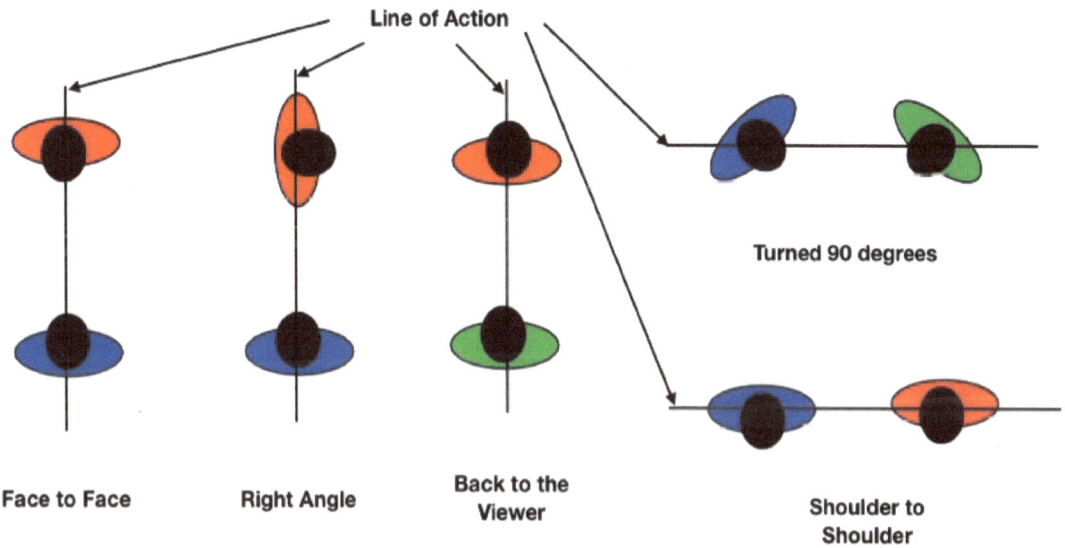

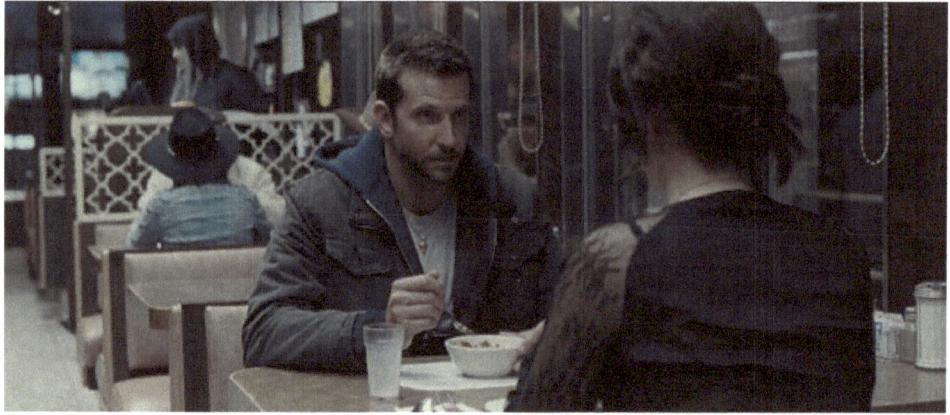

**1. Face to Face:** Two actors face each other. Below is a still from the movie The Silver Linings Playbook (2012) Bradley Cooper and Jennifer Lawrence are filmed facing each other. Despite the fact that Jennifer has her back turned to the camera (an over-the-shoulder shot), both actors are in a face-to-face position. When shooting a dialog sequence like this, think in terms of triangles to get all the coverage you'll need to edit later by utilizing three camera positions around the line-of-action. One camera shoots facing Brad Cooper (capturing singles, close-ups, and over-the-shoulder shots), the second shoots facing Jennifer Lawrence (capturing singles, close-ups, and over-the-shoulder shots), and the third captures two shots, perpendicular to the line-of-action.

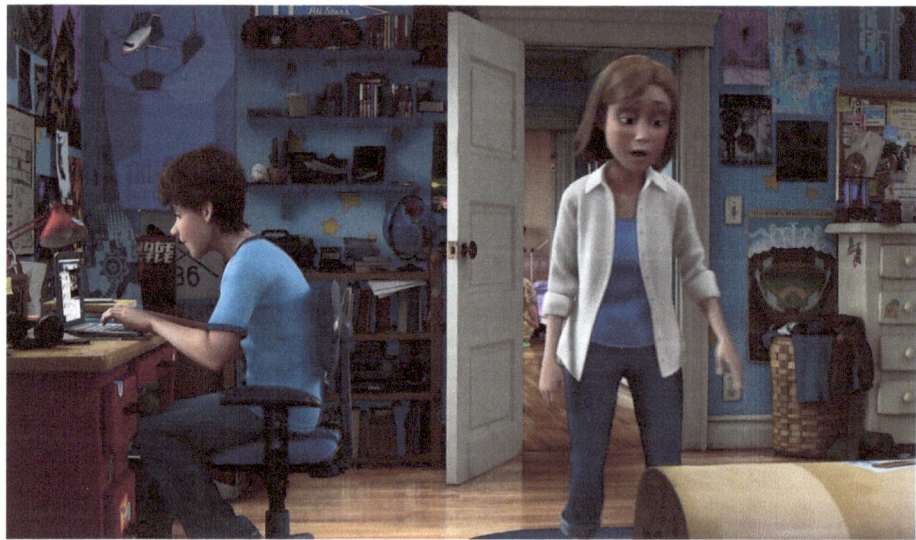

**2. Right Angle:** One actor stands sideways relative to the other. In Toy Story 3 (2010) below, the two characters are facing at right angles to each other. In this case neither is looking at the other.

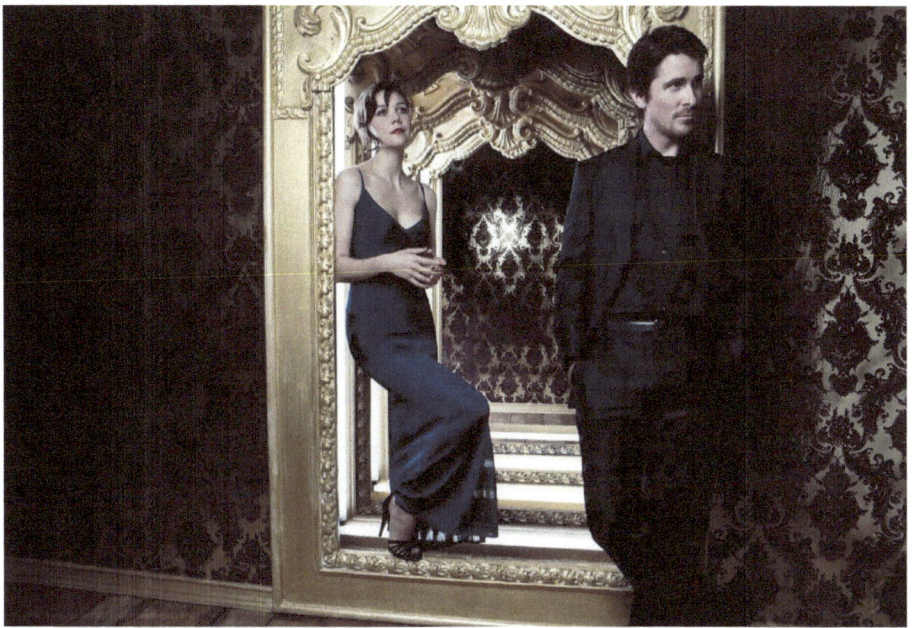

**3. Back Turned to the Other:** One actor's back is turned away from the other actor. In this still from the movie The Dark Knight (2008) Christian Bale has his back turned to Maggie Gyllenhaal. The director has used this staging to show Bale's emotional hesitancy and detachment.

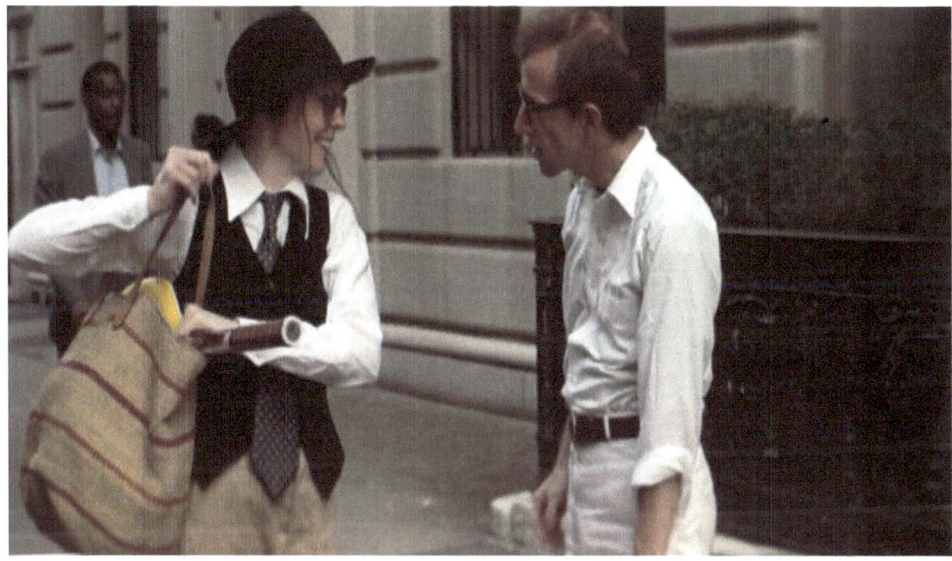

**4. 90°:** Each actor is turned 45° to each other. In the still below from Annie Hall (1977) Diane Keaton & Woody Allen stand partially turned toward each other in this intimate 90° position.

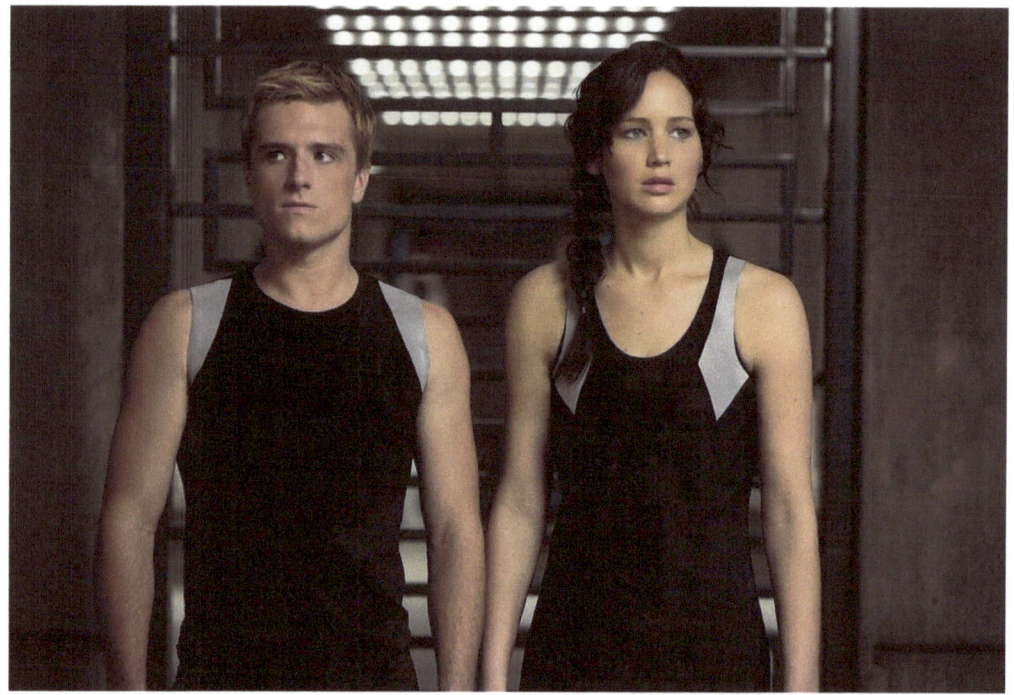

**5. Shoulder-to-Shoulder:** Both actors are standing shoulder-to-shoulder, facing in the same direction. In the The Hunger Games: Mockingjay (2014) below Jennifer Lawrence stands shoulder-to-shoulder with Josh Hutcherson. Both are together, yet separate at the same time.As you can see from the stills above, these images, in addition to being interesting arrangements, also convey emotional power. We'll discuss the psychological aspect of staging in the chapters to come. For now, its enough to absorb the concept of the relationship between the camera and five staging positions.

**Thee Tips:**

1. Write a short dialog scene and stage it using two of the five positions. To get enough coverage to edit each together, shoot each scene two to three time from start to finish. Positioning your camera in three different locations (in a triangular pattern) around the line-of-action. Edit each position separately and compare them. Which position enhances the emotional meaning of the scene? Why?

2. With the same dialog as in tip number one, but move the camera onto the line-of-action and film one of the actors in a close-up. This type of shot is considered a *subjective shot*, because you're see what the other actor sees.

3. Analyze how other filmmakers are utilize the five positions in their movies. This can be fun and a great learning experience.

# 30. WHERE DO I STAND? — Staging Actors Part 2

In addition to the *five basic positions*, that we discussed in the previous chapter, there are two additional *patterns* for *blocking* three or more principal actors' in a scene. (Please note: we are not talking about where the extras stand in a crowded scene, but how to arrange the key actors relative to each other.)

The *five basic positions* are the foundation for these other patterns. Each is based on what's called the *"I" Pattern*. Let's look at each pattern in detail:

**"I" Pattern:** the "I" pattern is the basis for all five of the positions we've discussed in the previous chapter. In the "I" pattern there can only be one *line-of-action* between the two actors regardless of how they are facing each other. (*see, Where do I stand –Staging Actors Part 1*)

**"A" pattern:** is a three actor pattern, arranged as an equilateral triangle w*ith an actor a*t each point. This pattern can have three different lines-*of-action*, see the diagram below. What we're about to cover can get complicated very quickly. Don't let it. Remember we're always dealing with an interchange between ONLY TWO ACTORS AT ONE TIME, regardless of how many actors are in the scene. And, the *line-of-action* is always between the actor who is speaking and the actor who is responding. Knowing that, you'll always know where to place the camera relative to the line-of-action.

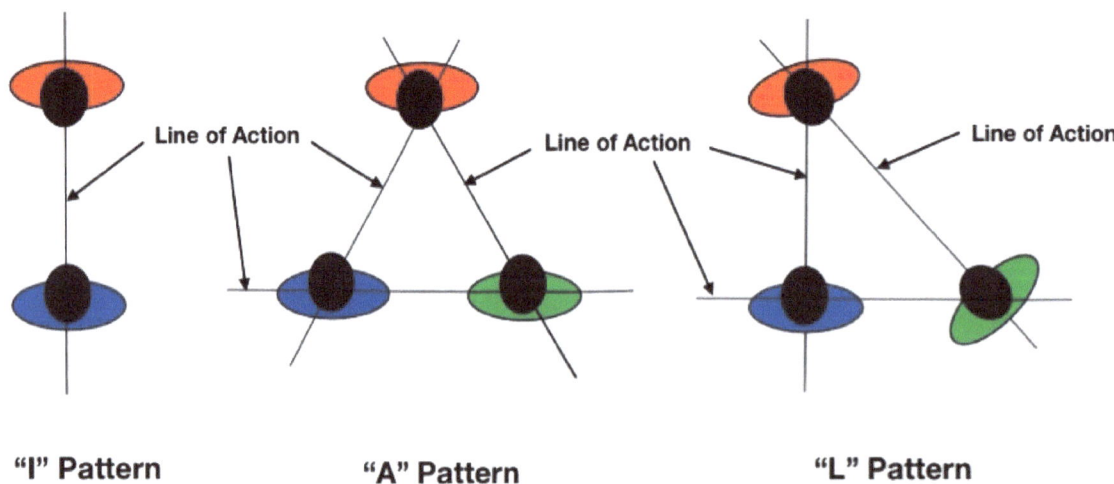

"I" Pattern          "A" Pattern          "L" Pattern

Many directors have chosen to simplify this model and kept the camera's position on one major *line-of-action* throughout the scene. See below for examples.

Obviously using less is easier. Despite that, it is worth understanding the principals behind these complicated patterns, because you'll never know when you'll need it.

**"L" pattern:** is also a three actor pattern, but is not symmetrical. As with the "A" pattern you can choose to simplify your camera set-ups and still get the coverage you need by positioning the camera around just one *line-of-action*.

Please note: When blocking the actors, and setting up the different camera angles for coverage within the scene, we must not cross the line-of-action. *([See The 180° Workspace for more details]*)

Lets take a look at how a sequence is shot using an "L" pattern staging with only one line-of-action. We'll examine a scene from M. Night Shyamalan's movie Unbreakable (2000). In the diagram below I've numbered four camera locations around the *line-of-action* for our sequence:

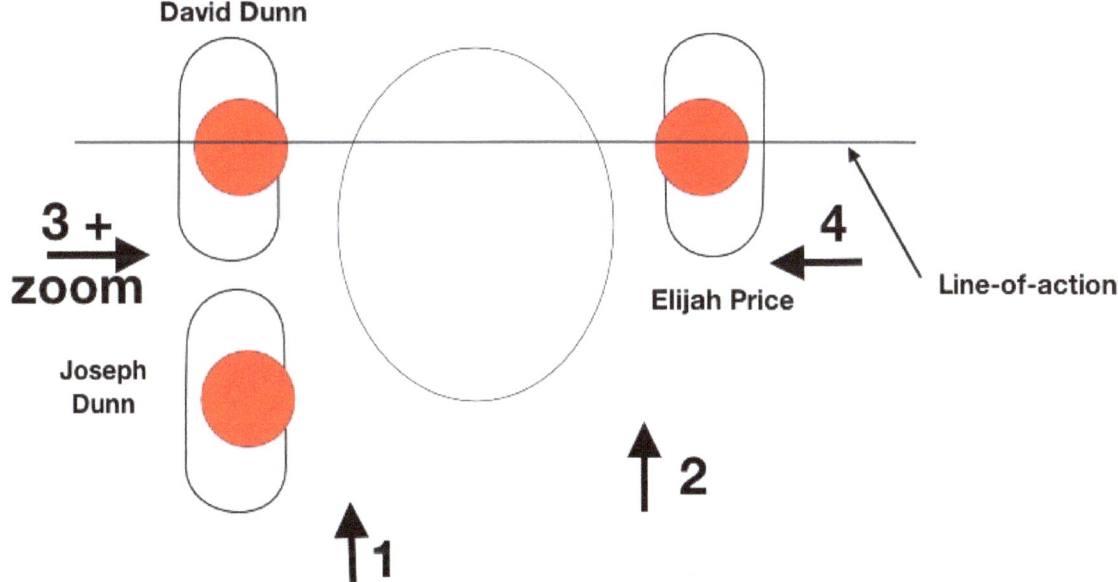

Here are the four camera positions:

1. Is a two shot of David Dunn and his son Joseph seen in profile

2. Is a close-up profile shot Elijah Prince

3. Is an over-the-shoulder shot of Elijah, which holds for a moment and then slowly zooms-in for a close-up (the fourth still in this sequence)

4. Is a two shot of David and Joseph.

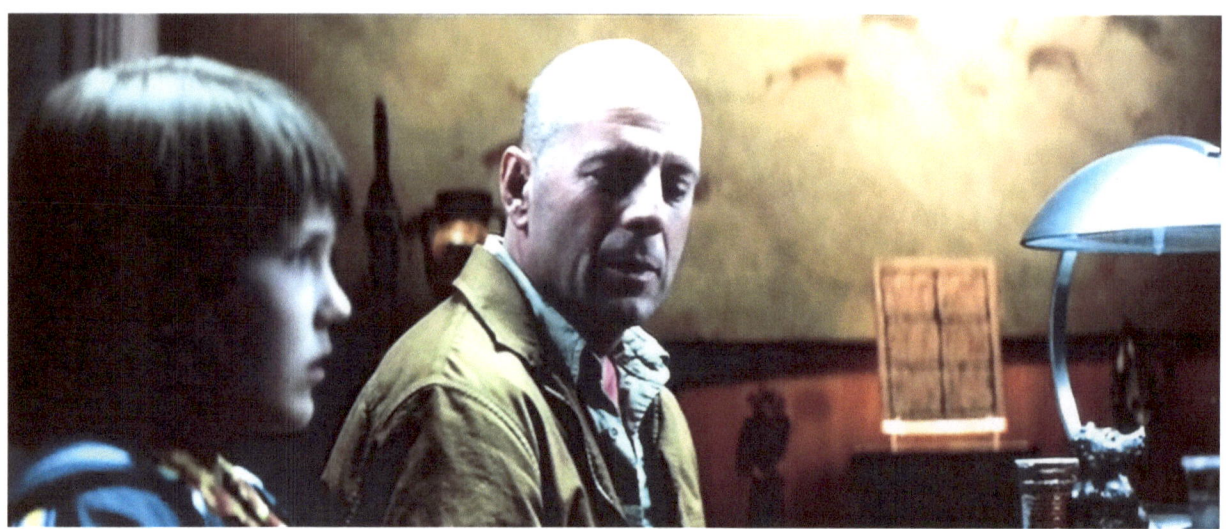

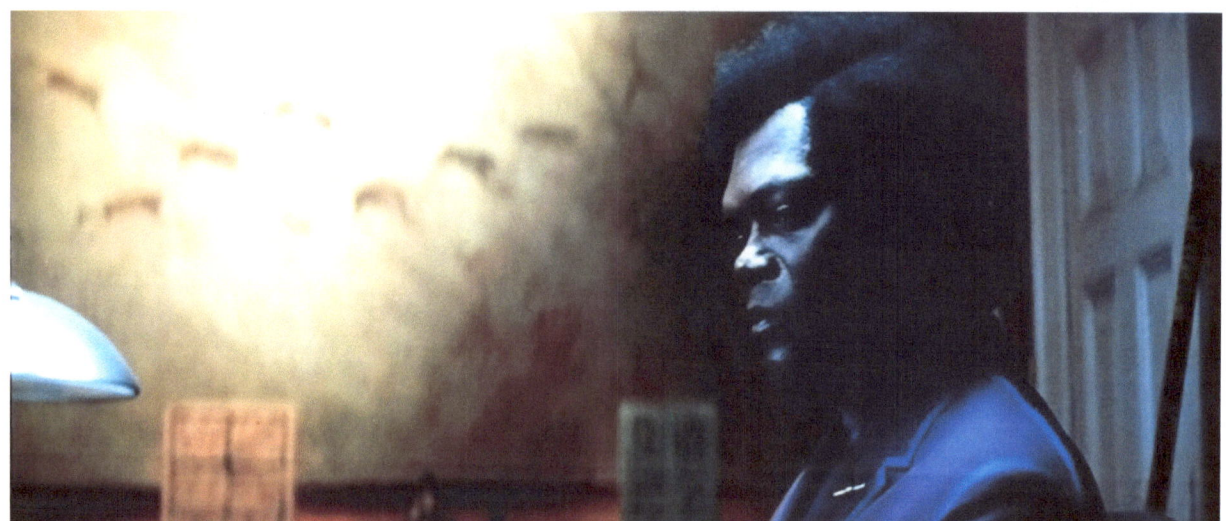

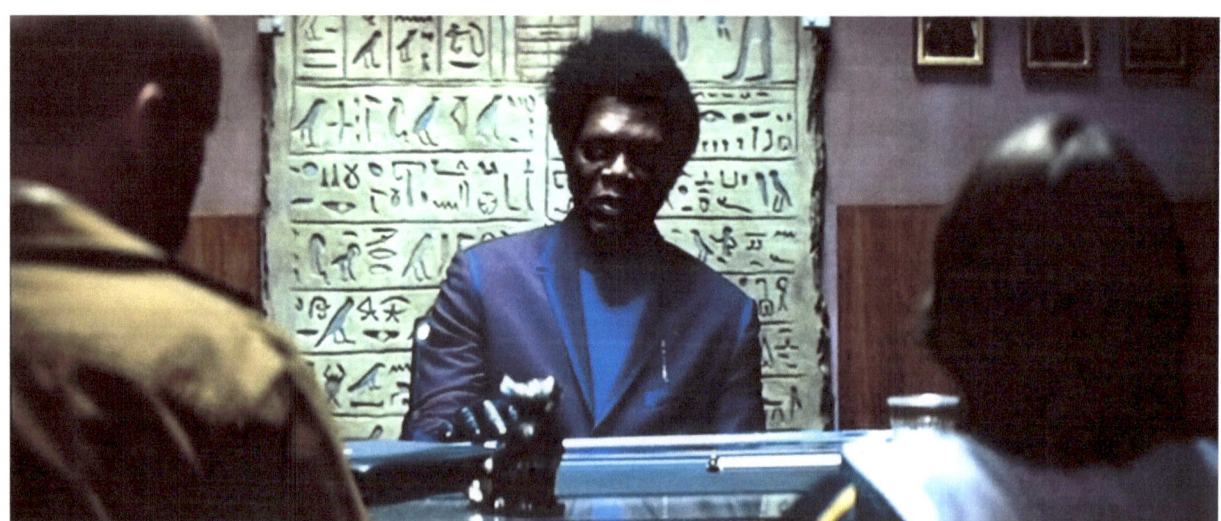

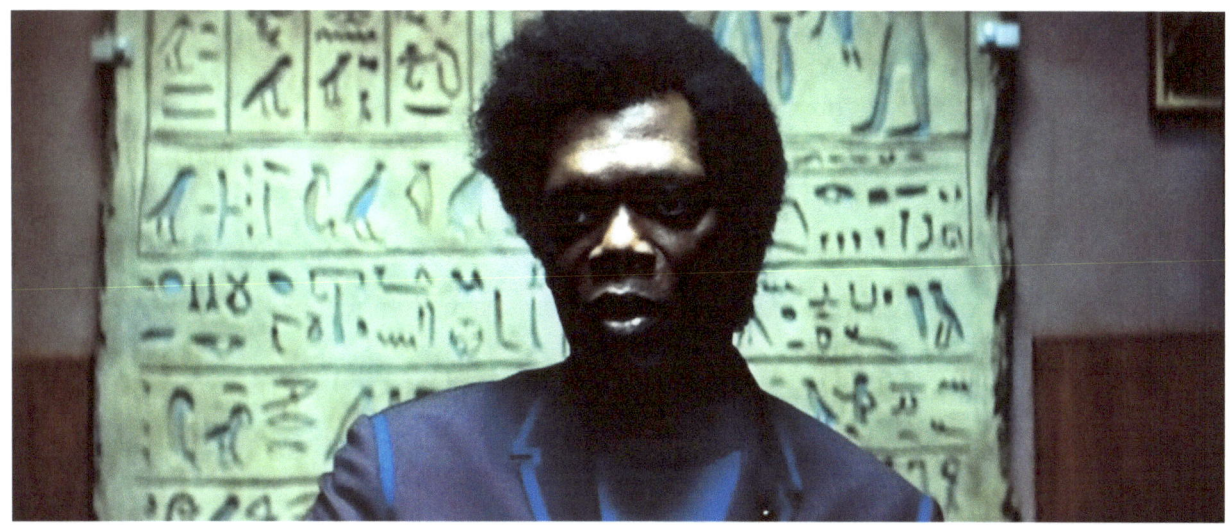

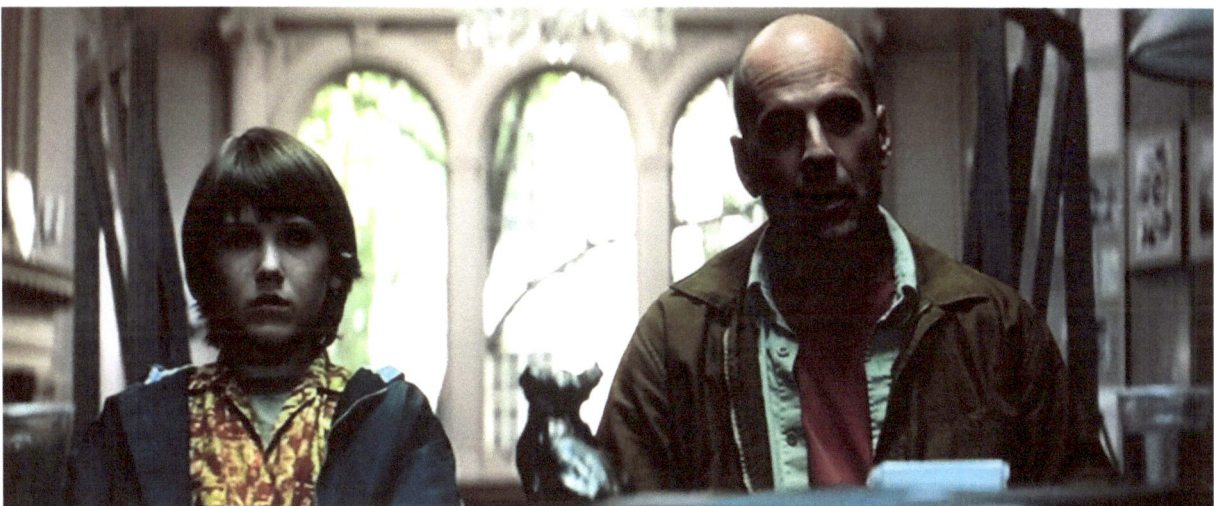

Another possible blocking for this sequence would have been to establish a *line-of-action* between David and Joseph, rather than between David and Elijah. In the example above, M. Night Shyamalan chose this particular blocking to emphases a contrasting symmetry of images between David and his son and the undiscovered evil of Elijah.

You'll be amazed at how many different ways you can shoot a scene by changing the camera's location around the *line-of-action*. We'll discuss the emotional and psychological implications of these arrangements in more depth in the chapter titled, *"The Eyes Have It"*

**Three tips:**

1. Experiment by blocking your actors. Shoot some of your footage from the wrong side of the line-of-action. How does that footage work with the rest.

2. Try shooting blocking with both wide angle and telephoto lenses. The telephoto will give you shallow space, while the wide angle creates depth.

3. Try having the actor(s) turn their head(s) in a different direction than their body is facing. How does this enhance or diminish the emotions you are trying to portray?

# 31. THE EYES HAVE IT

How do you know when someone is hiding something from you? Most people would agree, you can be pretty sure by watching their eyes. If you're watching a film and a character looks down, or away... or avoids making eye contact with the other actors in the scene... you'd know something is amiss with that person, not by what they've said, but by what their eyes have shown you.

One of the most powerful tools we have as filmmakers is our characters' eyes and what they do, or don't do. So let's talk about how to photograph eyes and use them to tell our story.

**Camera Position:** There are five *positions* we can locate the camera relative to our actors that are used to express our a subjects' thoughts, relationships, emotions, or the lack of them.

Each is a different angle of view of our character's face (especially their eyes) and body position. And, each has a specific psychological meaning for the audience and the other actors in the scene. Let's examine the five different *camera positions* by looking at how other filmmakers have incorporated these *camera positions* into their stories.

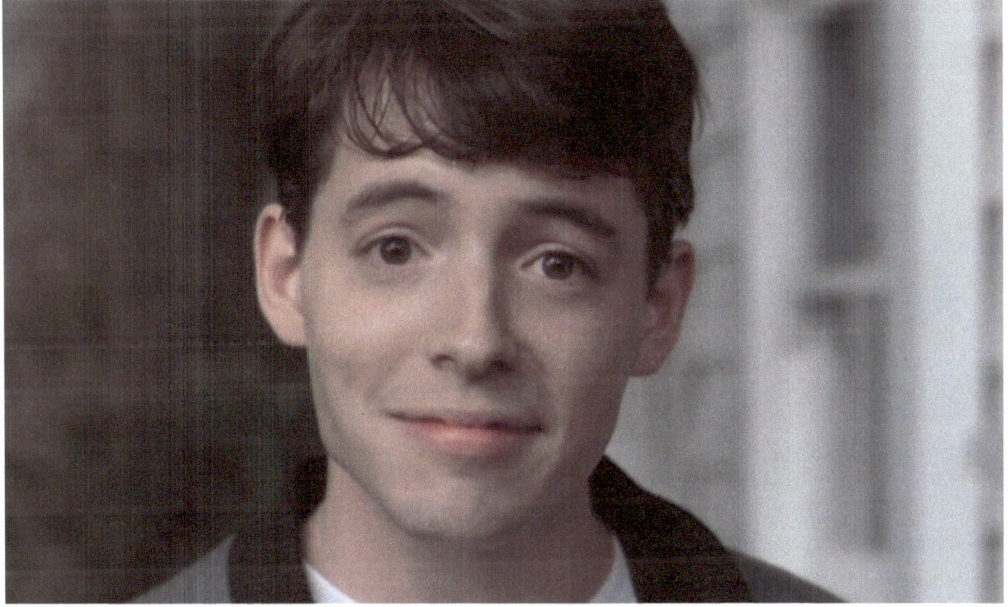

**1. Full-Front View: The actor looks straight into the camera lens.** In the still above Ferris Bueller (1986) is looking straight into the camera and talking directly to the audience. He is sharing his most intimate thoughts while inviting us to be a participant in whatever is going on. This camera position is used in newscasts, speeches, ads, and infomercials. It conveys the speaker's honesty and/or sincerity.

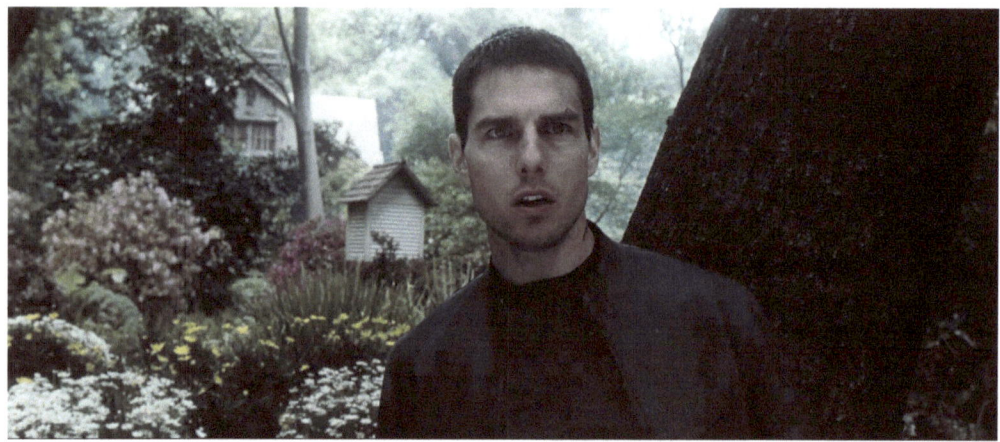

**Full-Front View — the actor does not look at the camera:** Above is a still from Minority Report (2002). This camera position allows us a very intimate view of the subject, who is not aware that they are being watched. An excellent position to capture close ups because we can clearly see any changes in expression or thought. This camera angle is often used in interviews. Usually, the interviewer is standing or sitting next to the camera, and the subject is looking just past the camera at the interviewer and not directly at or into the camera.

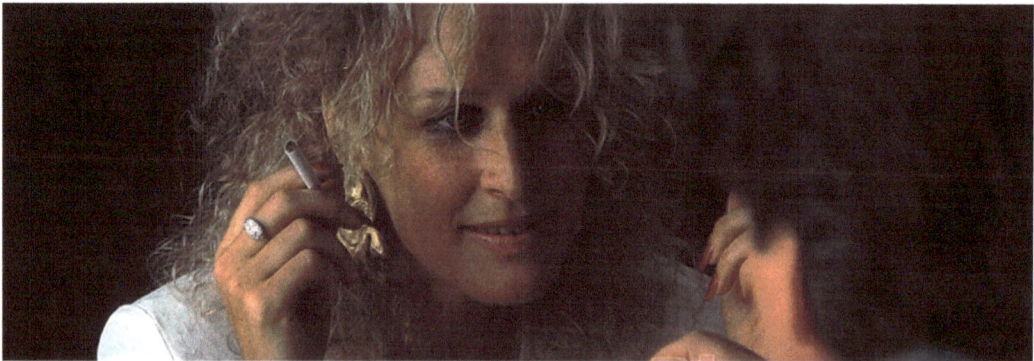

**3/4 Front View:** Excellent angle for *close up* and *over-the-shoulder* shots as seen in the still above from Fatal Attraction (1990). The subject is unaware that she is being watched. This allows the audience a great degree of intimacy. It is the equivalent of *personal space. ([See Character Space – Personal Space for details](#))* The audience can see the eyes in detail and all changes in facial expression. This is often used in a two subject interview, using either two or three cameras. (One camera for each subjects' *close up* and *over-the-shoulder* shot, and the third for either a profile *close up* or *two shot*.)

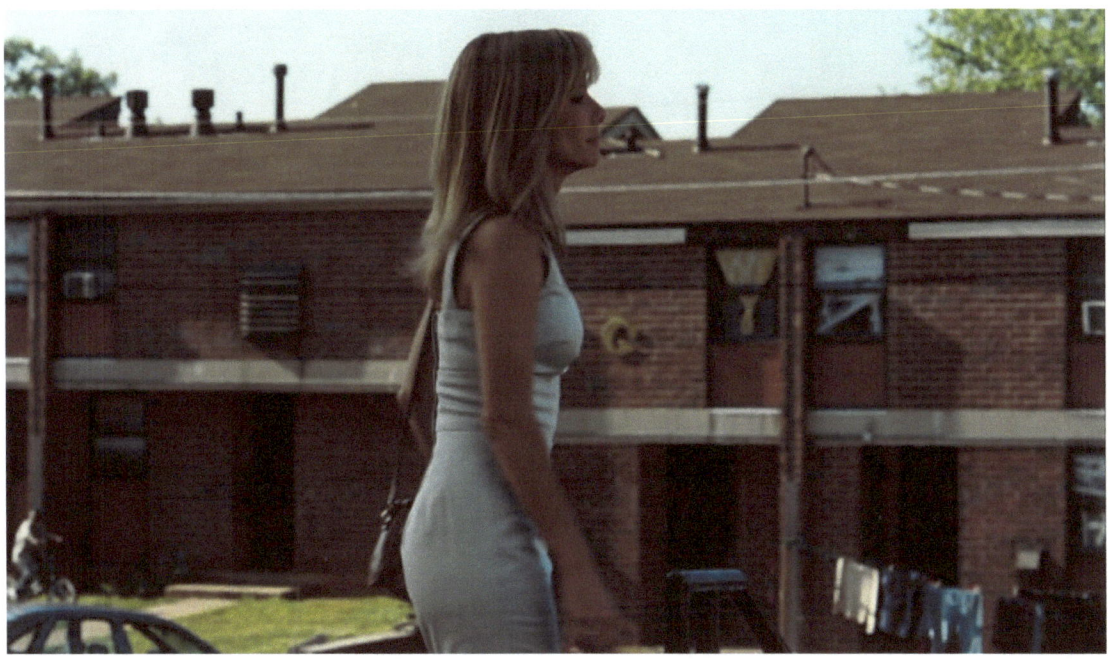

**Profile View:** the character is unaware of being observed. The further away from a frontal view we get the more emotionally distant the character is. This is true for both the audience and the actor's relationship to other actors in the scene. We are less able to read their emotions or thoughts. This is the equivalent of *social space*. (*see Character Space – Personal Space for details*)

The still above from the Blind Side (2009) shows Leigh Anne Touhy (Sandra Bullock) searching for Michael's mother in the Projects. She is looking straight ahead as she walks, not want to make eye contact with the toughs hanging out on the street.

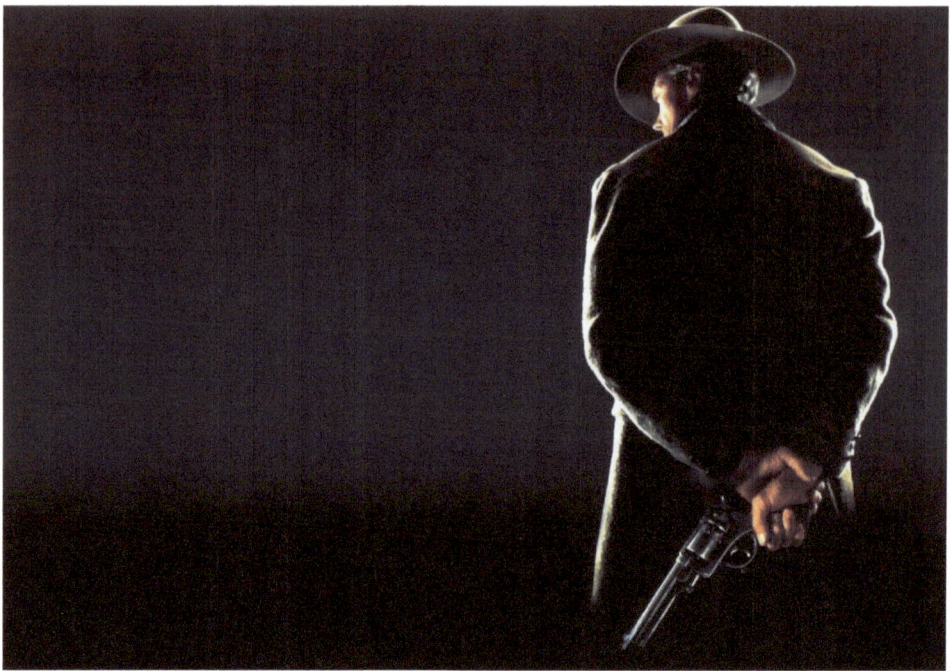

**3/4 Back View**: The character has partially turned his back to the viewer. This position can symbolize a character's rejection, unfriendliness, or antisocial feelings. Because we cannot see his eyes or face it is very difficult to read his thoughts or emotions. It also can imply concealment or mystery as in the still above of Clint Eastwood, from the movie The Unforgiven (1960), who is concealing a gun he doesn't want others to know about.

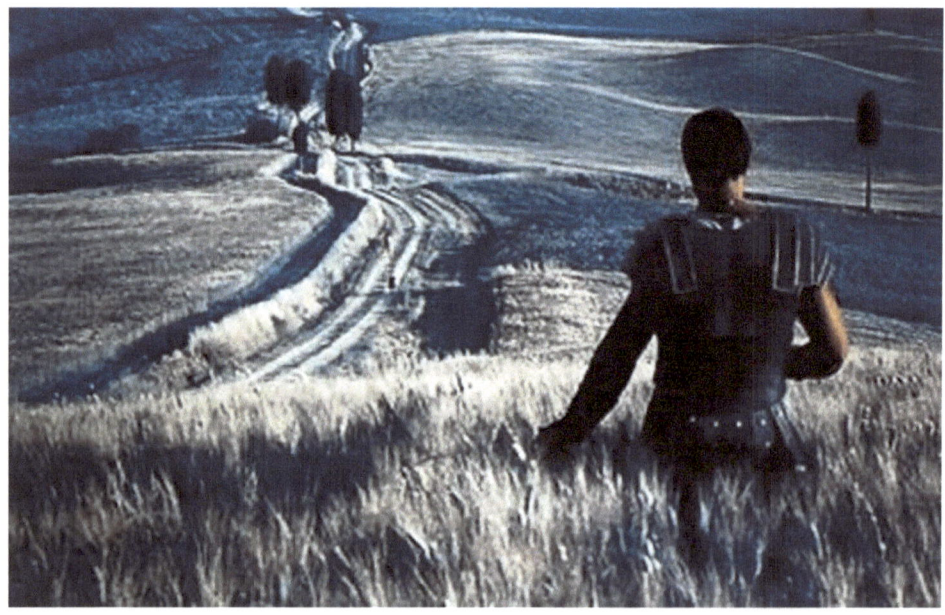

**Back to the Camera**: The most impersonal of all positions as seen in the still above from the Gladiator (2000). This position suggests a character's alienation from the world. When a character has his or her back to the camera, the audience can only guess at what the subject is feeling or thinking. It also can imply concealment or mystery.

As you can see, each *camera position* has a different view of the actors' eyes and body, which is a powerful tool you can use to express a characters emotions or psychological state.

## Three tips:

1. Experiment using the five camera positions to show joy, rage, or concealment. How do you show these intimate emotions as your camera moves further away from a full frontal view?

2. Experiment having a character look directly into the lens. Beside intimacy and trust, what else can you communicate?

3. Experiment and see happens when you combine these five camera positions with a low or high camera angle? When does the shot need to be kept at eyelevel? When not?

# 32. CHARACTER SPACE: Creating cinematic relationships

Someone has just invaded your personal space. Sticking their face so close to yours... you can smell their bad breath... and feel the heat coming off their body. There's a tightness in your chest... your breathing is shallow... do you fight or run? It's a real invasion of privacy and personal space, and you'll try to get away from it ASAP.

Cinema is different. It's a wonderful guilty pleasure. When this happens in a film, we as the audience feel our hero's discomfort, and enjoy the scene at the same time. As film viewers we inhabit the *character's space* and don't even give it a second thought. We can go anywhere, even into a couple's bedroom and watch, in close-up, their most intimate moments. Or, witness a birth, a catastrophe, a train wreck, and never blink an eye about it.

Creating *Character space* is one of the most powerful tools you have in your filmmakers' arsenal. As filmmakers our interest in *character space* has to do with how the distance between subjects effects our audience emotionally. The closer the characters are to each other, the more involved the viewer is with whatever is going on. Likewise, the further away, the more neutral. *Character space* deals with emotions in relationships. Not the filmmaker's, but the audiences'. As filmmakers, one of the major ways we can control how the audience feels, is simply by changing the distance between the camera and the subjects or between the subjects themselves. The still below of Tom Cruise and Samantha Morton from Minority Report (2002) illustrates the emotional power of intimate character space.

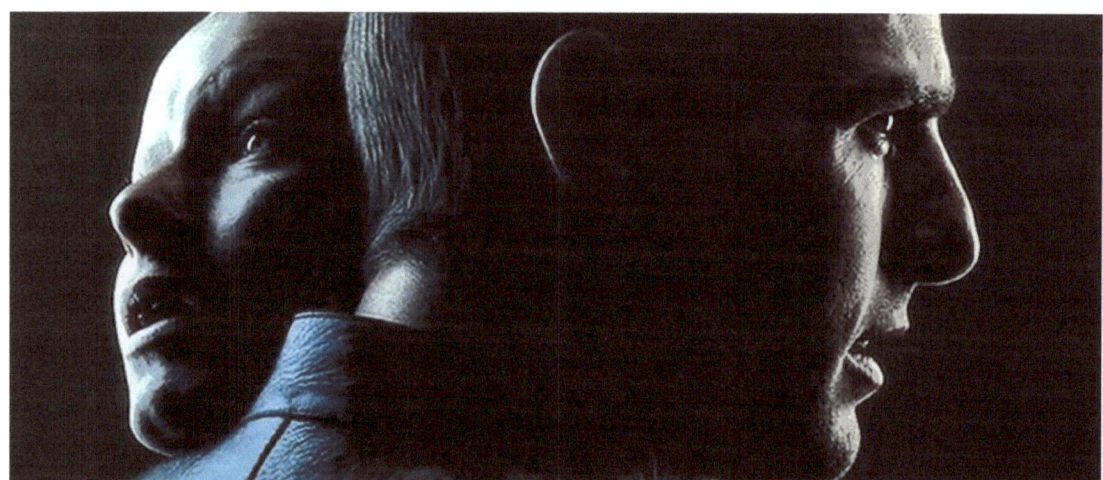

*Character space,* sometimes call *social space,* is the distance we maintain between ourselves and others. We all use *social space* as an unspoken way to establish boundaries between each other, allowing us either protection or intimacy, in our day-to-day interactions. By manipulating the distance between subjects and/or the camera, we as filmmakers, can get our audience to feel anything we want... Love, hate, rage, disgust, indifference.

The four types of *character space* are:

• INTIMATE — skin contact to eighteen inches away. It's the space we allow our loved ones to enter. Intimate space includes skin contact and up to eighteen inches away.

• PERSONAL — from eighteen inches to four feet. Personal space is the space we leave when talking with others. Personal space is from eighteen inches, arms length, to four feet apart.

• SOCIAL — four feet to twelve feet. Social space is from four feet to twelve feet. It is the space we maintain when we're in a social situation.

• PUBLIC — space varies depending on the situation, but includes avoiding eye contact, conversation, and touch.

We don't just let anyone into our intimate or personal space. As filmmakers we use *character space* to illuminate a subjects emotions and relationships, such as the "In-your-face" example above. We can choose to adhere to the social conventions, or break them. A powerful way to break a social convention is to exaggerate the space between subjects, moving them either closer or further away. Either way the audience experiences these relationships emotionally, without any dialog or words of explanation.

A wonderful example of how this works can be seen in the passage of time breakfast *montage* sequence in Orson Wells' movie Citizen Kanc (1941). (see below) In this scene we see Kane and his first wife at breakfast. As the sequence progresses, we experience how the couples relationship changes over a period of time, from intimate and happy to ambivalent and indifferent. This is accomplished entirely without dialog, by showing the change that occurs in the couples spatial relationship and body language at the breakfast table. The first still below shows Kane and his wife when they are first married. The montage sequence begins with the happy couple at breakfast, sitting close and leaning in towards each other, smiling, and making eye contact.

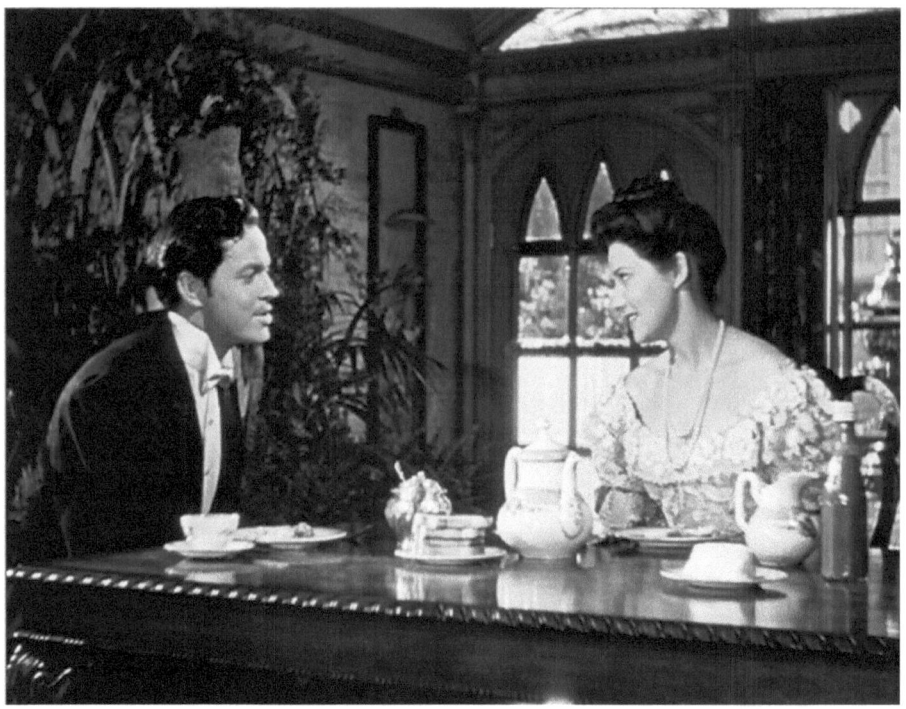

By the end of the sequence Kane and his wife are separated from each other by eight feet of breakfast table, each ignoring the other. There is no eye contact as they read their newspapers, their bodies are turned facing away from each other.

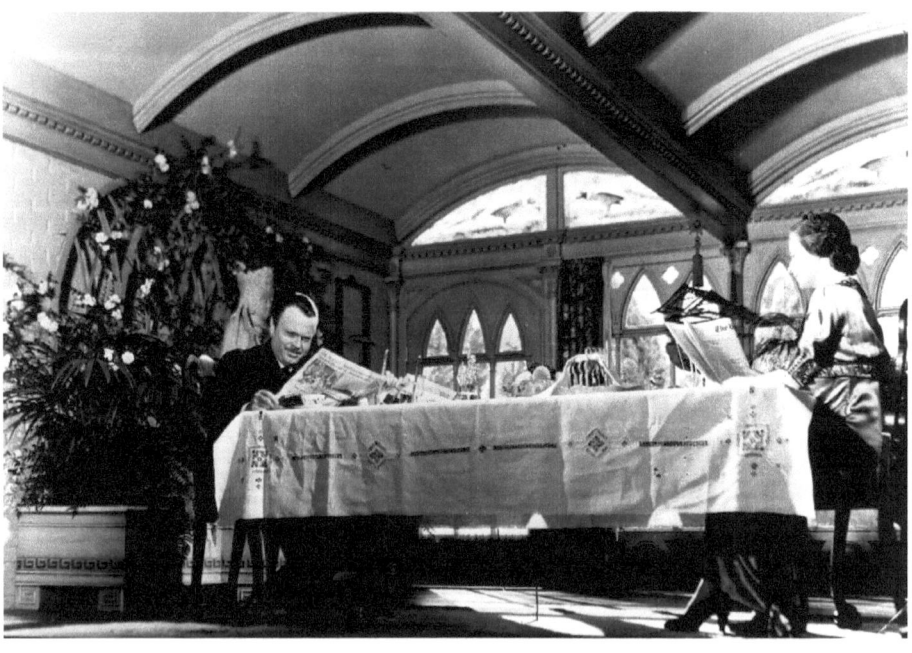

*Character space* is another powerful tool you can add to your filmmakers' arsenal. I'm not opposed to dialog, but I do feel that whenever possible try to eliminate dialog, and instead use *character space* and *body language* to convey meaning. I think they're much more powerful.

## Three tips:

1. Experiment shooting a short scene a few different times. Use the same staging for each version, but change the space between the actors. Were there any surprises when you did this? Emotional results you didn't expect? Understanding what emotion your creating for the audience with *character space* will help you, not only in blocking your subjects, but how you can control the meaning of a scene as well.

2. Experiment with different subject's blocking. What happens when you change a subjects distance in the scene, going from close together to far apart. How does, the change in distance between the subjects or the camera effect the impact of the scene?

3. Once you understand the basic rules of character space, how would you break them? For example: how would you show intimacy between two people who are fifteen feet apart? Or, how would you show indifference between two people who are embracing?

# 33.  CAMERA SPACE: Creating cinematic relationships

As a filmmaker your goal is to put your audience right in the middle of the action.  To do that we're going to move the camera, either closer or further away from our subjects, using what I call *camera space* to control what the audience sees and feels.  Think of the camera and audience as being interchangeable.  What the camera records is what the audience will see and feel.

*Camera space,* is related *to social space (see Character Space for details)* in that it is the distance that we maintain between ourselves and others as a form of protection or intimacy.  As filmmakers we manipulate this space, by moving the camera closer or further away from the action or the characters, so we can emotionally involve our audience with what is going on.  When I refer to moving the camera closer I'm using that description figuratively, meaning that the image fills the picture frame, thereby appearing closer.

There are two ways that *social space* is incorporated into cinematic language.  The first is *Character Space,* which is the distance between individual characters in a scene. *(see Character Space for more details) Camera space* is different.  It refers to the distance between the camera and the subject.  So that the closer the camera gets to the actor's face, especially the eyes, the greater is the involvement and emotions experienced by the audience.  The difference in shot types can be viewed as being the equivalent of the rules we defined for *social space.*

For example:

1.  THE CLOSEUP or EXTREME CLOSEUP is the equivalent of intimate space.  It's the space we allow our loved ones to enter.  Intimate space includes skin contact and up to eighteen inches away. All the examples below are from the movie Juno (2007)

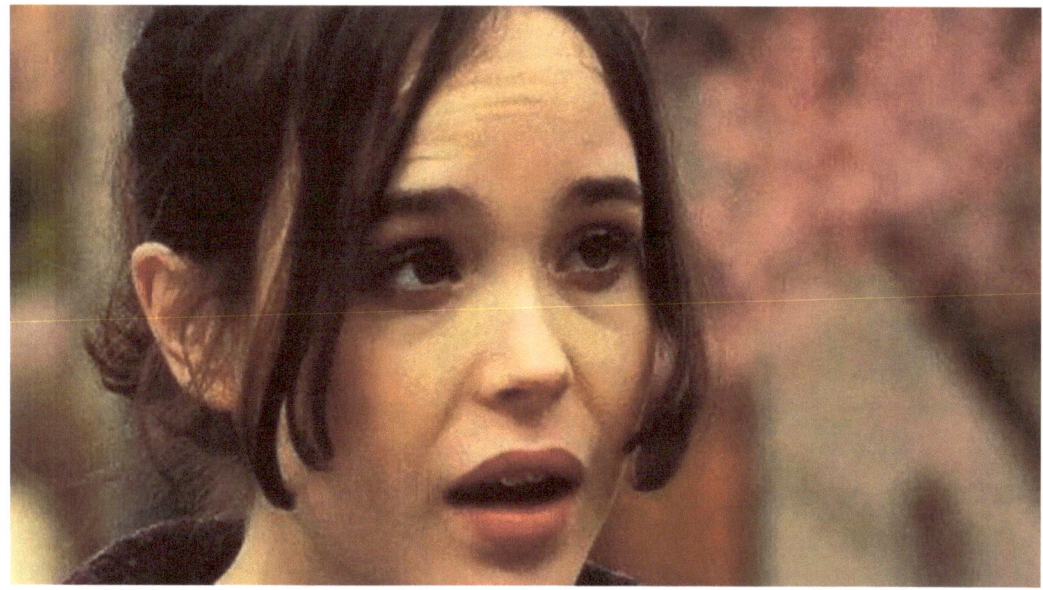

2. THE MEDIUM SHOT equals personal space. It is the space we leave when talking with others. Personal space is from eighteen inches to four feet apart.

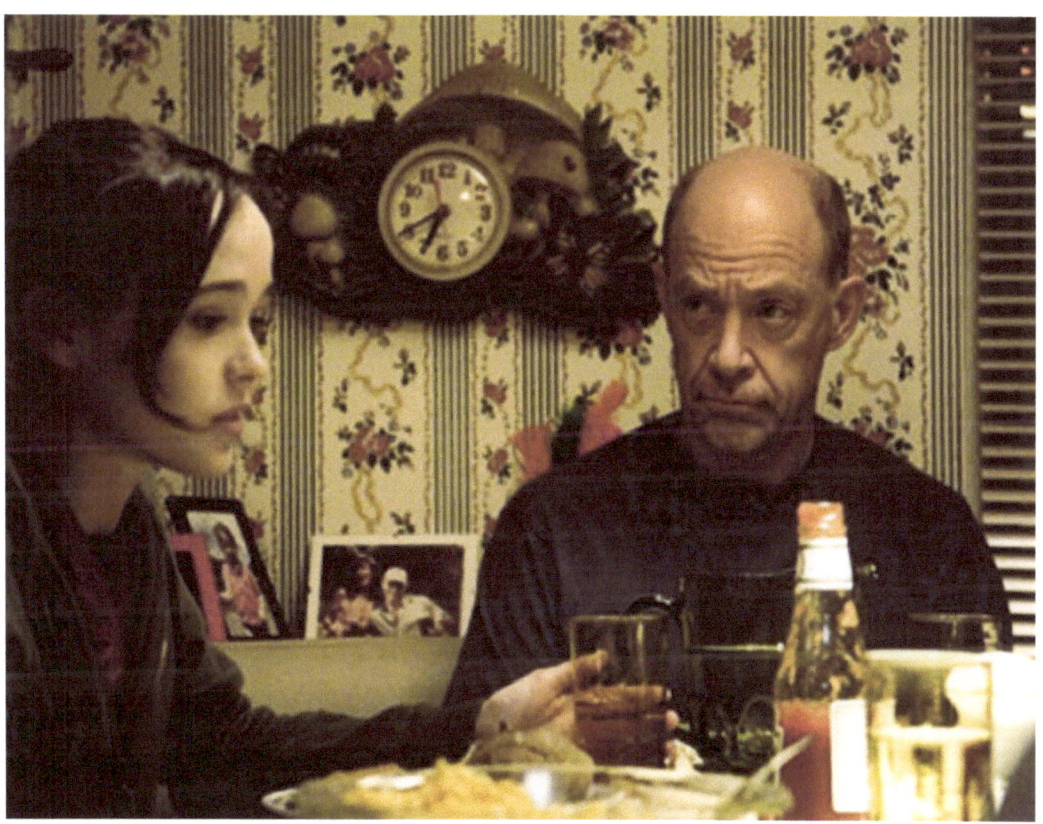

3. THE FULL SHOT equals social space. Social space is from four feet to twelve feet. It is the space we maintain when we're in a social situation.

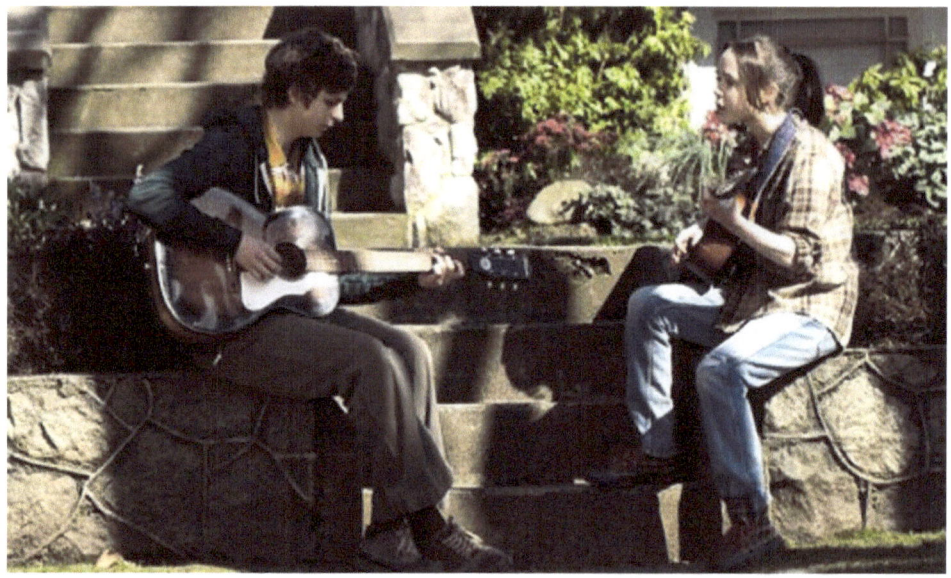

4. THE LONG SHOT or EXTREME LONG SHOT is equal to the public space. Public space varies depending on the situation, but includes avoiding eye contact, conversation, and touch.

The greater the distance between the camera and the subject, the more emotionally neutral the audience feels.

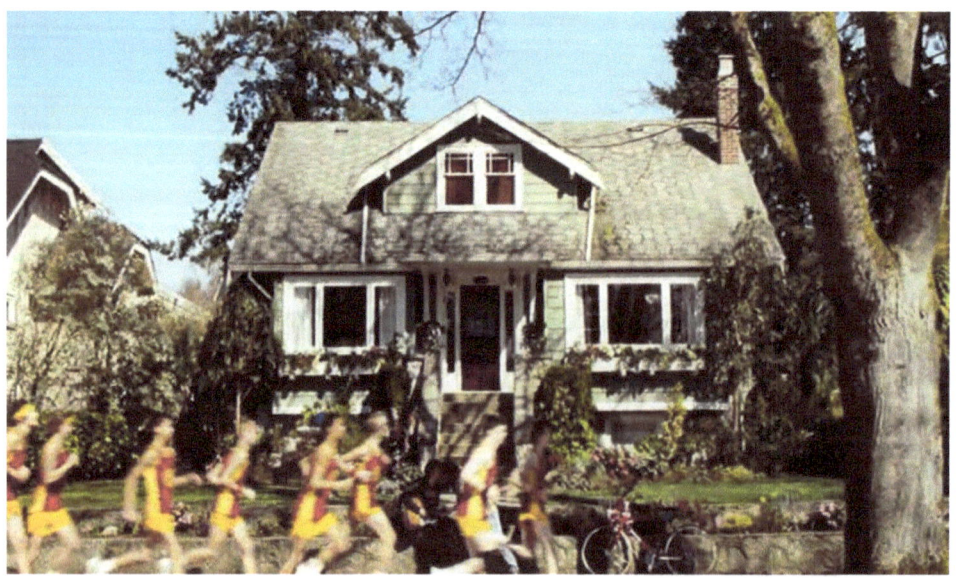

**Three tips:**

1. Get close. By close, I mean getting right up in someone's face with your camera. Your smartphone comes with a slightly wider than normal lens, so you need to get close. Probably closer than your comfortable doing. Don't be afraid... ask for permission... you're in the cinematic world now, not the social one. And that, allows you to get close whenever you need to. Another option is to use a telephoto lens to get closer. (see Lens Personalities for more details)

2. You don't always need a close-up in every scene. Experiment where the closest you get is a medium close-up, two shot, or over-the-shoulder shot.

3. Play with your audience by varying the camera space in a scene. Plan where you want to go and what emotion you want your audience to feel, but take your time getting there. Tease them. Give them a medium close-up, then back up to a medium shot, then medium close again, then get way back, and when they least expect it — go for the close-up. You're in control. So plan your shots so you take your audience on a ride. They'll love it.

# 34. INVISIBLE EDITING

Most amateur filmmakers are intimidated by the idea of editing. They wrongly believe that it's too complicated. It isn't. Consider this, many of the chapters you've already read in this book have been preparing you for the editing process. Here is a list of many of the editing concepts you've learned so far:

- Thinking in shots
- Using camera angles
- The emotional power of different kinds of shots (close-up, medium shots, etc)
- Using eye contact, or the lack of it, to express emotion
- How to build suspense
- CPR or how to utilizing Point-of-View shots
- Understanding the emotional power of camera and character space
- Continuity or how to cut a scene with actors using the 180° and 30° rule

The hard part of editing is knowing what, when, and why your cutting. Physically doing it is easy. If you can "Cut", "Paste", and "Delete with a word processing program you can edit a movie. The software can be as simple as iMovie, or as complicated as Final Cut Pro X or Adobe Premier. But, when push comes to shove in the editing world, it's all about "Selecting", "Trimming", "Pasting", "Moving", and "Deleting". Same as using a word processing program.

**Invisible Editing:** Invisible editing means that you mask every cut so the viewer forgets they're watching a film, they are immersed in the world of the movie and totally unaware of the change from one cut to another. Let's take a look at how it's done.

**Cutting:** this is done with a straight simple cut from one shot to another. Based on the concept of *continuity*, straight cutting incorporates an understanding of both the 180° and 30° rule regarding camera placement, shot size, and shot angle. The cut is always simply and clean, with no dissolve or fancy transition of any kind. This is the cut you'll be using 90% to 95% of the time when you edit.

The shots can be of a different object, angle, or camera framing. Examples are:

- cutting from a two shot to an over-the-shoulder shot.

- cutting from an over-the-shoulder shot to the reverse over-the-shoulder shot.
- cutting from one view of a subject or object to another.
- cutting from one location to another.

**Cutting on Action:** is a major aspect of invisible editing. *Cutting on action*, or *matching action*, gives life and vitality to a character's movements in a sequence. Vitality, that just wouldn't have been there had it been shown as just one continuous shot of the same action. *Cutting on action* is accomplished by matching the motion between two different shots so that they appear to be one fluid movement across the cut. This is accomplished by filming the action twice, using the same movement each time, but shot from a different angle, position, or shot size. It can be used with any movement or gesture, including subtle changes in a subjects gaze from one thing to another.

Let's see how this was done in the James Bond movie Skyfall (2012). In still number one below the cut is made part way through Bond's head movement as he turns to look at the spotter behind him.

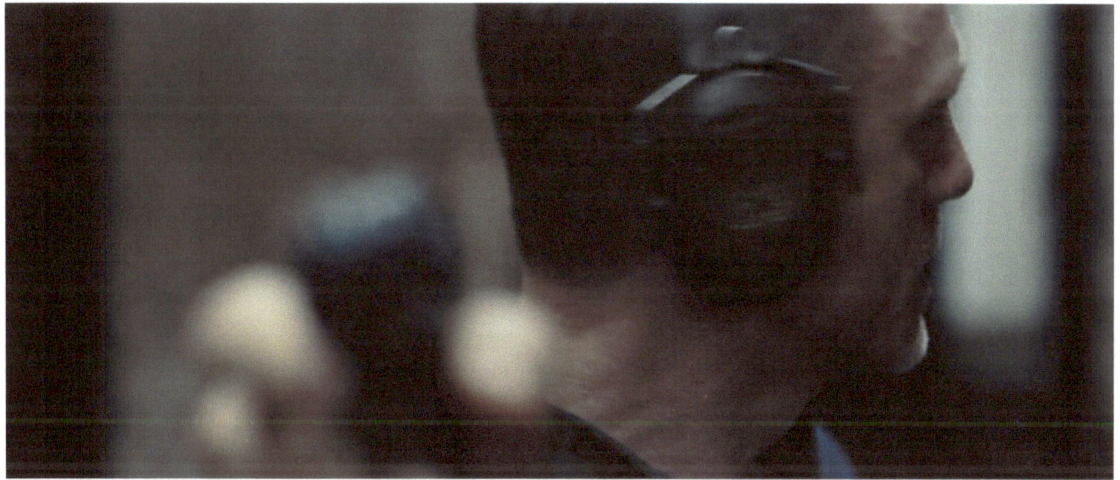

Shot 2 is aligned with shot 1, so it matches Bond's head movement as he turns to look at the spotter. Notice the change in size between the two shots.

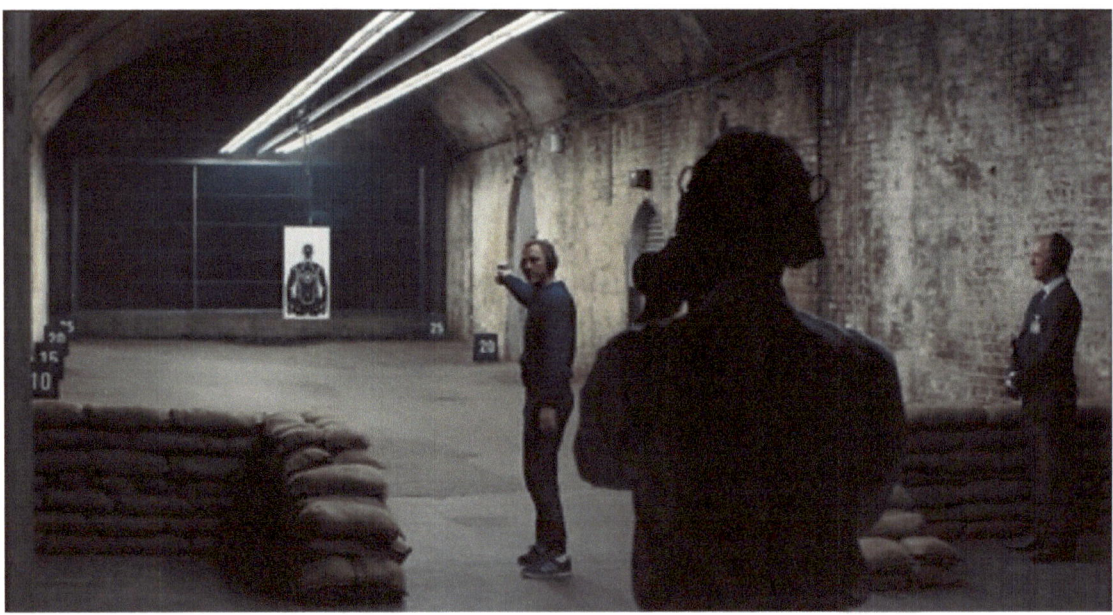

**Parallel Editing or Cross cutting:** utilizes combining alternating shots from two separate activities that are happening simultaneously, but in different locations, together to create interest and suspense. Usually at the end of the sequence the two activities meet and become one. For example, in a previous chapter we used a *cross cutting* structure to create a shot list for Bill and Nancy's 25th Anniversary Party. The Party's structure alternates between Bill and Nancy getting ready for the party upstairs and the food preparation downstairs. It culminates with their friends and guests applauding as they dance to their favorite song. (*see Developing Your Story - start at the end for details*).

**"B" roll:** "B" roll is footage of any kind that is inserted in between shots of the main subject. It can show:

• What a subject is talking about, say in an interview, or in conjunction with voice over narration.

• What a subject is thinking about or remembering.

• It can be of scenery or details of hands, feet, machinery, or any object or subject that relates to the main theme of the sequence.

**Transitions:** such as dissolves, wipes, page peels, slides, and mosaics are use to show transitions of time, location, subject, or theme. With the exception of the cross dissolve and the fade in or out, most transitions are considered decorative and playful and are rarely used on professional quality films. Below are the types of transitions available in the iMovie Editing App on an iPhone or iPad. "None" is actually a straight cut between shots.

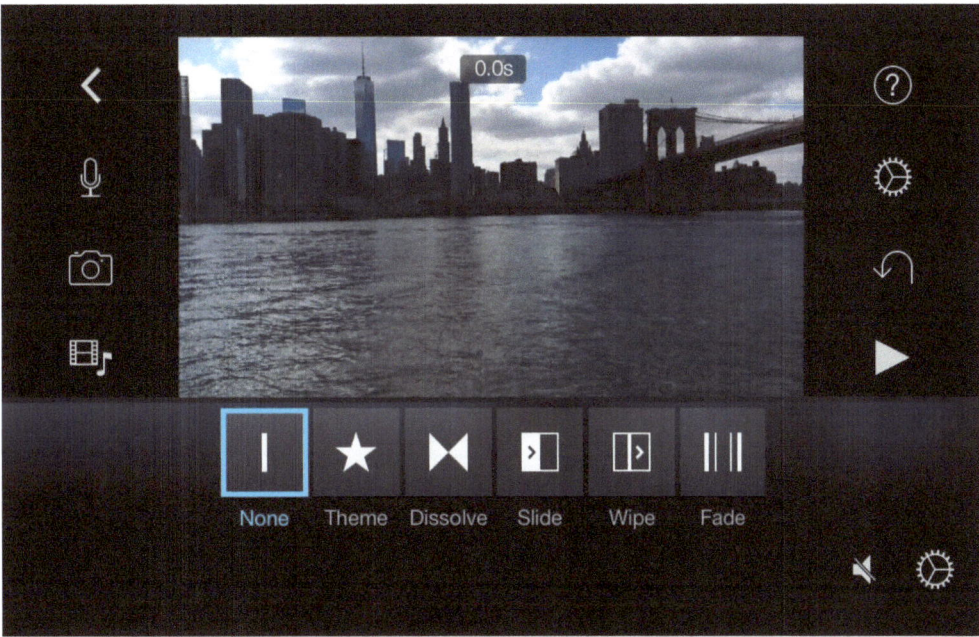

The screen shot below shows the use of two Dissolves and a Straight Cut on the timeline of an iMovie Project.

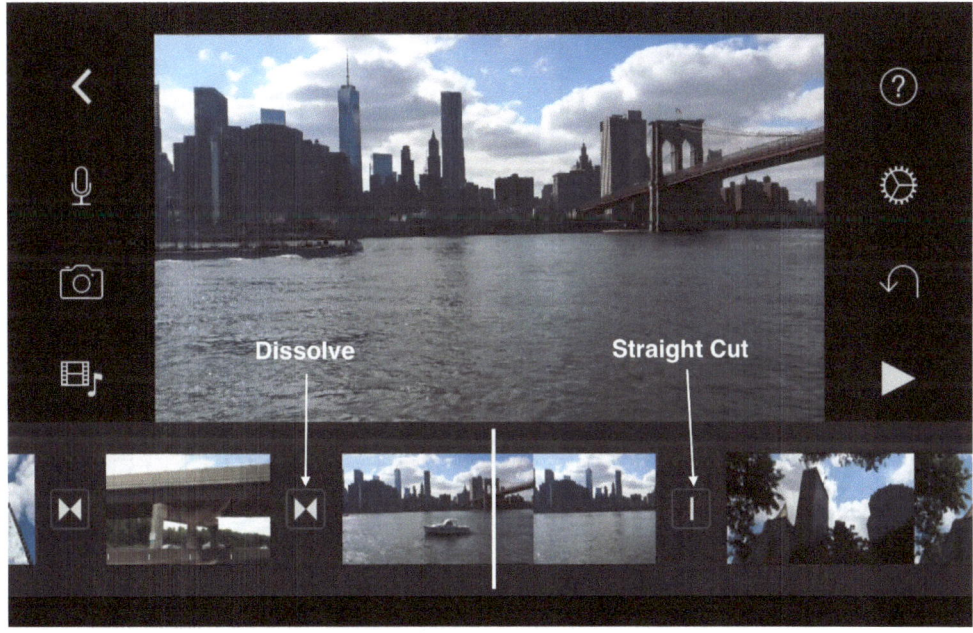

**Split Edit — "L" and "J" Cuts:** A Split edit is another powerful form of invisible editing. It uses the audio track to hide a cut by having the sound or dialog either precede or continue after the cut. In this way the sound carries the change in image across the cut, making it invisible to the audience. A "J" cut precedes the image, where we hear the audio first and then see the change. With an "L" cut the sound continues on into the next clip on the timeline.

A split edit can be any sound that carries across a cut, including environmental sounds like: a busy city street; the sound of a forest; waves washing up on a beach; sound effects; a music bed; or narration or dialog. As a matter of fact most dialog sequences are cut using split edits, which carry the speakers voice forward across the cut while we show the reaction of a listener or return back to a speaker. Like Cutting on Action, a dialog sequence is shot multiple times in order to get sufficient coverage especially for "L" and "J" edits. Below is a screen shot from an iPad showing "J" and "L" cuts. Notice the audio track from the Freeway clip precedes and follows the video image.

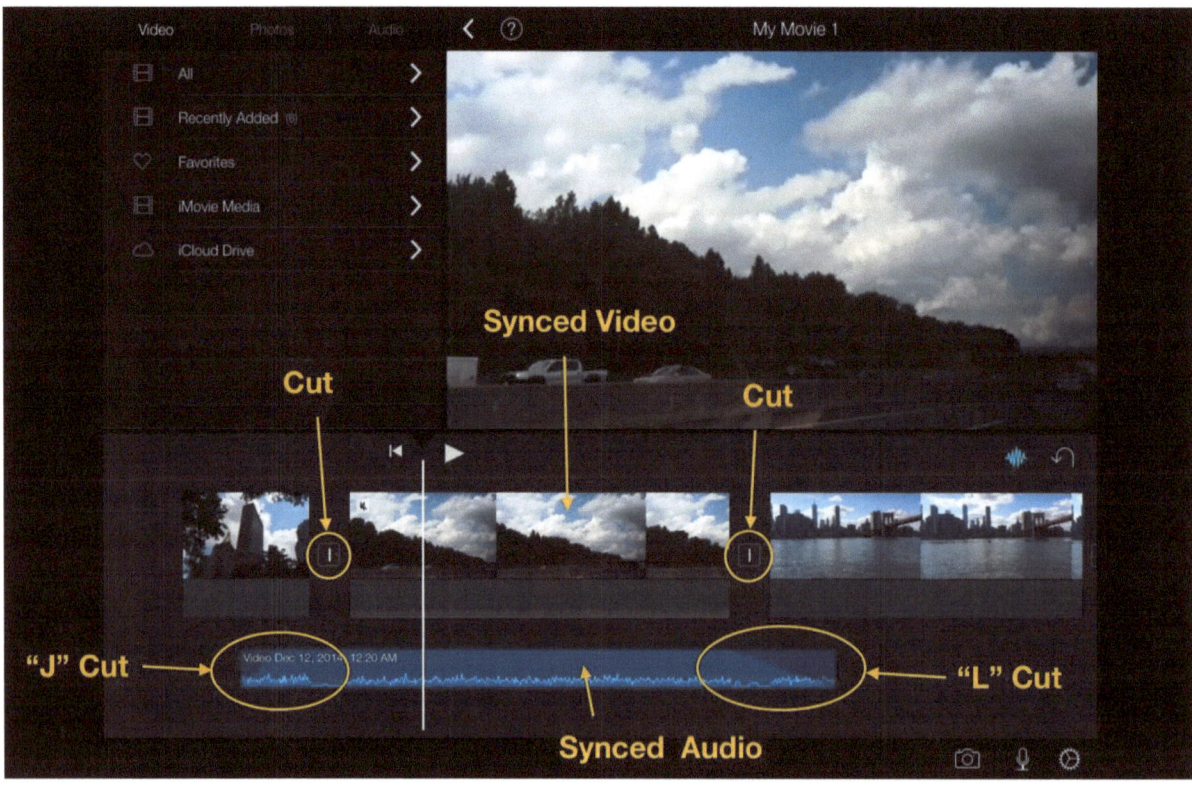

**Time Lapse, Slow Motion, and Stop Time Animation:** All have entered our movie and video lexicon and are synonymous with the compression or extension of time.

There are many inexpensive applications that will allow you to shoot time lapse, slow motion, or create stop time animations with a smartphone or tablet.

Below is a screen capture of a slow motion shot from an iPhone 5S Camera showing its total length and the speed adjustment handles which control either normal or 120 frames per second (Slow Motion). The distance between the vertical ticks can be adjusted and indicate the playback speed of the image. The further apart the ticks the slower is the motion.

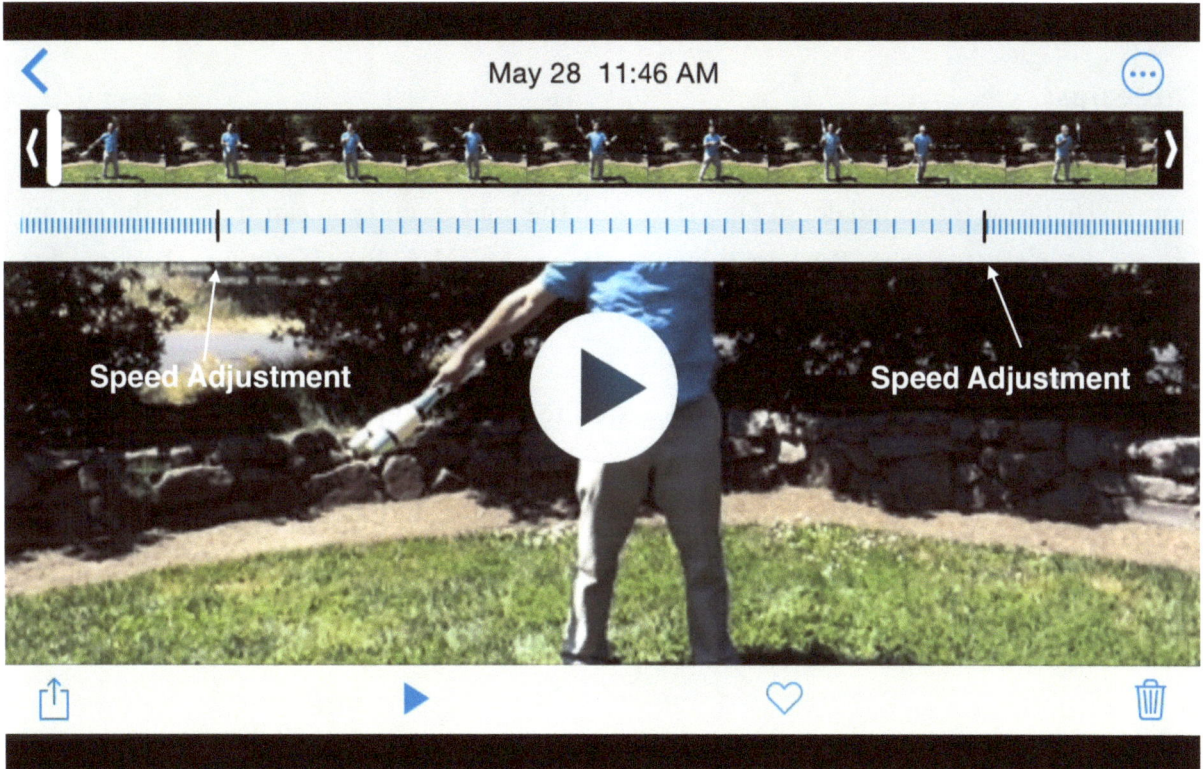

There will be times when you'll want to slow down or speed up the action of footage your cutting into a scene, to make the movement clearer. This type of speed change can work effectively as long as the change is not obvious to the audience. Slowing a bird's flight down, by say 50% is a good example of how to utilize this type of footage into your story. Please note, that controlling playback speed is limited on most smart device editing applications. For more flexibility, download your footage to your computer and edit on more robust application like iMovie, Final Cut Pro or Adobe Premiere.

**Jump-cut:** The advent of MTV and music videos has opened up a whole new type of editing that it now includes *jump-cuts*. A *jump-cut* is intentionally visible, and is the opposite of invisible editing and continuity, in that it uses the same size shot from one cut to the next, thereby creating the appearance of a gap or jump in the smooth flow of time of the scene. *Jump-cuts* by there nature call attention to themselves. It is a way of speeding up time, or creating a staccato effect. A wonderful use of *jump-cuts* can be seen in the movie Run Lola Run. The director, Tom Tykwer used dozens of jump cuts to speed up the movement of his main character Lola in a fresh and startling way.

**Three tips:**

1. Study other editors. The best way to do that is to turn off the sound in a movie or TV drama. That way, the sound doesn't interfere with the images, and you can see how the editor has put the movie together. Pay particular attention to how the editor is cutting. How is she editing? Are they using just straight cuts, dissolves, or are there other techniques they're using to engage the audience.

2. As you begin studying other directors and editor, notice how and when they cut on action. How would you use it in your productions?

3. Also notice how and when a director or editor incorporates jump cuts into his movie. How do they make you feel? When wouldn't you use them? Why?

# 35. SMART DEVICE EDITING — The basics

"It's in the "Can." Which is an old Hollywood saying that the footage has been shot, the film developed, and is now stored in light-proof metal cans waiting to be edited.

With digital cinematography, there is no can. But editing is as much a key activity as ever. Modern software makes getting the footage out of the can and up on the screen easy.

**The Basics**: Software applications have helped to simplify the video editing, making it an easy, intuitive, step-by-step process. It's not complicated. For example, you might be surprised to learn that almost all editing applications utilize the same basic type of interface and workflow. *(There always will be minor variations in how a software manufacturer names a specific function within its application, but regardless of what it's called, all editing programs function in same manner as described below.)*

Pretty much every video editing app contains the following:

**Media library:** that stores media in the form of video clip, photos, animation, music, audio tracks, and sound FX.

**Browser**: is designed for viewing your media prior to importing it into the project or timeline. Think of the browser as your private screening room.

**Timeline:** is where you build your movie. It contains video and audio clips, photographs, animations, titles, graphics, cuts, and transitions. Think of the Timeline as your workbench where you'll line up the shots, add audio, insert graphics, and create magical effects like dissolves.

**Viewer:** is your main viewing screen. It allows you to view clips played either from the browser or the timeline.

**Play head:** indicates the precise location on the timeline that is being displayed in the viewer — both visually and auditoriually.

**Video Clip:** each clip is displayed as a thumbnail on the timeline, showing the length of each clip and where on the timeline it is located.

**Transitions:** ranging from cross-dissolves to wipes, they are displayed in-between clips on the timeline.

**Tool Bar:** is revealed when a clip, or audio track, is highlighted. The tool bar contains a variety of options for changing transitions, trimming clips, using different types of titles, clip speed changes, audio volume controls, and other effects.

Below is a screen capture of the iMovie editing screen on an iPhone 5S. Many functions listed above, like the Media Library, require clicking on an icon to get to them. Or, the tool bar is revealed when a clip, audio track, or transition is highlighted by tapping it.

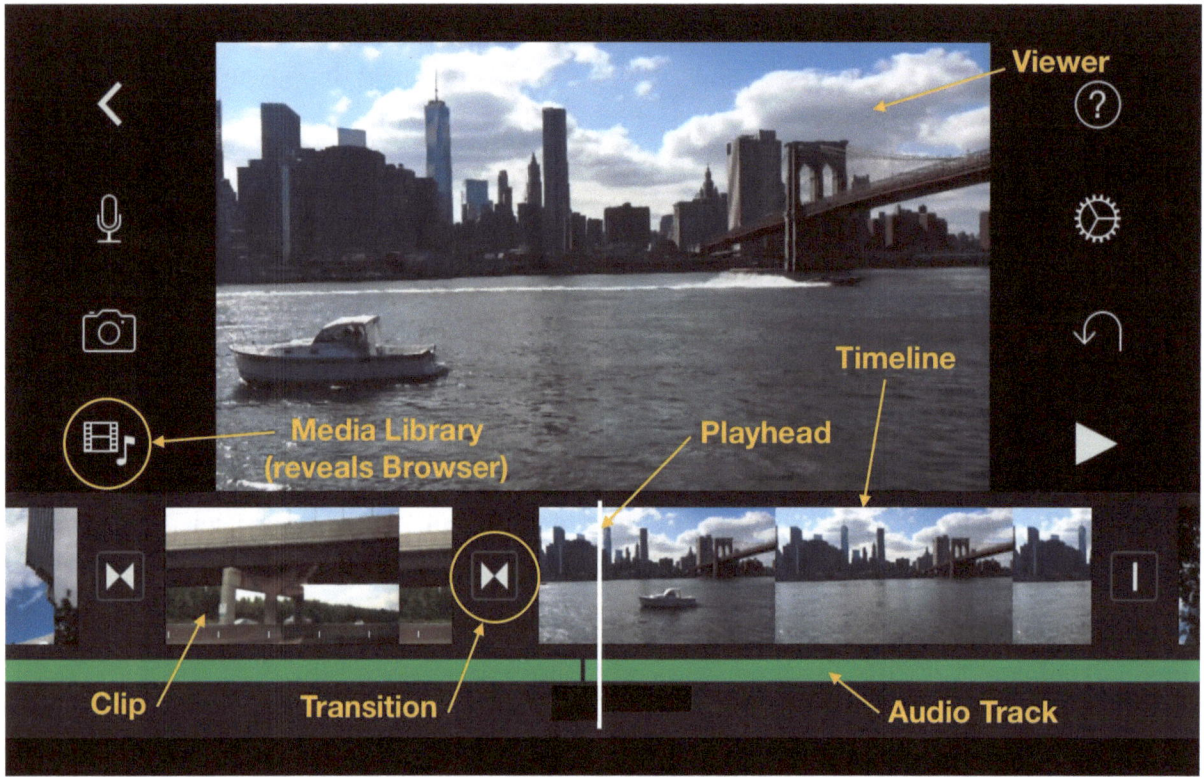

Working with a new editing app is like moving to a new apartment. Apartments may different in size and design, but just about every apartment will have a kitchen, bathroom, bedroom, etc. The light switches and refrigerator maybe found in a different location, and possibly have more features, but they all function the same.

**Note to Computer Editors:** this chapter focuses on how to edit on a smart device, to illustrate how easy it is. I believe that many of you will choose to edit on your computer instead. Please keep in mind, that when you do, you'll find that your computer editing application utilizes the same basic interface and workflow as we've described above.

**Importing Footage** — most applications have a *Media Library* containing video, audio, and pictures. On a smartphone tapping on the *Media Library* icon will bring up a second window offering you choices for "Video", "Photos", and "Audio". Choosing one, such as "Artists" from the "Audio" window, will bring you to the specific "Browser" window for that type of media.

Below is the iMovie Media Library screen on an iPad Mini. Notice the "Video, "Photos" and "Audio" tabs at the top of the window. The current screen shot is displaying the "Audio" options window.

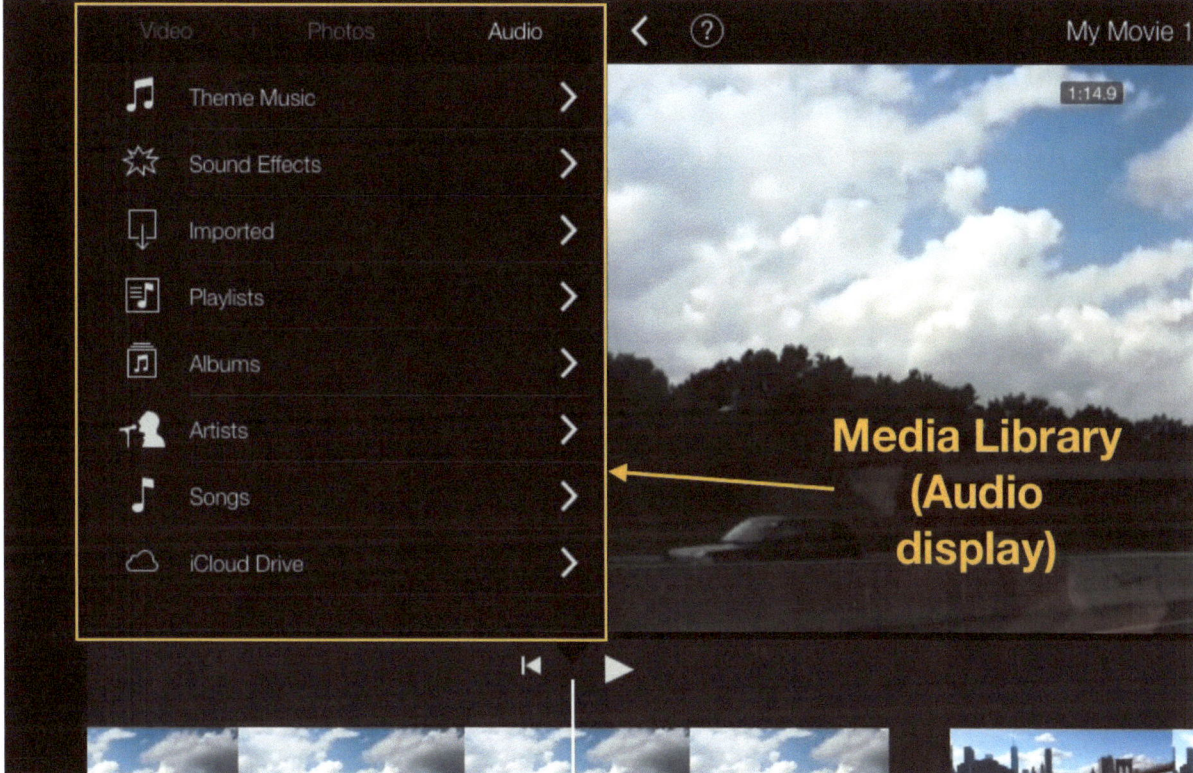

Below is the Audio Browser Screen on the iPhone 5S. From the Media Library Audio screen we've tapped "Artist", which brought up another screen showing all the recording artist in my iTunes collection. Choosing "The Beatles" brought up a song list, where we chose the song "Blackbird" by tapping on it, revealing the tool bar which allows us to either listen to the selection or add the song to the timeline at the play head.

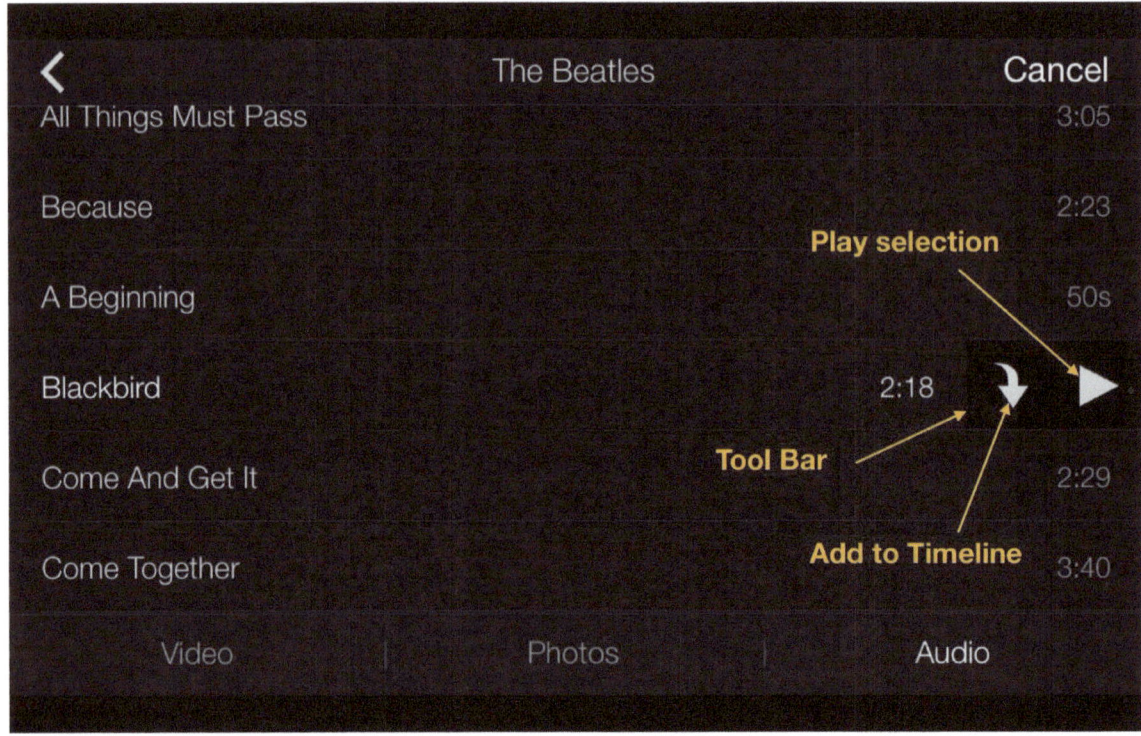

To choose a video clip from your camera roll tap "Video" in the iMovie Browser screen. That will bring up all the videos in your camera roll. Then tapping on a clip will reveal all the tool bar options.

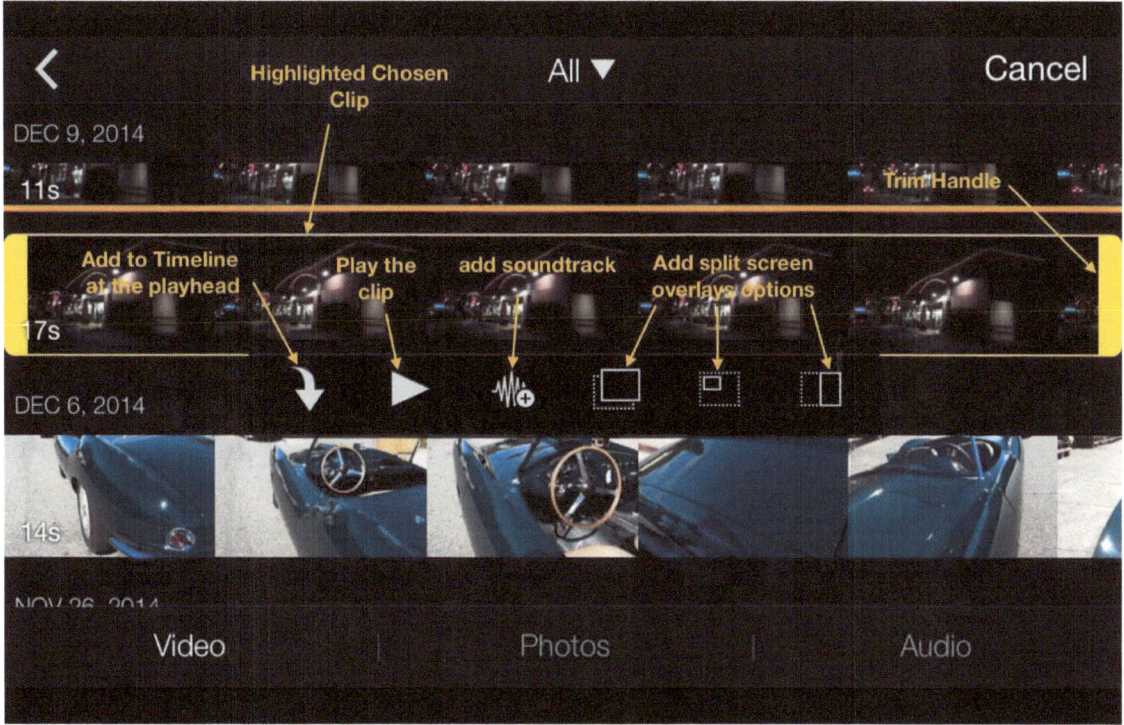

**Editing in the Timeline** This is where the fun starts. Choosing clips from your Media Library and its various browsers, adding them to the timeline, thereby creating a rough arrangement of what your movie is eventually going to look like.

The second step is making what's called a rough cut, where you'll begin moving, trimming, duplicating, deleting, and adding new clips, until they're in an arrangement that you like and seem to flow from beginning to end. Most applications allow you to perform what is called non-destructive editing. Which means that regardless of how you trim, split, or delete the clip on the timeline, the original clip remains pristine and untouched in your library.

Your goal is to created a rhythm and flow to your project so that it has its own internal logic. Video editing is much like writing, it's a process of discovery through rewriting and polishing.

Remember, like a word processor, you're not stuck with the first arrangement of clips you've put on the timeline. You can change... anything...everything. Add music, sound FX, split screen, photos, and even apply Ken Burns type effects.

To make changes to your clip, photo, audio track, or title, just tap that specific element on the timeline and its tool bar will appear.

**Clip Editing:** The screen capture below shows details of the iMovie Video Clip Editing Tool Bar.  The highlighted scissors (bottom left) is the Trimming Tool option which offers "Split", "Duplicate", and "Delete" functions.  In addition, the clip's length can be trimmed by sliding the front or rear yellow trim handles left or right.  You can repositioned a clip by holding and sliding the clip to a new position.

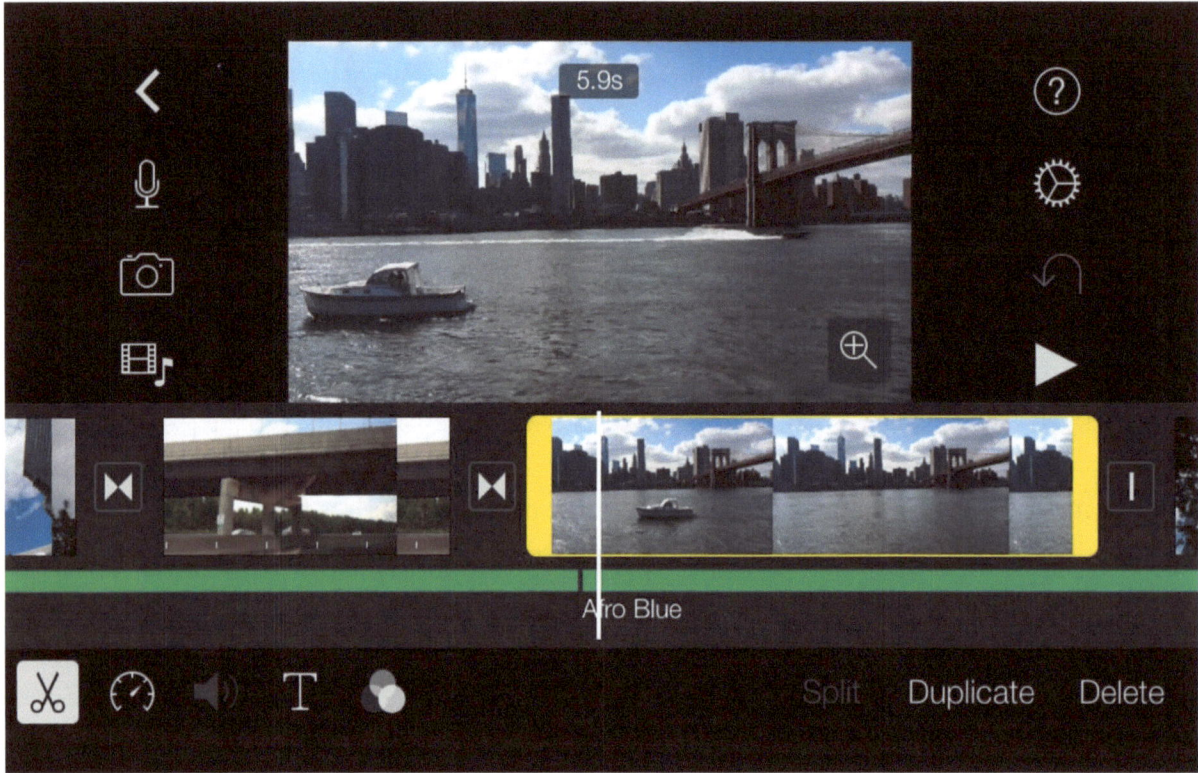

**Speed Changes:**  Below is the iMovie Speed Change Tool Bar. The highlighted clock (bottom left) is the Speed Change Tool which offers speed changes from 2x faster to 1/8th slow motion playback, freeze frame, and reset functions.  The speed and freeze frame functions are indicated by the highlighted bar with tick marks.  Trimming is done using the yellow trimming handles.

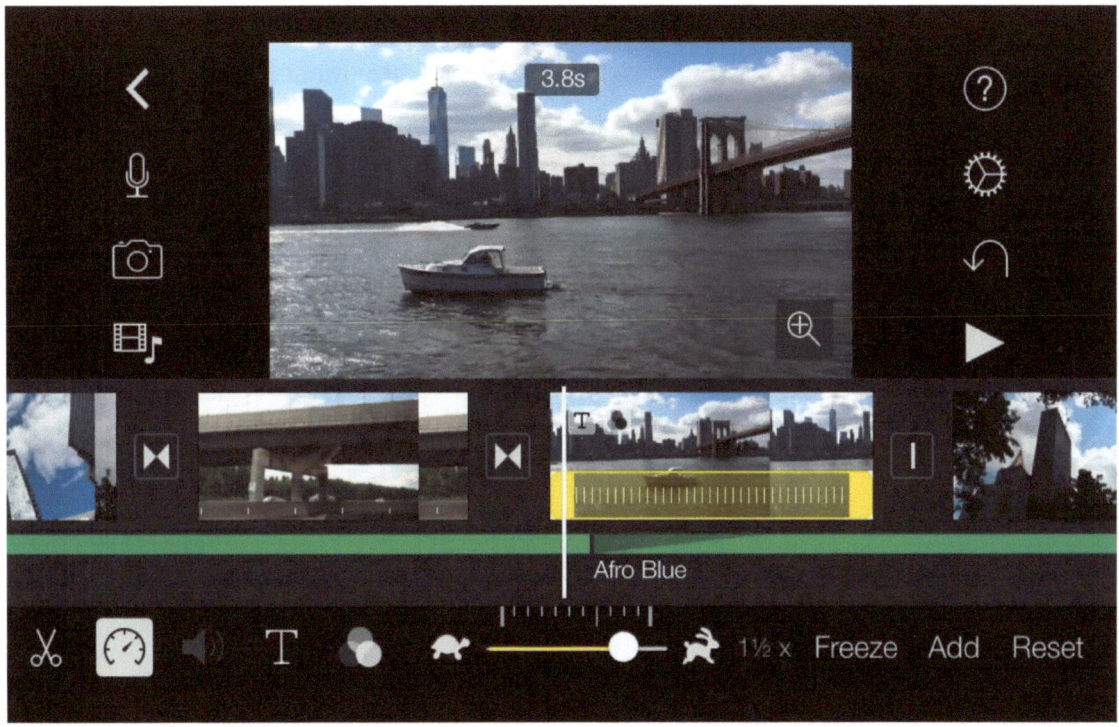

**Sound Editing:** The Sound Editing Tool Bar icon seen below is the highlighted speaker (bottom left which offers volume (from 0 to 500%) and fade in and out functions.

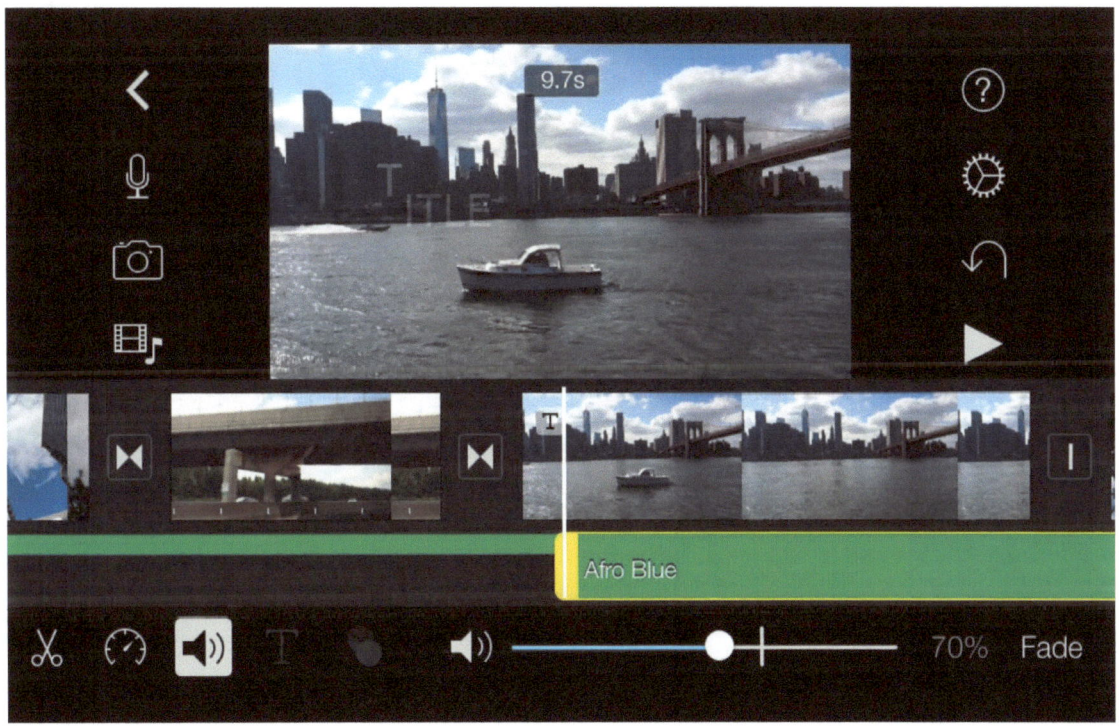

**Title Tool Bar**:  The highlighted "T" icon (bottom left) is the Title bar which offers both animated and stationary titles in a variety of different type faces. It allows you to either "Center" the text or use the "Lower" 3rds function, which is meant for subjects names and titles.

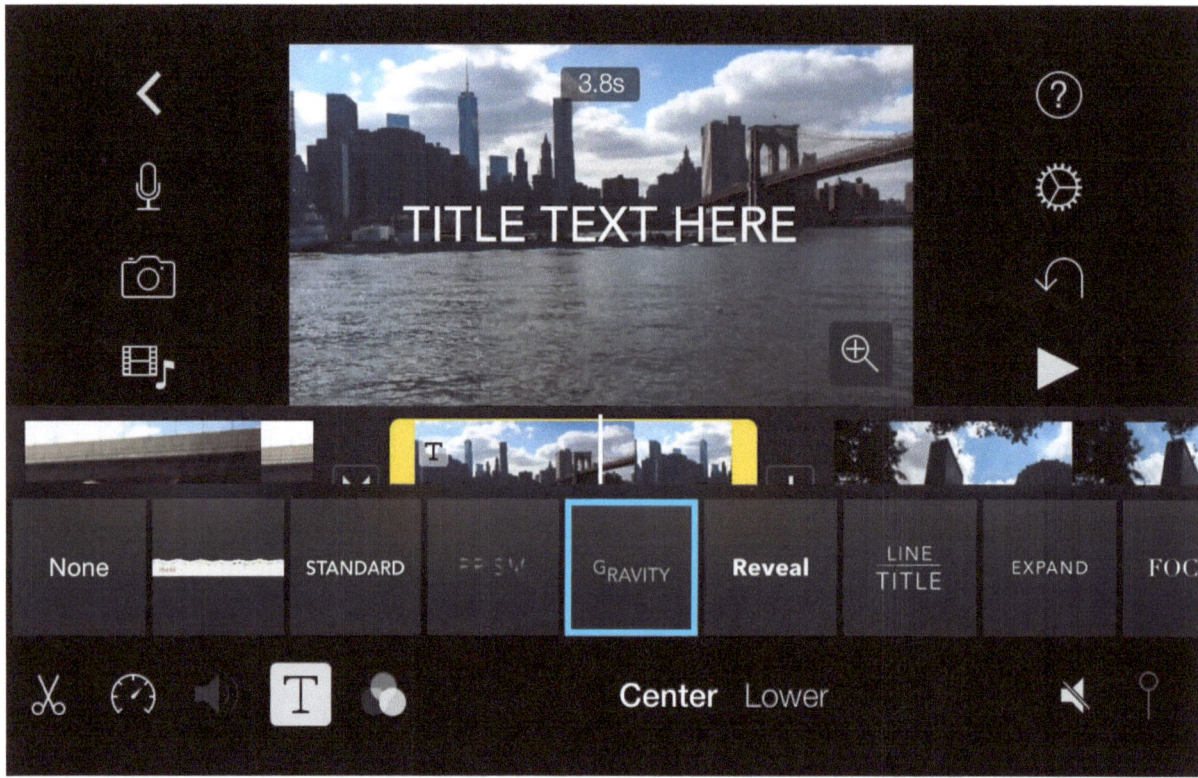

**Filter Tool Bar:**  The highlighted three circles icon (bottom left) is the Filter Tool which offers you a variety of filters to modify the look of either a single clip or your whole project.

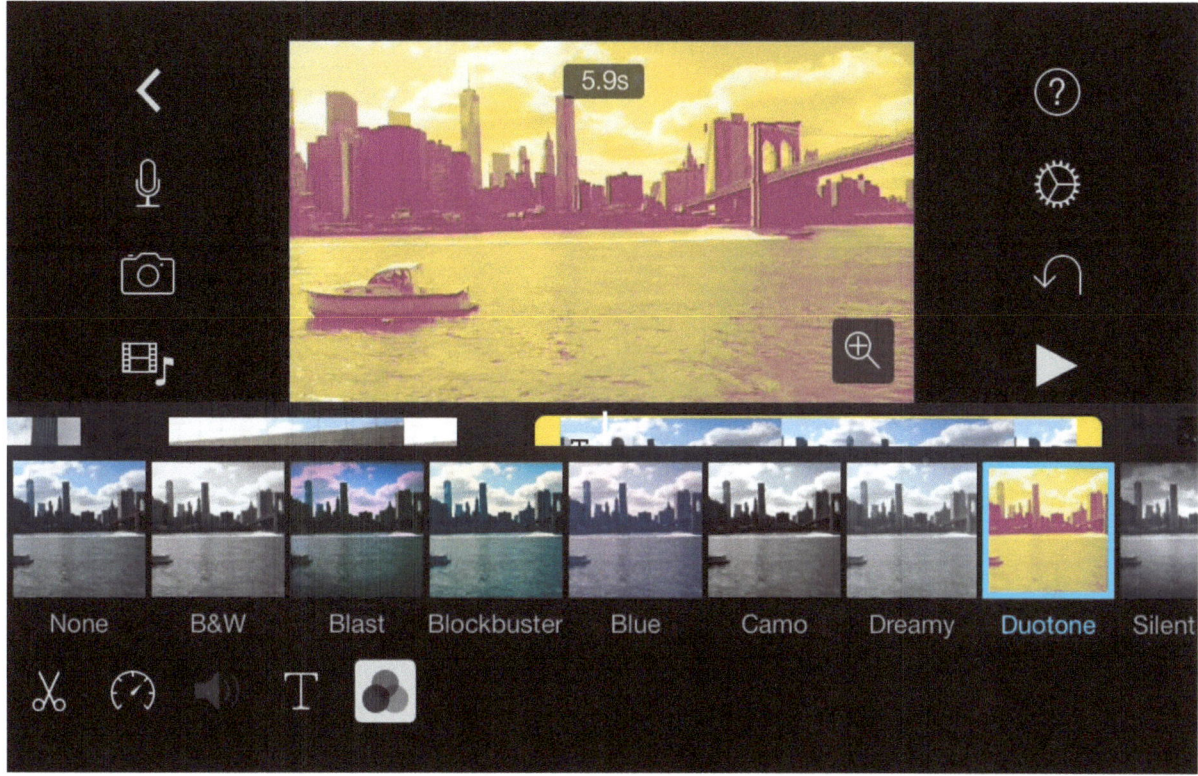

**Audio Record** (Microphone icon) **and Camera** (Camera icon) **Options** allow you to record audio or video directly to the timeline using the built in audio recorder or camera. If you want to use this it's fine, but I personally would not use these functions, because they don't offer you the same control that you would have if you recorded them on a separate application and added them to the timeline later.

**Saving and Sharing:** Sharing is incredibility easy to do. Start by touching the *back arrow*, (circled in red in the screen below) located at the top left hand corner of your editing screen, this will take you to the Video, Projects, and Theater window. There you can choose:

- **Video** to review your video footage
- **Projects** which will display all your projects
- **Theater** where you can watch all your completed projects and other imported movies.

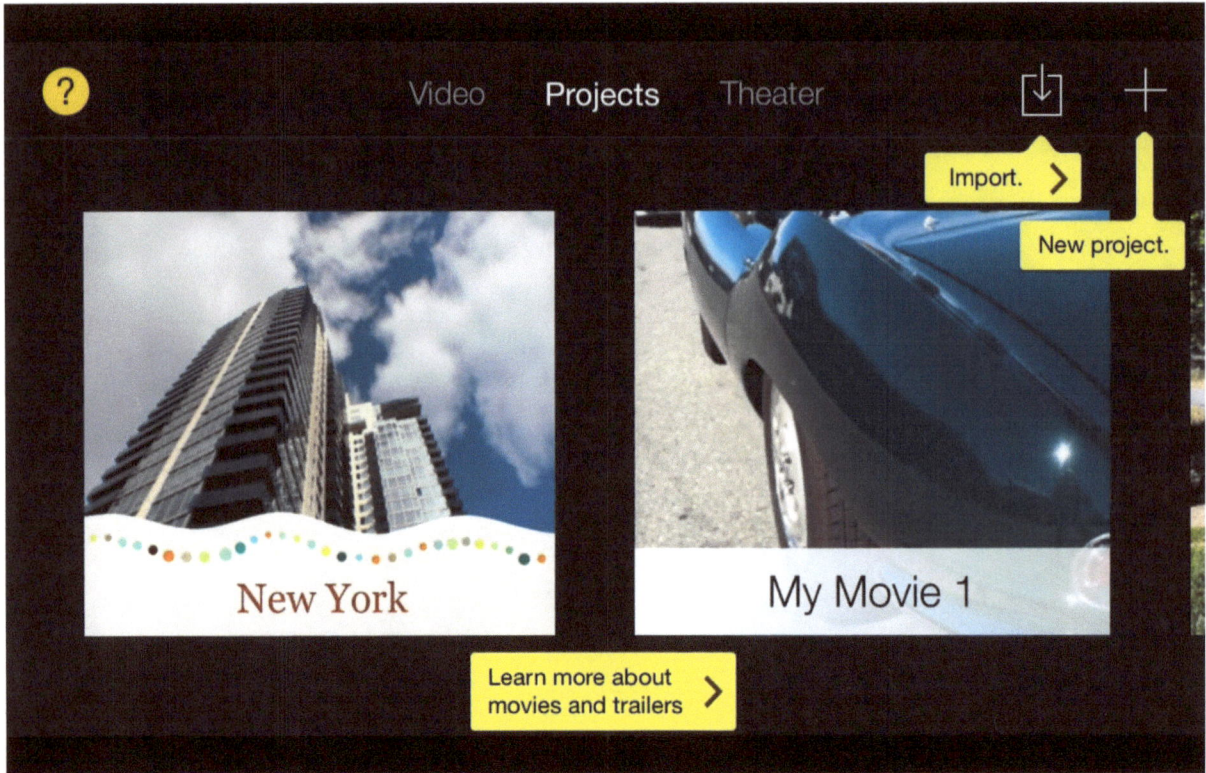

To share the movie in the Project Window tap the movie you want to share, which will take you to the individual project screen.

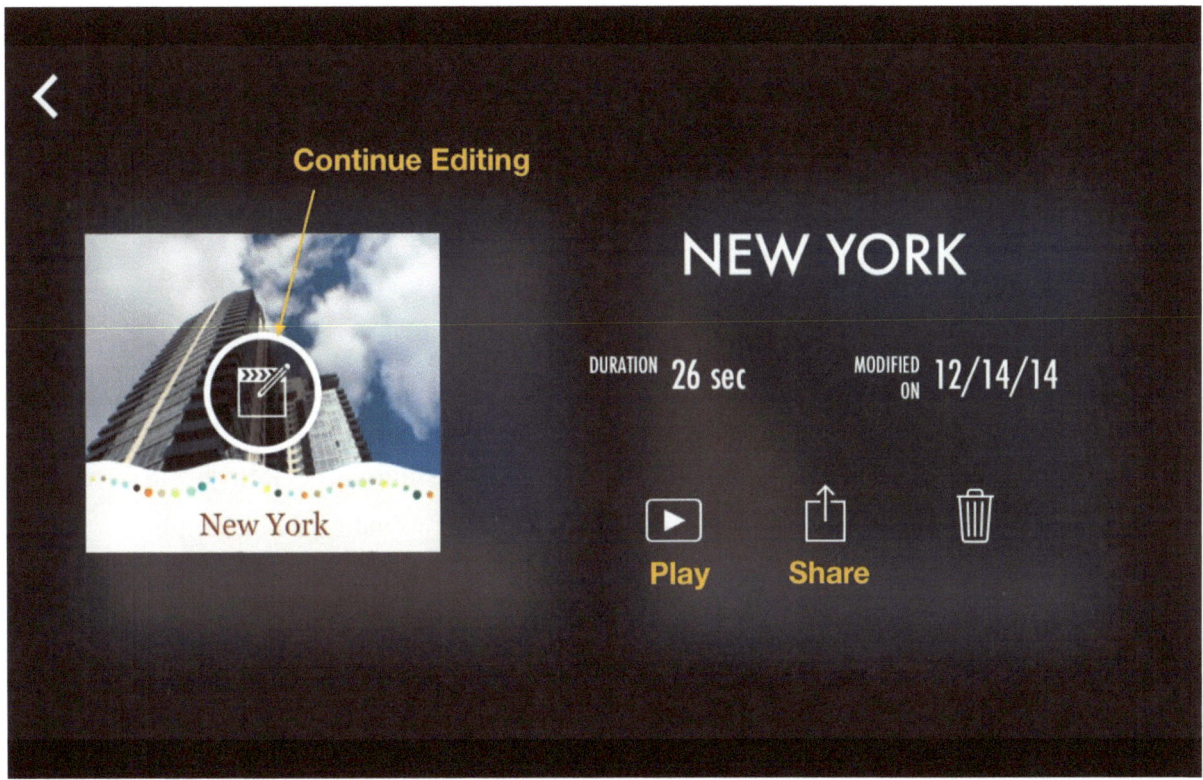

Tapping the share icon, in the Project screen, takes you to the Share Selection window, where you can choose from a variety of venues for displaying your work, including email.

**How to Save and Share Your Work**

**AirDrop and programs like SHAREit allow you** to share with a nearby device. using Wi-Fi and Bluetooth technology. Your appliances must be on the same Wi-Fi network, or within approximately 30 feet (10 meters) of the other device. Transfers are encrypted for security.

**Save to Camera Roll** (iOS and Android devices) Tap the share button, then tap "Save Video", tap the size you want to export. You can access your Camera Roll within the Photos app on your device.

**Save to iTunes** (or the Android or Windows equivalent) Tap the share button, then tap "Save to iTunes", then choose either Video File or iMovie Project, and tap to save. You can download your project to your computer through iTunes.

**Save to iMovie Theater** (or Android or Windows equivalent)  One way to save your completed  film is by tapping the "iMovie Theater" icon, which will automatically render it into a QuickTime .MOV file. The movie appears in iMovie Theater. If you have an iCloud account set up, the movie automatically appears in iMovie Theater on your other devices, including your Mac, iOS devices, and Apple TV.

**Save to YouTube, Vimeo, FaceBook, DropBox and More**  Tapping on the YouTube, Vimeo, or other icon, in the share selection window, will take you to the that websites Share Project window, where you can  sign in and complete the  questionnaire.  iMovie will automatically render and upload your project to that website.   What could be simpler!

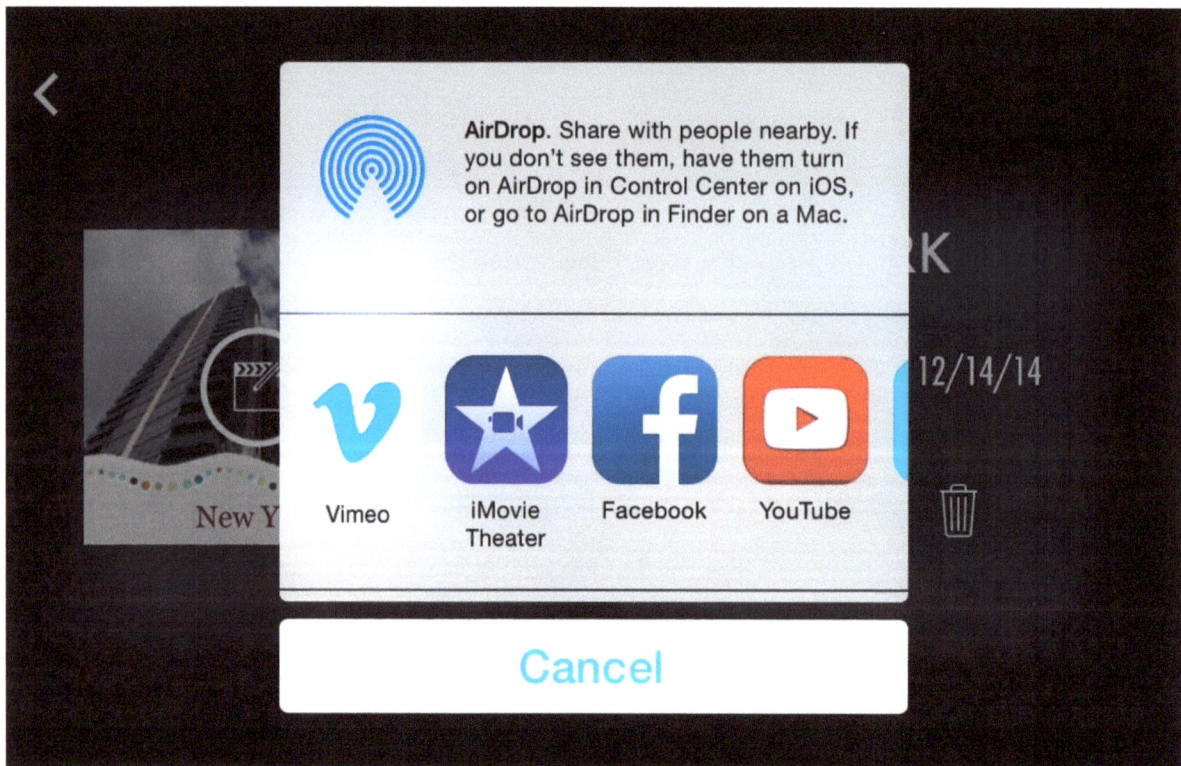

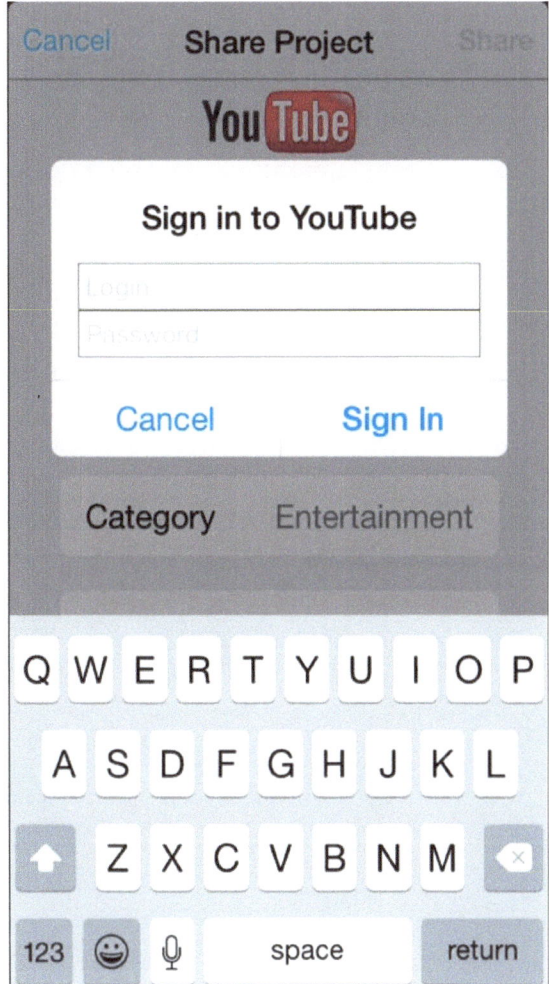

Here is a list of recommended smart device video editing applications

- iMovie – iOS
- Pinnacle Studio — IOS  $12.99
- TouchEdit — iPad Video Editing App  (Designed by famous Hollywood film editor Dan Lebental) $24.95
- KineMaster Pro — Android Video Editing (Supports Samsung but not Motorola devices) $2.99
- Movie Edit Touch for Windows 8 — Free, but do purchase the $2.49 in-app purchase for full functionality

**Free Computer Editing Tutorials** for many of the major video editing applications can be found at:

• **Ripple Training** — Offers free tutorials on Final Cut Pro, Motion, and DaVince Resolve. They have also developed a $4.99 training app for iMovie called, "Lessons for iMovie" available on Apple App Store.

• **Larry Jordan.biz** — Offers free tutorials on Final Cut Pro, Motion, Adobe Premier Pro, and other Adobe Applications.

• **YouTube** — Type in "Tutorial" and the name of the app you're interested in to bring up their tutorials.

Both Larry Jordan and Ripple Training have terrific free online tutorials on almost aspect of video editing.  I highly recommend signing up for their free Newsletters.

# 36. SOUND IS HALF THE PICTURE – Using Music and SFX (Sound Effects)

Sound is so important to modern day film and video we'd be lost without it. To give you an idea of how powerful the relationship between sound and image is, watch this award winning short titled, _The Other Side_, with the sound off.

https://vimeo.com/94527506

Now go ahead and play it again, this time with the sound turned on. I especially enjoy the narrator's deep gravely voice as he introduces us to The Other Side, in complete darkness. Notice the spooky music (called a sound bed) under the opening credits. And, as the movie opens we hear the scraping sound of a match being lit, see a candle, and hear a piano playing a repetitive plaintive melody, we hear something banging and see a crucifix, hung on a wall, jump each time we hear the sound.

Notice: how the sound works with the images; how the music reflects the character's change in mood; and how the sound effects (SFX) enhance the tension and suspense. This is not some haphazard arrangement, but a carefully built collaboration of sound, music, and image meant to create a complete emotional experience for the audience.

Music and SFXs are powerful. whether we consciously recognize them or not, they have an effect on us. They stimulate our emotions in ways we don't understand intellectually. With sound it's more a matter of feeling than knowing. Many talented movie composers know this and use it to effect the emotional centers of the brain.

> _"I feel that music on the screen can seek out and intensify the inner thoughts of the characters. It can invest a scene with terror, grandeur, gaiety, or misery. It can propel narrative swiftly forward, or slow it down. It often lifts mere dialogue into the realm of poetry. Finally, it is the communicating link between the screen and the audience, reaching out and enveloping all into one single experience."_ — Film composer Bernard Herrmann (composer for the movie Psycho)

Even the simplest video, say a travelogue, can be enhanced by adding sounds and music. If it's about a city, adding the sounds of that location mixed with music helps to give the audience the flavor of that place.

179

**Sound Effects (SFX)** — Adding SFX is like adding spices to food; it brings out the flavor and enhances the experience. SFX can be anything: birds singing, leaves rustling, cars backfiring, water bubbling, doors squeaking, anything and everything. You don't have to go crazy and add a lot. Sometimes just a little goes a long way.

iMovie's library is limited, but most editing programs come with an assortment of audio options including Theme Music and SFX. Below is the screen capture of iMovie's Sound Effects screen. Tapping on an effect will bring up the tool bar, which allows you to listen to the effect, or add it to your timeline at the play head.

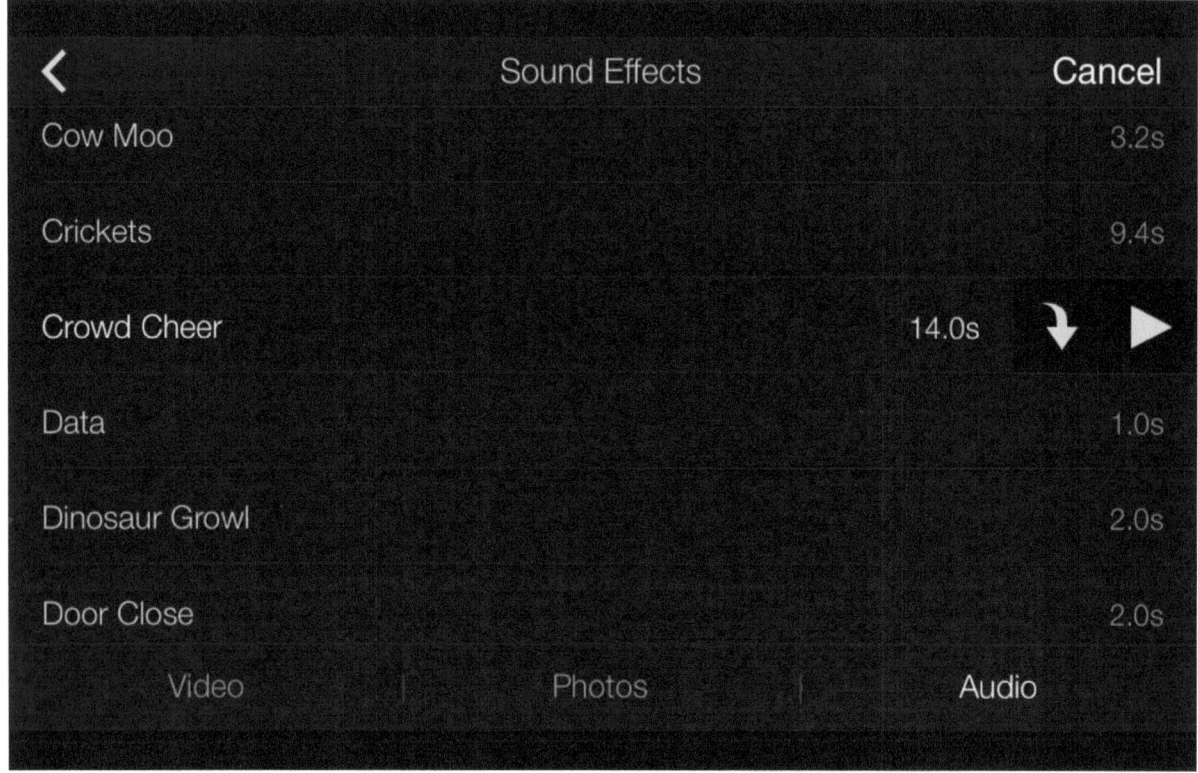

**Editing Sound and Picture** The image below is not a seismographic record of an earthquake, but the waveform of a recording of my voice saying, *"This is what a waveform looks like."* Compared to the thumbnail of a video clip, the waveform is a very abstract representation of sound. Regardless, the waveform is what gets displayed for any sound or music on the editing timeline. With a little experience, you'll find that it's not difficult to identify individual words and sounds on the waveform, thereby allowing you to eliminate unwanted sounds, edit dialog, SFX, and add a music tracks.

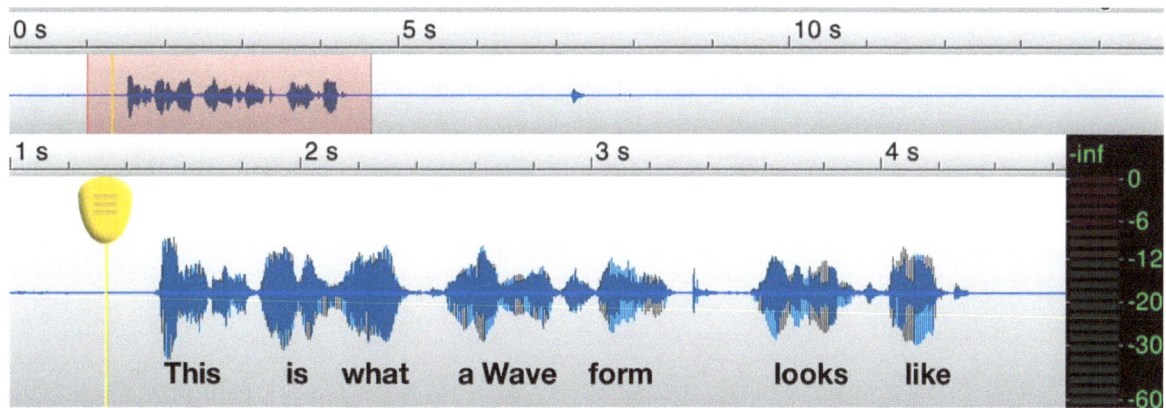

A sound clip can be trimmed and moved in the same manner as a video clip. Using the "Scissors", "Clock", and "Speaker" icons, you can split, duplicate, delete, change the playback speed, adjust the volume, and add a fade to the beginning and end of a clip. Repositioning a sound clip works the same way as moving a video clip does, just tap and slide.

Most editing apps will allow you to add multiple layers of sound, music, and narration tracks to the timeline, so, if you want, you can create a multi-dimensional sound track. In the iMovie Timeline on my iPhone 5s below has multiple audio tracks: Music is green; SFX light blue; and the synced sound track for the video clip is dark blue.

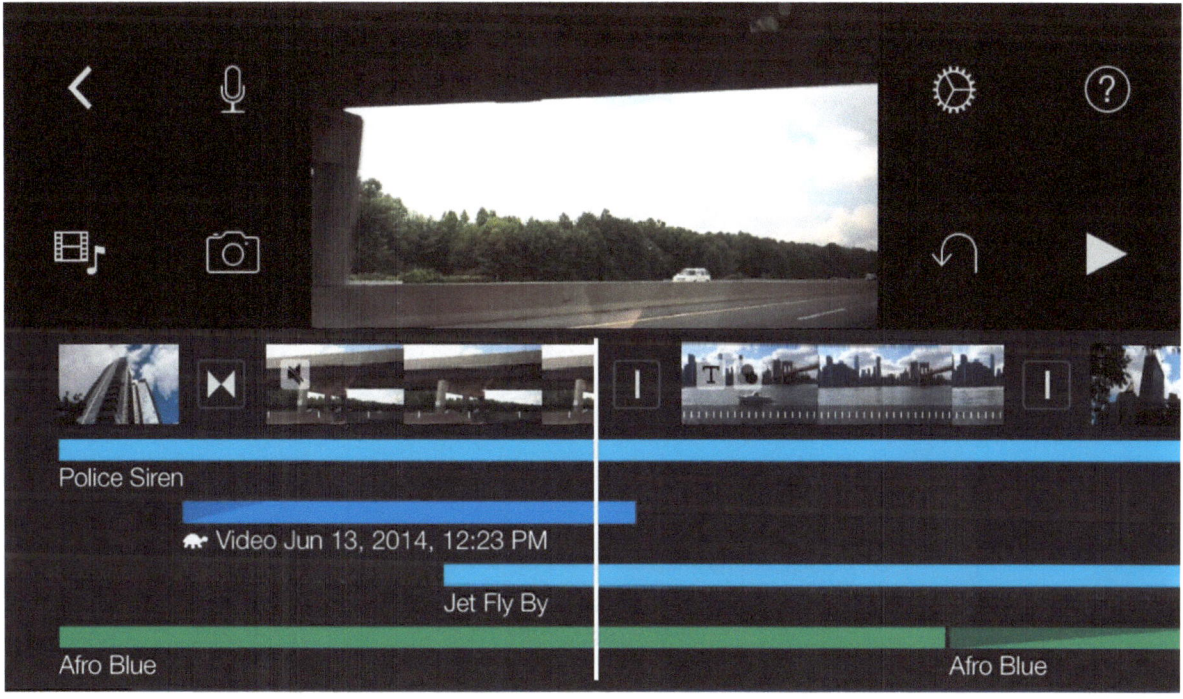

**Sound Design:** In Hollywood movies creating a believable  sound track is the responsibility of the the Sound Designer.  He'll add all sorts of sounds to the movie.  For example a Sound Designer creating an explosion for a scene will mix many different sound effects together to sell the experience.  He might combine the following sounds:

- breaking glass
- metal crashing to the ground
- high pitched whistles
- low pitched rumbles
- multiple clips of  different explosions
- and any other sound that will enhance the experience for the viewer.

Sound Design is a fascinating topic.  Movies like "Star Wars", "Citizen Kane", "Apocalypse Now", "Never Cry Wolf", and "Once Upon a Time in the West" are groundbreaking examples of how sound, music, and picture can work together in new and exciting ways.

**Royalty Free Audio** - You can also purchase royalty free audio and music files on-line. (Royalty free means the royalty fee is waived, you can use the sound as often as you like once you've paid for it. I know that confusing, but the idea is you purchase it once an it's yours, you don't have to pay an additional royalty every time it's shown.)

Any music or SFX purchased can be downloaded to iTunes on your computer, or saved to a cloud storage App like DropBox,  which will allow you store all types of files, including audio and video.  From DropBox you add saved files directly into your editing program.  One website I like for music and SFX is AudioJungle.  It has a large selection at very reasonable prices.

http://audiojungle.net/

**Three Tips and a bonus**

1.  Spend some time listening to a sequence from one of your favorite movies.   Pay close attention to when and how music is used to create mood, indicate a change, or is associated with a specific character.  *(Think of Laura's theme in Dr. Zhivago. )*

2.  Watch and listen, especially to action movies, especially to fight, car chase, and battle scenes.  You'd be surprised at how many unusual effects are used to create a sound environment that the audience will believe.

3.  Use your smart device to record your own sound effects.  In addition to shooting video,

consider recording live sounds, that you'll later incorporate into your video.

Bonus: Many editors' like to cut their shows to music, making edits (cuts) that follow along with the beat of a song.  In the waveform below it is easy to see the peaks in the waveform that represent the beat in this Blue Guitar song.

# CLOSING THOUGHTS

We've come a long way together. I hope you've enjoyed the process and feel more knowledgeable about how to make movies everyone will love.

I'd love to hear from you! Mail me at, guru@mobilemoviemaking.com

Also, please visit our website, http://www.MobileMovieMaking.com. There you'll find articles on every aspect of iPhone movie making including: contests, product reviews, how-to-do-it articles, and works from award winning smartphone filmmakers.

By the way, one of the outcomes of writing this book is that I've started giving hands-on workshops so people can have the experience of trying out some of the tools and techniques we've explored in this book. In addition, I'm also working with small business owners who are interested in making their own movies rather than paying some else to do it. Below is a link to my workshop page and email. Let me know if you're interested in attending a workshop. Who knows, maybe we can arrange one near you. Write me:

guru@mobilemoviemaking.com

or visit our workshop page.

http://mobilemoviemaking.com/bronsein-home-page/

# ABOUT THE AUTHOR

Allen Bronstein is co-founder and Chief Content Officer of MobileMovieMaking.com a online magazine devoted to making movies with a smartphone or tablet. Over the past 35 years as an artist, filmmaker, and teacher Allen has developed the ability to make technical and artistic topics understandable to everyone. He brings this skill to his new book *Make iPhone Movies Everyone Loves*, his iPhone Video Guru workshops at,

http://mobilemoviemaking.com/bronstein-home-page/

and his individual consulting practice for business owners who want to create their own videos. He is an award-winning video producer and director who has worked for commercial clients such as Google, E-Bay, and Foster Farms; he has also produced two nature videos under the Magic Journey Cinema label. Mr. Bronstein has a Masters of Fine Arts degree from Mills College in Oakland, California and lives in the San Francisco Bay Area.

www.ingramcontent.com/pod-product-compliance
Lightning Source LLC
Chambersburg PA
CBHW050712180526
45159CB00003B/1008